Supercharged JavaScript Graphics

Supercharged JavaScript Graphics

Raffaele Cecco

O'REILLY®

Beijing · Cambridge · Farnham · Köln · Sebastopol · Tokyo

Supercharged JavaScript Graphics

by Raffaele Cecco

Published by O'Reilly Media, Inc., 1005 Gravenstein Highway North, Sebastopol, CA 95472.

O'Reilly books may be purchased for educational, business, or sales promotional use. Online editions are also available for most titles (*http://my.safaribooksonline.com*). For more information, contact our corporate/institutional sales department: (800) 998-9938 or *corporate@oreilly.com*.

Editor: Simon St. Laurent
Production Editor: Holly Bauer
Copyeditor: Rachel Monaghan
Proofreader: Genevieve d'Entremont

Indexer: Ellen Troutman Zaig
Cover Designer: Karen Montgomery
Interior Designer: David Futato
Illustrator: Robert Romano

Printing History:

July 2011:   First Edition.

ISBN: 978-1-449-39363-2

[LSI]

1309960268

Table of Contents

Preface

Having been a video game developer for many years and being used to working with high-performance programming languages and hardware, I initially had modest expectations of graphics programming with JavaScript. What I actually found was an excellent and efficient programming language that is continually being leveraged with better browsers, performance enhancements, and exciting new facilities. Combined with features such as Canvas, JavaScript offers web developers a truly viable alternative to plug-ins such as Adobe Flash, and features such as WebGL ensure a very bright future for graphics programming using JavaScript and a browser.

This book is for those who have a good working knowledge of JavaScript and would like to experiment with graphics programming that goes beyond simple hover effects or relying purely on the animation facilities of libraries such as jQuery. Within these pages, I cover various graphics-related subjects, including:

- Reusing and optimizing code, including inheritance techniques and performance tips
- Taking advantage of the surprising graphics power of regular DOM manipulation (DHTML)
- Using the Canvas element for additional graphics power
- Creating video games
- Using math for creative graphics and animation
- Presenting your data in creative ways with the Google Visualizations API and Google Chart Tools
- Using jQuery effectively and developing graphically oriented jQuery plug-ins
- Creating graphically rich web applications suitable for mobile devices using jQuery Mobile
- Using PhoneGap to create native Android applications from your web applications

This fast-paced book will give you a broad kick-start into various graphics techniques, hopefully whetting your appetite for further exploration of the subjects covered.

Experiment and have fun!

Audience and Assumptions

Readers of this book should have a good working knowledge of creating websites and web applications—and in particular, the use of JavaScript.

I like jQuery because it speeds up development, and many of the code samples include this library by default. In general, any external libraries and associated files are included from a reliable content delivery network such as Google's, thus avoiding the need for you to copy files to your own web space.

Math has been kept to a minimum, although some of the examples use basic vectors and trigonometry.

Organization

The book is fast paced, with the first graphics programming examples appearing in Chapter 1.

In the subsequent chapters, I cover a variety of graphics-oriented topics, focusing primarily on subjects that can add impressive visual impact and interactivity to your web applications.

No book about interactive graphics would be complete without a discussion of video games. We'll explore this subject in depth by developing a full video game application, as well as examining features that are useful for games projects, such as sprites and scrolling.

The topics covered in each chapter can be summarized as follows:

Chapter 1, *Code Reuse and Optimization*
> Covers JavaScript object-oriented programming techniques as well as code optimizations (including jQuery optimizations) that are useful where performance is important in graphics-based applications. We'll also discuss the little-used JavaScript binary operators and how you can use them for optimization.

Chapter 2
> Shows how regular DOM manipulation (DHTML) can be used for fast-moving graphics. We'll develop a sprite system (useful for games and other effects) and see how it works within the context of a jQuery plug-in.

Chapter 3, *Scrolling*
> Covers basic CSS scrolling techniques, including parallax effects. We'll then move on to JavaScript-controlled scrolling and finally to a fast, tile-based parallax scrolling system. I'll introduce you to the powerful Tiled map editor, showing you how to create tile-based maps.

Chapter 4, *Advanced UI*

Includes coverage of the user interface libraries jQuery UI and Ext JS. We'll explore the differing approaches of the two libraries and their respective suitabilities for various types of applications. In addition to using existing UI libraries, we'll build a 3D carousel from scratch.

Chapter 5, *Introduction to JavaScript Games*

Demonstrates how to build fun and playable games without resorting to external plug-ins such as Flash. Subjects covered include collision detection and object handling. We'll also develop a full retro-style arcade game to illustrate in action the techniques we've discussed.

Chapter 6, *HTML5 Canvas*

Examines the Canvas element in depth, with numerous examples—including how to develop a graphical chat application using Canvas and WebSockets. Canvas topics include an introduction to basic drawing, strokes, fills, gradients, recursive drawing, bitmaps, and animation.

Chapter 7, *Vectors for Games and Simulations*

Covers the myriad uses for 2D vectors in graphical applications and games, proving that a little bit of math can go a long way. Code examples include cannon and rocket simulations with realistic movement.

Chapter 8, *Google Visualizations*

Explores Google Chart Tools, an expansive resource of data visualization tools that can put an exciting spin on most kinds of data. From bar charts to Google-O-Meter gauges, this chapter covers the implementation of both static and interactive charts and other graphical visualizations in your applications. It includes the crucial topic of formatting your data in the correct way for Chart Tools to use.

Chapter 9, *Reaching the Small Screen with jQuery Mobile*

Describes jQuery Mobile, a framework built on top of jQuery to provide a unified user interface to mobile-targeted web applications. jQuery Mobile turns regular HTML pages into an interactive and animated mobile experience. This chapter covers the development of a graphical sliding puzzle game specifically geared to the jQuery UI and mobile devices.

Chapter 10, *Creating Android Apps with PhoneGap*

Want to create a native mobile application using your usual web development skills? PhoneGap comes to the rescue. This chapter explains how to install and configure PhoneGap to create native Android applications. After we walk through installation and configuration, we'll convert the sliding puzzle game we developed in Chapter 9 into a native app ready for deployment to mobile devices.

Conventions Used in This Book

The following typographical conventions are used in this book:

Italic

> Indicates new terms, URLs, email addresses, filenames, and file extensions.

`Constant width`

> Indicates computer code in a broad sense, including commands, arrays, elements, statements, options, switches, variables, attributes, keys, functions, types, classes, namespaces, methods, modules, properties, parameters, values, objects, events, event handlers, XML tags, HTML tags, macros, the contents of files, and the output from commands.

`Constant width bold`

> Shows commands or other text that should be typed literally by the user.

`Constant width italic`

> Shows text that should be replaced with user-supplied values or by values determined by context.

> This icon signifies a tip, suggestion, or general note.

> This icon indicates a warning or caution.

Websites and pages are mentioned in this book to help you locate online information that might be useful. Normally I specify both the address (URL) and the name (title, heading) of a page. Some addresses are relatively complicated, so you can probably locate the pages more easily by using your favorite search engine to find a page by its name, typically by entering it inside quotation marks. This method may also help if you can't find the page by its address; it may have simply moved elsewhere, so the name could still work.

Using Code Examples

This book contains many code snippets and examples, along with several complete and substantial applications. Some of these will be laborious to enter manually, so I would recommend copying the code from the book's code repository. Larger portions of code may be interspersed with regular copy text. This helps provide a fluid narrative through the code, rather than requiring you to constantly cross-reference code to text in different locations.

Where an example HTML page is featured, most of the examples use the HTML5 doctype:

```
<!DOCTYPE html>
```

For convenience, any CSS styles used in the examples are embedded within the HTML of the page. This is not necessarily the approach that you should take with production web applications, as external style sheets are recommended. However, within the context of a book, it makes sense to keep things together where possible. You can find the code examples here:

http://www.professorcloud.com/supercharged

Target Browsers

Most of the example code in this book will work on reasonably up-to-date browsers, such as:

- Firefox 3.6x+
- Safari 4.0x+
- Opera 10.x+
- Chrome 5.x+
- Internet Explorer 8+

In fact, some of the examples work even in IE6 and IE7, although I don't recommend using these browsers.

The examples were fully tested on Windows machines using XP, Vista, and Windows 7, and partially tested on iOS. In theory, the examples should also work on Linux versions of the supported browsers.

Use of the Canvas tag is limited to browsers that support it, so for Internet Explorer, this means version 9 only (for native support without any additional plug-ins or libraries).

A handful of the examples require a specialized environment to work, such as a mobile development environment (PhoneGap), server language (PHP), or a specific browser. Where this is the case, I cover setting up and configuring the environment.

Safari® Books Online

Safari. Safari Books Online is an on-demand digital library that lets you easily search over 7,500 technology and creative reference books and videos to find the answers you need quickly.

With a subscription, you can read any page and watch any video from our library online. Read books on your cell phone and mobile devices. Access new titles before they are available for print, and get exclusive access to manuscripts in development and post feedback for the authors. Copy and paste code samples, organize your favorites, download chapters, bookmark key sections, create notes, print out pages, and benefit from tons of other time-saving features.

O'Reilly Media has uploaded this book to the Safari Books Online service. To have full digital access to this book and others on similar topics from O'Reilly and other publishers, sign up for free at *http://my.safaribooksonline.com*.

How to Contact Us

Please address comments and questions concerning this book to the publisher:

O'Reilly Media, Inc.
1005 Gravenstein Highway North
Sebastopol, CA 95472
(800) 998-9938 (in the United States or Canada)
(707) 829-0515 (international or local)
(707) 829-0104 (fax)

We have a web page for this book, where we list errata, examples, and any additional information. You can access this page at:

http://www.oreilly.com/catalog/9781449393632

To comment or ask technical questions about this book, send email to:

bookquestions@oreilly.com

For more information about our books, courses, conferences, and news, see our website at *http://www.oreilly.com*.

Find us on Facebook: *http://facebook.com/oreilly*

Follow us on Twitter: *http://twitter.com/oreillymedia*

Watch us on YouTube: *http://www.youtube.com/oreillymedia*

Acknowledgments

It takes a lot more than an author to get a book to print, so I'd like to thank the following people:

- Simon St.Laurent, who was nothing but enthusiastic, encouraging, and helpful throughout the development of this book.
- All those who contributed time and expertise to review the book—especially Shelley Powers, who provided lots of insightful comments and suggestions.

- My copyeditor, Rachel Monaghan, and others in the production staff who smoothed out the last push to this book's completion.
- The generous community of developers who freely share their work, hints, and tips to help move the Web forward.
- My wife and daughter, Rebecca and Sofia, who were worried that my laptop had become a permanent appendage.

CHAPTER 1

Code Reuse and Optimization

JavaScript has an undeservedly dubious reputation. Many people have written about its limitations as an object-oriented programming (OOP) language, even questioning whether JavaScript is an OOP language at all (it is). Despite JavaScript's apparent syntactic resemblance to class-based OOP languages like C++ and Java, there is no Class statement (or equivalent) in JavaScript, nor any obvious way to implement popular OOP methodologies such as inheritance (code reuse) and encapsulation. JavaScript is also very loosely typed, with no compiler, and hence offers very few errors or warnings when things are likely to go wrong. The language is too forgiving in almost all instances, a trait that gives unsuspecting programmers a huge amount of freedom on one hand, and a mile of rope with which to hang themselves on the other.

Programmers coming from more classic and strictly defined languages can be frustrated by JavaScript's blissful ignorance of virtually every programming *faux pas* imaginable: global functions and variables are the default behavior, and missing semicolons are perfectly acceptable (remember the rope mentioned in the previous paragraph?). Of course, any frustration is probably due to a misunderstanding of what JavaScript is and how it works. Writing JavaScript applications is much easier if programmers first accept a couple of foundational truths:

- JavaScript is not a class-based language.
- Class-based OOP is not a prerequisite for writing good code.

Some programmers have attempted to mimic the class-based nature of languages like C++ in JavaScript, but this is analogous to pushing a square peg into a round hole: it can be done (sort of), but the end result can feel contrived.

No programming language is perfect, and one could argue that the perceived superiority of certain programming languages (or indeed, the perceived superiority of OOP itself) is a good example of the emperor's new clothes.*In my experience, software written in C++, Java, or PHP generates no fewer bugs or problems than projects created with

---

* *http://en.wikipedia.org/wiki/Emperor%27s_new_clothes*

JavaScript. In fact (cautiously sticking my neck out), I might suggest that due to Java-Script's flexible and expressive nature, you can develop projects in it more quickly than in other languages.

Luckily, most of JavaScript's shortcomings can be mitigated, not by forcibly contorting it into the ungainly imitation of another language, but by taking advantage of its in-herent flexibility while avoiding the troublesome bits. The class-based nature of other languages can be prone to unwieldy class hierarchies and verbose clumsiness. Java-Script offers other inheritance patterns that are equally useful, but lighter-weight.

If there are many ways to skin a cat, there are probably even more ways to perform inheritance in JavaScript, given its flexible nature. The following code uses *prototypal inheritance* to create a Pet object and then a Cat object that inherits from it. This kind of inheritance pattern is often found in JavaScript tutorials and might be regarded as a "classic" JavaScript technique:

```
// Define a Pet object. Pass it a name and number of legs.
var Pet = function (name, legs) {
    this.name = name; // Save the name and legs values.
    this.legs = legs;
};

// Create a method that shows the Pet's name and number of legs.
Pet.prototype.getDetails = function () {
    return this.name + ' has ' + this.legs + ' legs';
};

// Define a Cat object, inheriting from Pet.
var Cat = function (name) {
    Pet.call(this, name, 4); // Call the parent object's constructor.
};

// This line performs the inheritance from Pet.
Cat.prototype = new Pet();

// Augment Cat with an action method.
Cat.prototype.action = function () {
    return 'Catch a bird';
};

// Create an instance of Cat in petCat.
var petCat = new Cat('Felix');

var details = petCat.getDetails();    // 'Felix has 4 legs'.
var action = petCat.action();         // 'Catch a bird'.
petCat.name = 'Sylvester';            // Change petCat's name.
petCat.legs = 7;                      // Change petCat's number of legs!!!
details = petCat.getDetails();        // 'Sylvester has 7 legs'.
```

The preceding code works, but it's not particularly elegant. The use of the new statement makes sense if you're accustomed to other OOP languages like C++ or Java, but the prototype keyword makes things more verbose, and there is no privacy; notice how petCat has its `legs` property changed to a bizarre value of 7. This method of inheritance offers no protection from outside interference, a shortcoming that may be significant in more complex projects with several programmers.

Another option is not to use `prototype` or `new` at all and instead take advantage of JavaScript's ability to absorb and augment instances of objects using *functional inheritance*:

```
// Define a pet object. Pass it a name and number of legs.
var pet = function (name, legs) {
    // Create an object literal (that). Include a name property for public use
    // and a getDetails() function. Legs will remain private.
    // Any local variables defined here or passed to pet as arguments will remain
    // private, but still be accessible from functions defined below.
    var that = {
        name: name,
        getDetails: function () {
            // Due to JavaScript's scoping rules, the legs variable
            // will be available in here (a closure) despite being
            // inaccessible from outside the pet object.
            return that.name + ' has ' + legs + ' legs';
        }
    };
    return that;
};

// Define a cat object, inheriting from pet.
var cat = function (name) {
    var that = pet(name, 4); // Inherit from pet.
    // Augment cat with an action method.
    that.action = function () {
        return 'Catch a bird';
    };
    return that;
};

// Create an instance of cat in petCat2.
var petCat2 = cat('Felix');

details = petCat2.getDetails();    // 'Felix has 4 legs'.
action = petCat2.action();         // 'Catch a bird'.
petCat2.name = 'Sylvester';        // We can change the name.
petCat2.legs = 7;                  // But not the number of legs!
details = petCat2.getDetails();    // 'Sylvester has 4 legs'.
```

There is no funny `prototype` business here, and everything is nicely encapsulated. More importantly, the `legs` variable is private. Our attempt to change a nonexistent public `legs` property from outside `cat` simply results in an unused public `legs` property being created. The real `legs` value is tucked safely away in the closure created by the get Details() method of pet. A closure preserves the local variables of a function—in this case, pet()—after the function has finished executing.

In reality, there is no "right" way of performing inheritance with JavaScript. Personally, I find functional inheritance a very natural way for JavaScript to do things. You and your application may prefer other methods. Look up "JavaScript inheritance" in Google for many online resources.

 One benefit of using prototypal inheritance is efficient use of memory; an object's prototype properties and methods are stored only once, regardless of how many times it is inherited from.

Functional inheritance does not have this advantage; each new instance will create duplicate properties and methods. This may be an issue if you are creating many instances (probably thousands) of large objects and are worried about memory consumption. One solution is to store any large properties or methods in an object and pass this as an argument to the constructor functions. All instances can then utilize the one object resource rather than creating their own versions.

Keeping It Fast

The concept of "fast-moving JavaScript graphics" may seem like an oxymoron.

Truth be told, although the combination of JavaScript and a web browser is unlikely to produce the most cutting-edge arcade software (at least for the time being), there is plenty of scope for creating slick, fast-moving, and graphically rich applications, including games. The tools available are certainly not the quickest, but they are free, flexible, and easy to work with.

As an interpreted language, JavaScript does not benefit from the many compile-time optimizations that apply to languages like C++. While modern browsers have improved their JavaScript performance enormously, there is still room to enhance the execution speed of applications. It is up to you, the programmer, to decide which algorithms to use, which code to improve, and how to manipulate the DOM in efficient ways. No robot optimizer can do this for you.

A JavaScript application that only processes the occasional mouse click or makes the odd AJAX call will probably not need optimization unless the code is horrendously bad. The nature of applications covered in this book requires efficient code to give the user a satisfactory experience—moving graphics don't look good if they are slow and jerky.

The rest of this chapter does not examine the improvement of page load times from the server; rather, it deals with the optimization of running code that executes after the server resources have loaded. More specifically, it covers optimizations that will be useful in JavaScript graphics programming.

What and When to Optimize

Of equal importance to optimization is knowing when *not* to do it. Premature optimization can lead to cryptic code and bugs. There is little point in optimizing areas of an application that are seldom executed. It's a good idea to use the Pareto principle, or 80–20 rule: 20% of the code will use 80% of the CPU cycles. Concentrate on this 20%, 10%, or 5%, and ignore the rest. Fewer bugs will be introduced, the majority of code will remain legible, and your sanity will be preserved.

Using profiling tools like Firebug will quickly give you a broad understanding of which functions are taking the most time to execute. It's up to you to rummage around these functions and decide which code to optimize. Unfortunately, the Firebug profiler is available only in Firefox. Other browsers also have profilers, although this is not necessarily the case on older versions of the browser software.

Figure 1-1 shows the Firebug profiler in action. In the Console menu, select Profile to start profiling, and then select Profile again to stop profiling. Firebug will then display a breakdown of all the JavaScript functions called between the start and end points. The information is displayed as follows:

Function
    The name of the function called

Percent
    Percentage of total time spent in the function

Call
    How many times the function was called

Own time
    Time spent within a function, excluding calls to other functions

Time
    Total time spent within a function, including calls to other functions

Average
    Average of Own times

Min
    Fastest execution time of function

Max
    Slowest execution time of function

File
    The JavaScript file in which the function is located

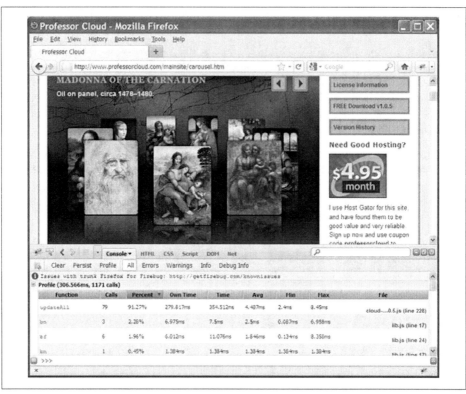

Figure 1-1. Firebug profiler in action

Being able to create your own profiling tests that work on all browsers can speed up development and provide profiling capabilities where none exist. Then it is simply a matter of loading the same test page into each browser and reading the results. This is also a good way of quickly checking micro-optimizations within functions. Creating your own profiling tests is discussed in the upcoming section "Homespun Code Profiling" on page 7.

 Debuggers like Firebug can skew timing results significantly. Always ensure that debuggers are turned off before performing your own timing tests.

"Optimization" is a rather broad term, as there are several aspects to a web application that can be optimized in different ways:

The algorithms

Does the application use the most efficient methods for processing its data? No amount of code optimization will fix a poor algorithm. In fact, having the correct algorithm is one of the most important factors in ensuring that an application runs quickly, along with the efficiency of DOM manipulation.

Sometimes a slow, easy-to-program algorithm is perfectly adequate if the application makes few demands. In situations where performance is beginning to suffer, however, you may need to explore the algorithm being used.

Examining the many different algorithms for common computer science problems such as searching and sorting is beyond the scope of this book, but these subjects are very well documented both in print and online. Even more esoteric problems relating to 3D graphics, physics, and collision detection for games are covered in numerous books.

The JavaScript
Examine the nitty-gritty parts of the code that are called very frequently. Executing a small optimization thousands of times in quick succession can reap benefits in certain key areas of your application.

The DOM and jQuery
DOM plus jQuery can equal a brilliantly convenient way of manipulating web pages. It can also be a performance disaster area if you fail to observe a few simple rules. DOM searching and manipulation are inherently slow and should be minimized where possible.

Homespun Code Profiling

The browser environment is not conducive to running accurate code profiling. Inaccurate small-interval timers, demands from events, sporadic garbage collection, and other things going on in the system all conspire to skew results. Typically, JavaScript code can be profiled like this:

```
var startTime = new Date().getTime();
// Run some test code here.
var timeElapsed = new Date().getTime() - startTime;
```

Although this approach would work under perfect conditions, for reasons already stated, it will not yield accurate results, especially where the test code executes in a few milliseconds.

A better approach is to ensure that the tests run for a longer period of time—say, 1,000 milliseconds—and to judge performance based on the number of iterations achieved within that time. Run the tests several times so you can perform statistical calculations such as mean and median.

To ensure longer-running tests, use this code:

```
// Credit: based on code by John Resig.

var startTime = new Date().getTime();
for (var iters = 0; timeElapsed < 1000; iters++) {
    // Run some test code here.
```

```
        timeElapsed = new Date().getTime() - startTime;
    }
    // iters = number of iterations achieved in 1000 milliseconds.
```

Regardless of the system's performance, the tests will run for the same amount of time. Very fast systems will simply achieve more iterations. In practice, this method returns nicely consistent results.

The profiling tests in this chapter run each test five times, for 1,000 milliseconds each. The median number of iterations is then used as the final result.

Optimizing JavaScript

Strictly speaking, many optimizations that can be applied to JavaScript can be applied to any language. Going down to the CPU level, the rule is the same: minimize work. In JavaScript, the CPU-level work is so abstracted from the programmer that it can be difficult to ascertain how much work is actually going on. If you use a few tried-and-tested methods, it is a safe bet that your code will benefit, although only performing empirical tests will prove this conclusively.

Lookup Tables

Computationally expensive calculations can have their values precalculated and stored in a lookup table. You can then quickly pull the values out of the lookup table using a simple integer index. As long as accessing a value from the lookup table is a cheaper operation than calculating the value from scratch, an application will benefit from better performance. JavaScript's trigonometry functions are a good example of where you can use lookup tables to speed things up. In this section, the Math.sin() function will be superseded by a lookup table, and we'll build an animated graphical application to utilize it.

The Math.sin() function accepts a single argument: an angle, measured in radians. It returns a value between –1 and 1. The angle argument has an effective range of 0 to 2π radians, or about 6.28318. This is not very useful for indexing into a lookup table, as the range of just six possible integer values is too small. The solution is to dispense with radians completely and allow the lookup table to accept integer indexes of between 0 and 4,095. This granularity should be enough for most applications, but you can make it finer by specifying a larger steps argument:

```
var fastSin = function (steps) {
    var table = [],
        ang = 0,
        angStep = (Math.PI * 2) / steps;
    do {
        table.push(Math.sin(ang));
        ang += angStep;
    } while (ang < Math.PI * 2);
```

```
        return table;
    };
```

The `fastSin()` function divides 2π radians into the number of steps specified in the argument, and stores the `sin` values for each step in an array, which is returned.

Testing the JavaScript `Math.sin()` against a lookup table yields the results shown in Figure 1-2.

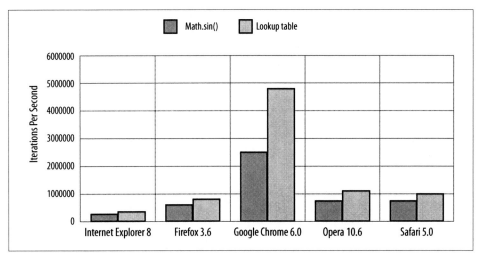

Figure 1-2. Math.sin() versus lookup table performance. Bigger is better.

Across most browsers, there appears to be an approximately 20% increase in performance, with an even more pronounced improvement in Google Chrome. If the calculated values within the lookup table had come from a more complex function than `Math.sin()`, then the performance gains would be even more significant; the speed of accessing the lookup table remains constant regardless of the initial work required to fill in the values.

The following application uses the `fastSin()` lookup table to create a hypnotic animated display. Figure 1-3 shows the output.

```html
<!DOCTYPE html>
<html>

    <head>
        <title>
            Fast Sine Demonstration
        </title>
        <script type="text/javascript"
            src="http://ajax.googleapis.com/ajax/libs/jquery/1.4.2/jquery.min.js">
        </script>
        <style type="text/css">
            #draw-target {
                width:480px; height:320px;
```

```
                background-color:#000; position:relative;
            }
        </style>
        <script type="text/javascript">
            $(document).ready(function() {
                (function() {
                    var fastSin = function(steps) {
                        var table = [],
                            ang = 0,
                            angStep = (Math.PI * 2) / steps;
                        do {
                            table.push(Math.sin(ang));
                            ang += angStep;
                        } while (ang < Math.PI * 2);
                        return table;
                    };
```

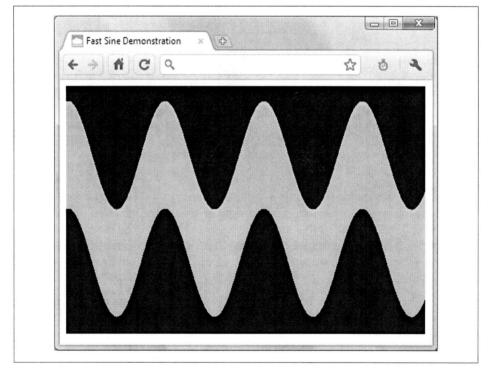

Figure 1-3. Sine lookup table used in an animated application

The fastSin() function is called, and the created sine lookup table is referenced in sinTable[].

```
                var sinTable = fastSin(4096),
                    $drawTarget = $('#draw-target'),
                    divs = '',
                    i, bars, x = 0;
```

The drawGraph() function draws a sine wave by updating the height and position of numerous one-pixel-wide divs. Table 1-1 shows the arguments.

```
var drawGraph = function(ang, freq, height) {
    var height2 = height * 2;
    for (var i = 0; i < 480; i++) {
        bars[i].style.top =
        160 - height + sinTable[(ang + (i * freq)) & 4095]
            * height + 'px';
        bars[i].style.height = height2 + 'px';
    }
};
```

Table 1-1. Arguments passed to drawGraph()

Argument	Description
ang	The start angle for the sine wave.
freq	The frequency of the sine wave. Defines the "tightness" of the wave.
height	The height (amplitude) of the wave; also affects the thickness of the lines drawn.

The following loop creates 480 one-pixel vertical div elements. The divs are then appended to $drawTarget. All the divs are then referenced in the bars[] array for use in drawGraph().

```
for (i = 0; i < 480; i++) {
    divs +=
        '<div style = "position:absolute;width:1px;height:40px;'
        + 'background-color:#0d0; top:0px; left: '
        + i + 'px;"></div>';
}
$drawTarget.append(divs);
bars = $drawTarget.children();
```

setInterval() repeatedly calls drawGraph() with continuously changing parameters to create an animated effect:

```
setInterval(function() {
    drawGraph(x * 50, 32 - (sinTable[(x * 20) & 4095] * 16),
        50 - (sinTable[(x * 10) & 4095] * 20));
    x++;
}, 20);
})();

            });
        </script>
    </head>

    <body>
        <div id="draw-target">
        </div>
    </body>

</html>
```

Bitwise Operators, Integers, and Binary Numbers

In JavaScript, all numbers are represented in a floating-point format. In contrast to languages such as C++ and Java, int and float types are not explicitly declared. This is a surprising omission, and a legacy of JavaScript's early years as a simple language intended for web designers and amateurs. JavaScript's single number type does help you avoid many numeric type errors. However, integers are fast, CPU-friendly, and the preferred choice for many programming tasks in other languages.

> JavaScript's number representation is defined in the ECMAScript Language Specification as "double-precision 64-bit format IEEE 754 values as specified in the IEEE Standard for Binary Floating-Point Arithmetic." This gives a (somewhat huge) range of large numbers ($\pm 1.7976931348623157 \times 10^{308}$) or small numbers ($\pm 5 \times 10^{-324}$). Beware, though: floating-point numbers are subject to rounding errors; for example, alert(0.1 + 0.2) displays 0.30000000000000004, not 0.3 as expected!

However, a closer look at the ECMAScript Standard reveals that JavaScript has several internal operations defined to deal with integers:

ToInteger
> Converts to an integer

ToInt32
> Converts to a signed 32-bit integer

ToUint32
> Converts to an unsigned 32-bit integer

ToUint16
> Converts to an unsigned 16-bit integer

You cannot use these operations directly; rather, they are called under the hood to convert numbers into an appropriate integer type for JavaScript's rarely used bitwise operators. Though sometimes incorrectly dismissed as slow and irrelevant to web programming, some of these operators possess quirky abilities that can be useful for optimization.

> Bitwise operators convert numbers into 32-bit integers, with a numerical range of –2,147,483,648 to 2,147,483,647. Numbers outside this range will be adjusted to fit.

A quick recap of binary numbers

During the halcyon days of computing, when 16 KB of RAM was considered a lot, binary numbers were a programmer's staple diet. The sort of low-level programming used for the computers of the day required a good understanding of binary and hexa-decimal notation. Binary numbers are rarely used in web programming, but they still have their place in areas such as hardware drivers and networking.

Everyone is familiar with the base-10 number system. In the first row of Table 1-2, each column from right to left represents an increasing power of 10. By multiplying the numbers in the second row by their corresponding power of 10 and then adding all the results (or products) together, we end up with a final number:

$$(3 \times 1,000) + (9 \times 1) = 3,009$$

Table 1-2. Base-10 number system

10,000	1,000	100	10	1
0	3	0	0	9

The principle is exactly the same for base-2, or binary, numbers. However, instead of the columns increasing in powers of 10, they increase in powers of 2. The only digits required in the second row are either 0 or 1, also known as a *bit*. The simple on-off nature of binary numbers is perfect for emulating in digital electronic circuits. Table 1-3 shows the binary representation of the base-10 number 69:

$$(1 \times 64) + (1 \times 4) + (1 \times 1) = 69$$

Table 1-3. The 8-bit binary representation of base-10 number 69

128	64	32	16	8	4	2	1
0	1	0	0	0	1	0	1

How can a binary number be negated (sign change)? A system called *twos comple-ment* is used as follows:

1. Invert each bit in the binary number, so 01000101 becomes 10111010.
2. Add 1, so 10111010 becomes 10111011 (–69).

The topmost bit acts as a sign, where 0 means positive and 1 means negative. Go through the same procedure again, and we are back to +69.

JavaScript's bitwise operators

JavaScript's bitwise operators act on the binary digits, or bits, within an integer number.

Bitwise AND (x & y). This performs a binary AND on the operands, where the resultant bit will be set only if the equivalent bit is set in both operands. So, 0x0007 & 0x0003 gives 0x0003. This can be a very fast way of checking whether an object possesses a desired set of attributes or flags. Table 1-4 shows the available flags for a pet object. For example, a small, old, brown dog would have a flags value of 64 + 16 + 8 + 2 = 90.

Table 1-4. Binary flags of a pet object

Big	Small	Young	Old	Brown	White	Dog	Cat
128	64	32	16	8	4	2	1

Searching for pets with certain flags is simply a case of performing a bitwise AND with a search value. The following code searches for any pet that is big, young, and white (it may be either a cat or dog, as this is not specified):

```
var searchFlags = 128 + 32 + 4;
var pets = []; // This is an array full of pet objects.
var numPets = pets.length;
for (var i = 0; i < numPets; i++) {
    if (searchFlags & pets[i].flags === searchFlags) {
        /* Found a Match! Do something. */
    }
}
```

With a total of 32 bits available in an integer to represent various flags, this can be much faster than checking flags stored as separate properties or other types of conditional testing; for example:

```
var search = ['big','young','white'};
var pets = []; // This is an array full of pet objects.
var numPets = pets.length;
for (var i = 0; i < numPets; i++) {
    // The following inner loop makes things much slower.
    for(var c=0;c<search.length;c++) {
        // Check if the property exists in the pet object.
        if ( pets[i][search[c]] == undefined) break;
    }
    if( c == search.length ) {
        /* Found a Match! Do something. */
    }
}
```

The & operator can also act in a similar way to the modulus operator (%), which returns the remainder after division. The following code will ensure that the variable value is always between 0 and 7:

```
value &= 7; // Equivalent to value % 8;
```

The equivalence to the % operator works only if the value after the & is 1, or a power of 2 less 1 (1, 3, 7, 15, 31...).

Bitwise OR (x | y). This performs a binary OR on the operators, where the resultant bit will be set if the equivalent bit is set in either operand. So, 0x0007 | 0x0003 gives 0x0007. Effectively, it merges the bits together.

Bitwise XOR (x ^ y). This performs a binary exclusive OR on the operators, where the resultant bit will be set if only one of the equivalent bits is set in either operand. So, 0x0000 ^ 0x0001 gives 0x0001, and 0x0001 ^ 0x0001 gives 0x0000. This can act as a shorthand way of toggling a variable:

```
toggle ^= 1;
```

Each time `toggle ^= 1;` is executed, the `toggle` value will flip between 1 and 0 (assuming it is 1 or 0 to start with). Here is the equivalent code using `if-else`:

```
if (toggle) {
    toggle = 0;
}else {
    toggle = 1;
}
```

or using the ternary operator (`?`):

```
toggle = toggle ? 0:1;
```

Bitwise NOT (~x). This performs a ones complement, or inversion of all bits. So, in binary, 11100111 would become 00011000. If the number in question is a signed integer (where the topmost bit represents the sign), then the `~` operator is equivalent to changing the sign and subtracting 1.

Shift left (x << numBits). This performs a binary shift left by a specified number of bits. All bits are moved to the left, the topmost bit is lost, and a 0 is fed into the bottommost bit. This is the equivalent of an unsigned integer multiplication of x by `2^numBits`. Here are some examples:

```
y = 5 << 1; // y = 10; Equivalent to Math.floor(5 * (2^1)).
y = 5 << 2; // y = 20; Equivalent to Math.floor(5 * (2^2)).
y = 5 << 3; // y = 40; Equivalent to Math.floor(5 * (2^3)).
```

Tests reveal no performance benefit over using the standard multiply operator (`*`).

Shift right with sign (x >> numBits). This performs a binary shift right by a specified number of bits. All bits are moved to the right, with the exception of the topmost bit, which is preserved as the sign. The bottommost bit is lost. This is the equivalent of a signed integer division of x by `2^numBits`. Here are some examples:

```
y = 10 >> 1; // y = 5; Equivalent to Math.floor(5 / (2^1)).
y = 10 >> 2; // y = 2; Equivalent to Math.floor(5 / (2^2)).
y = 10 >> 3; // y = 1; Equivalent to Math.floor(5 / (2^3)).
```

Tests reveal no performance benefit over using the standard divide operator (`/`).

The following code looks pretty useless:

```
x = y >> 0;
```

However, it forces JavaScript to call its internal integer conversion functions, resulting in the fractional parts of the number being lost. Effectively, it is performing a fast `Math.floor()` operation. Figure 1-4 shows that for Internet Explorer 8, Google Chrome, and Safari 5.0, there is a speed increase.

Shift right with zero fill (x >>> y). Rarely used, this is similar to the `>>` operator, but the topmost bit (sign bit) is not preserved and is set to 0. The bottommost bit is lost. For positive numbers, this is the same as the `>>` operator. For negative numbers, however, the result is a positive number. Here are some examples:

```
y = 10 >>> 1; // y = 5;
y = -10 >>> 2; // y = 1073741821;
y = -10 >>> 3; // y = 536870910;
```

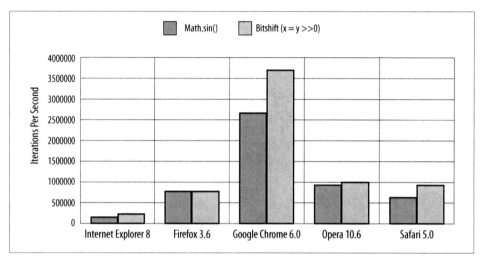

Figure 1-4. Math.floor() versus bitshift. Bigger is better.

Loop unrolling: An inconvenient truth

Looping in any programming language adds a certain amount of overhead beyond the code within the loop. Loops usually maintain a counter and/or check for the termination condition, both of which take time.

Removing the loop overhead provides some performance benefits. A typical JavaScript loop looks like this:

```
for (var i = 0; i < 8; i++) {
    /*** do something here  **/
}
```

By executing this instead, you can completely eliminate the loop overhead:

```
/*** do something here  ***/
/*** do something here  ***/
/*** do something here  ***/
/*** do something here  ***/
/*** do something here  ***/
/*** do something here  ***/
/*** do something here  ***/
/*** do something here  ***/
```

However, with a loop of just eight iterations, the improvement is not worth the effort. Assuming do something here is a simple statement (e.g., x++), removing the loop might execute the code 300% faster, but this is at the microsecond level; 0.000003 seconds versus 0.000001 seconds is not going to make a noticeable difference. If do something here is a big and slow function call, then the figures read more like 0.100003 seconds versus 0.100001 seconds. Again, too small an improvement to be worthwhile.

There are two factors that determine whether loop unrolling will provide a tangible benefit:

- The number of iterations. In practice, many iterations (probably thousands) are needed to make a difference.
- The proportion of time the inner loop code takes versus the loop overhead. Complex inner loop code that is many times slower to execute than the loop overhead will show a smaller improvement. This is because most of the time is being spent inside the inner loop code, not the loop overhead.

It is not practical to entirely unroll loops that require hundreds or thousands of iterations. The solution is to use a technique that is a variation of *Duff's device*. This works by performing partial unrolling of a loop. For example, a loop of 1,000 iterations can be broken into 125 iterations of code that is unrolled eight times:

```
// Credit: from Jeff Greenberg's site via an anonymous donor.
var testVal = 0;
var n = iterations % 8
while (n--)
{
    testVal++;
}

n = parseInt(iterations / 8);
while (n--)
{
    testVal++;
    testVal++;
    testVal++;
    testVal++;
    testVal++;
    testVal++;
    testVal++;
    testVal++;
   }
}
```

The first while loop takes into account situations where the number of iterations is not divisible by the number of unrolled code lines. For example, 1,004 iterations requires a loop of 4 normal iterations (1004 % 8), followed by 125 unrolled iterations of 8 each (parseInt(1004 / 8)). Here is a slightly improved version:

```
var testVal = 0;
var n = iterations >> 3; // Same as: parseInt(iterations / 8).
while(n--){
    testVal++;
    testVal++;
    testVal++;
    testVal++;
    testVal++;
```

```
        testVal++;
        testVal++;
        testVal++;
}
n = iterations - testVal; // testVal has kept a tally, so do the remainder here.
while(n--) {
        testVal++;
}
```

 Duff's device refers to a specific C-language optimization for unrolling loops that was developed by Tom Duff in 1983. He does not claim credit for loop unrolling as a general principle. Loop unrolling is common practice in assembly language, where tiny optimizations can make a difference in areas such as large memory copies and clears. Optimizing compilers may also perform automatic loop unrolling.

For loops of 10,000 iterations with trivial code, this returns significant performance gains. Figure 1-5 shows the results. Should we now optimize all our loops like this? No, not yet. The test is unrealistic: it is unlikely that incrementing a local variable is all we want to do within a loop.

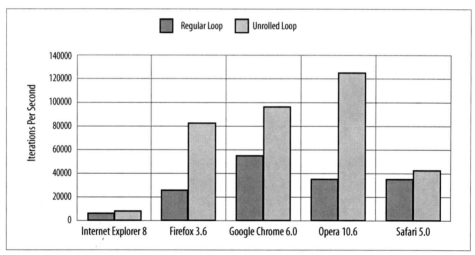

Figure 1-5. Unrolled loop with trivial inner loop code (10,000 iterations). Great results, but don't get too excited. Bigger is better.

A better test involves iterating through an array and calling a function with the array contents. This is much more along the lines of what will happen inside real applications:

```
// Initialize 10000 items.
var items = [];
for (var i = 0; i < 10000; i++) {
    items.push(Math.random());
}
```

```
// A function to do some useful work.
var processItem = function (x) {
    return Math.sin(x) * 10;
};

// The slow way.
var slowFunc = function () {
    var len = items.length;
    for (var i = 0; i < len; i++) {
        processItem(items[i]);
    }
};

// The 'fast' way.
var fastFunc = function () {
    var idx = 0;
    var i = items.length >> 3;
    while (i--) {
        processItem(items[idx++]);
        processItem(items[idx++]);
        processItem(items[idx++]);
        processItem(items[idx++]);
        processItem(items[idx++]);
        processItem(items[idx++]);
        processItem(items[idx++]);
        processItem(items[idx++]);
    }
    i = items.length - idx;
    while (i--) {
        processItem(items[idx++]);
    }
};
```

Figure 1-6 shows the improvement. Ouch. The real work within the loops has made the loop unrolling benefit a drop in the ocean. It is somewhat akin to ordering the 4,000-calorie Mega Burger Meal and hoping the diet soda will make things less fattening. Considering the 10,000 iterations, this is a disappointing set of results.

The moral of this story is that JavaScript loops are actually rather efficient, and you need to place micro-optimizations within the context of real application behavior to realistically test their benefits.

Optimizing jQuery and DOM Interaction

jQuery is an extensively used JavaScript library and provides a concise, convenient, and flexible way of accessing and manipulating elements within the DOM. It is designed to mitigate cross-browser issues, allowing you to concentrate on core application development rather than fiddling with browser quirks. jQuery is built around a *selector engine*, which allows you to find DOM elements using familiar CSS-style selector

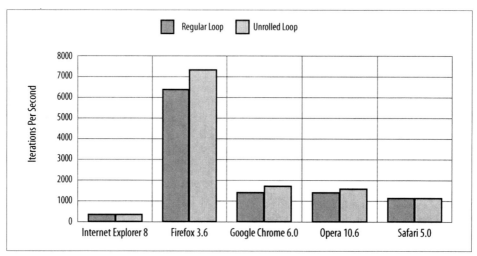

Figure 1-6. Unrolled loop with nontrivial inner loop code (10,000 iterations). A disappointing turnout. Bigger is better.

statements. For instance, the following code returns a jQuery object (a kind of array) containing all image elements with a CSS class of `big`:

```
$images = jQuery('img.big');
```

or the jQuery shorthand notation way:

```
$images = $('img.big');
```

The `$images` variable is just that, a normal variable. The preceding `$` is simply a reminder that it references a jQuery object.

There is one caveat to jQuery's power: an apparently small and innocuous jQuery statement can do a lot of work behind the scenes. This might not be significant if a small number of elements is being accessed only occasionally. However, if many elements are being accessed on a continuous basis—for example, in a highly animated page—there can be serious performance implications.

Optimizing CSS Style Changes

A fundamental part of creating JavaScript graphics using DHTML is being able to quickly manipulate the CSS style properties of DOM elements. In jQuery, you can do this like so:

```
$('#element1').css('color','#f00');
```

This would find the element whose `id` is `element1` and change its CSS `color` style to red.

Scratching beneath the surface, there is a lot going on here:

- Make a function call to jQuery and ask it to search the DOM for an element with id of `element1`. Apart from doing the search itself, this involves performing regular expression tests to determine the type of search required.
- Return the list of items found (in this case, one item) as a special jQuery array object.
- Make a function call to the jQuery `css()` function. This performs various checks such as determining whether it is reading or writing a style, whether it is being passed a string argument or object literal, and more. It finally updates the style of the element itself.

Performing this type of work many times in succession will be slow, regardless of how efficient jQuery is under the hood:

```
$('#element1').css('color','#f00');     // Make red.
$('#element1').css('color','#0f0');     // Make green.
$('#element1').css('color','#00f');     // Make blue.
$('#element1').css('left','100px');     // Move a bit.
```

Each of the preceding lines performs a search for the element with id of `element1`. Not good.

A faster method is to specify a context within which jQuery should search for elements. By default, jQuery begins its searches from the `document` root, or the topmost level within the DOM hierarchy. In many instances, starting from the root level is unnecessary and makes jQuery do more searching than is required. When you specify a context, jQuery has less searching to do and will return its results in less time.

The following example searches for all elements with a CSS class of `alien`, beginning the search within the DOM element referenced in `container` (the context):

```
$aliens = $('.alien', container); // Search within a specific DOM element.
```

The context parameter type is flexible and could have been another jQuery object or CSS selector:

```
// Start search within the elements of the jQuery object, $container.
$aliens = $('.alien', $container);

// Look for an element with id of 'container' and start the search there.
$aliens = $('.alien', '#container');
```

Make sure that searching for the context is not slower than searching for the elements within it! It is better to reference the context DOM element directly where possible.

Ideally, once elements have been found, you should not search for them again at all. We can cache (reuse) the search results instead:

```
var $elem = $('#element1');     // Cache the search results.
$elem.css('color','#f00');      // Make red.
$elem.css('color','#0f0');      // Make green.
$elem.css('color','#00f');      // Make blue.
$elme.css('left','100px');      // Move a bit.
```

This still leaves the jQuery `css()` function call, which is doing more work than is necessary for our purposes. We can dereference the jQuery search results right down to the actual style object of the DOM element:

```
// Get the first element ([0]) from the jQuery search results and store
// a reference to the style object of that element in elemStyle.

var elemStyle = $('#element1')[0].style;

// It is now quicker to manipulate the CSS styles of the element.
// jQuery is not being used at all here:

elemStyle.color = '#f00';     // Make red.
elemStyle.color = '#0f0';     // Make green.
elemStyle.color = '#00f';     // Make blue.
elemStyle.left = '100px';     // Move a bit.
```

Figure 1-7 shows the performance results of setting a CSS style for one DOM element via an uncached `jQuery.css()`, a cached `jQuery.css()`, or a direct write to the `style` object of the DOM element. The differences would be even more significant in more complex pages with slower CSS selectors—for example, `$('.some-css-class')`.

Where speed is of the essence, manipulating an element's properties directly will be faster than going through jQuery. For example, the `jQuery.html()` method can be considerably slower than using an element's `innerHTML` object directly.

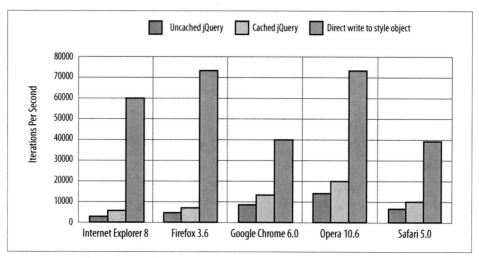

Figure 1-7. Speed comparison of using uncached jQuery, cached jQuery, and direct write to update an element's CSS style. Bigger is better.

Do the results in Figure 1-7 imply that we shouldn't be using jQuery at all? Not so; jQuery is far too good a library to reject, and it is understandably slow in certain circumstances. The rule is to be wary of how jQuery is used in time-critical areas of your application. This will usually be a small percentage of the total code. The majority of your application can and should use jQuery for quicker development, convenience, and fewer cross-browser issues.

Optimizing DOM Insertion

If you need to add a large number of elements into the DOM in your application, there can be performance implications. The DOM is a complex data structure that prefers being left alone. Of course, this is not really feasible in dynamic web pages, so you need an efficient way of inserting elements.

You can insert an element into the DOM with jQuery like this:

```
$('#element1').append('<p>element to insert</p>');
```

This is perfectly adequate for a few elements, but when you need to add hundreds or thousands of elements, inserting them individually can be too slow.

A better way is to build up all the intended elements into one big string and insert them simultaneously as a single unit. For each element, this prevents the overhead of the jQuery call and the various internal tests it performs:

```
var    elements = '';

// First build up a string containing all the elements.
for (var i = 0; i < 1000; i++) {
    elements += '<p>This is element ' + i + '</p>';
}

// They can now be inserted all at once.
$('#element1').append(elements);
```

Other Resources

Here's some suggested reading for those wanting to expand their knowledge of Java-Script:

- *JavaScript: The Definitive Guide* by David Flanagan (O'Reilly; *http://oreilly.com/catalog/9780596101992*)
- *JavaScript: The Good Parts* by Douglas Crockford (O'Reilly; *http://oreilly.com/catalog/9780596517748*)

CHAPTER 2

DHTML Essentials

DHTML seems like a curiously old-fashioned term these days, especially within the context of more modern browser facilities such as HTML5 Canvas, SVG, and Flash. However, rather like the tortoise and the hare,* DHTML will always be the more reliable (if slower) contender when the other, more exciting methods are not guaranteed to be available.

Actually, in many cases you don't need anything other than DHTML; the use of other methods can often be attributed simply to developer "wants" rather than "needs." Casual games, image zooms, and many other effects are perfectly feasible without resorting to the "power tools." Libraries like jQuery can make implementation even easier. A little thought and delicate manipulation of the DOM will ensure that DHTML graphics can move quickly and smoothly.

In this chapter, we'll develop a fast sprite system using vanilla JavaScript and DHTML. For the sake of compatibility, we'll avoid the latest bleeding-edge developments in the language and instead focus on the effective use of core JavaScript.

Creating DHTML Sprites

In computer graphics, *sprites* are two-dimensional bitmap objects that can be moved around under software control. Until the advent of three-dimensional polygon graphics, video game consoles used sprites almost exclusively for generating their moving characters. Mobile devices have prompted a resurgence in the use of sprite-like graphics for casual games and other user interface effects. You can emulate sprite functionality by using DHTML. In the following section, we'll create a `DHTMLSprite` object for use in a variety of applications. Although there are newer and faster methods of creating sprite-like effects (such as the HTML5 Canvas element), regular DHTML provides solid cross-browser compatibility and in many situations is a perfectly viable alternative to using plug-ins such as Adobe Flash.

---

* *http://en.wikipedia.org/wiki/The_Tortoise_and_the_Hare*

Sprites in this context are subtly different from CSS sprites, a popular web design technique. CSS sprites refer to altering only the CSS background position of an HTML element, thus allowing the element to show a small portion of a larger background image for the purpose of animation effects. In computer graphics parlance, this is known as *dynamic texture coordinates*. For our purposes, a sprite maintains its original meaning of a movable graphic object, although we will use the CSS sprite technique to change its image.

DHTMLSprite should be versatile enough to use in a variety of applications, and offer the following capabilities:

- Change its image (animation) with a simple function call and image index.
- Manage its own DOM element internally.
- Hide and show itself without altering the DOM.
- Remove its DOM element and perform any cleanup.

Image Animation

Sprites would be pretty boring without animation, so we need a neat method of changing the image used for the sprite. Although using an img element for sprite drawing seems like an obvious choice, it involves loading a different image file for each animation frame. There is a more efficient way to handle multiple sprite images while also reducing the number of image files required.

The CSS background-position property allows HTML elements (a div, in this case) to show a small portion of a larger image. A single container image can therefore act as a repository for numerous smaller sprite images. To use these sprite images, we must define the horizontal and vertical pixel offsets of the background-position property within the div, as well as the width and height. Unfortunately, this can be a fiddly and nonintuitive way of animating. It would be much better if we could reference the sprite images with a simple index number. For example, in Figure 2-1, the five sprite images that make up a cog animation are represented by indexes 0, 1, 2, 3, and 4. The first box sprite image is represented by index 5, and so on.

We need to convert the index number into pixel offsets within the container image. One option is to manually create a table that references the sprite image index numbers to the pixel offsets required. Although this is a valid solution, it would be very tedious to enter the offsets manually and keep the table updated if the sprite images changed position. A more elegant solution is to calculate the offsets.

Converting from an index number to horizontal and vertical pixel offsets involves some simple arithmetic. In Figure 2-1, the container image is 256 pixels wide, and each sprite image within it (ignoring the small ones at the bottom) is 64 pixels square. The pixel offsets can be calculated in JavaScript like this:

```
// This code is unoptimized, but illustrates the calculations required.
var vertOffset = -Math.floor (index * 64 / 256) * 64; // 64 is the sprite height.
var horizOffset = -(index * 64 % 256);               // 64 is the sprite width.
```

Notice how the values calculated are negated. Imagine that the div element is a fixed, 64-pixel-square aperture above the first cog image (index = 0). To show the next cog image (index = 1), the container image must be moved to the left by 64 pixels (negative horizontal offset). If the index were set to the last cog image (index = 4), the container image would need to move up by 64 pixels (negative vertical offset).

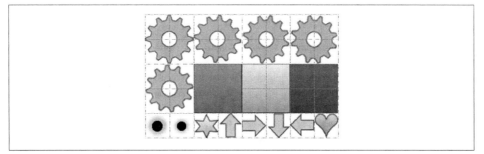

Figure 2-1. Animation images embedded into a single container image; each dotted grid square represents 32 pixels

How are sprites of different sizes handled? In Figure 2-1, there are some smaller 32-pixel sprite images at the bottom of the container image. The calculation to determine the pixel offsets is the same as before, but we use the required sprite size of 32 pixels instead:

```
// This code is unoptimized, but illustrates the calculations required.
var vertOffset = -Math.floor (index * 32 / 256) * 32; // 32 is the sprite height.
var horizOffset = -(index * 32 % 256);               // 32 is the sprite width.
```

The index numbers also need to take into account that the sprite sizes are now 32 pixels. The first 32-pixel sprite image in Figure 2-1 (the first small black circle) has an index of 32. As long as sprite images appear in the container image at pixel boundaries that are a multiple of their size, they can be accessed using the indexing calculations.

The container image in Figure 2-1 is a 32-bit PNG file, which allows millions of colors and an alpha channel for smooth transparency. Unfortunately, 32-bit PNGs don't work very well in IE6, because the transparent areas become an opaque gray. One solution is to save the image as an 8-bit paletized PNG. In IE6, this will display correctly, although any semitransparent areas will disappear completely and show a coarser edge.

Encapsulation and Drawing Abstraction (aka Hiding Stuff)

Hiding all the DOM manipulation shenanigans within DHTMLSprite and away from the application using it allows for cleaner and more maintainable code; the application can focus on logic rather than the mechanics of drawing. Converting the application to use another sprite drawing method such as the HTML5 Canvas element or SVG becomes simpler. Alternatively, the application could choose an appropriate drawing method based on the browser's capabilities.

Minimizing DOM Insertion and Deletion

Repeatedly adding, removing, and destroying DOM elements can have detrimental effects on performance, as well as forcing JavaScript's garbage collector to work overtime. To mitigate these undesirable effects, maintain a list of initialized but hidden sprites. When a sprite is required, you can take it from the list and make it visible without actually inserting anything into the DOM. When the sprite is no longer needed, you can hide it and place it back on the list. Providing a show and hide method within DHTMLSprite will allow an application to implement this technique if required.

If a DHTMLSprite is to be removed permanently, it should remove its own DOM element and perform any other associated cleanup.

The Sprite Code

Rather than passing several separate arguments to the sprite, we pass all setup parameters inside a single object called params. As well as making the order of parameters noncritical, this also allows other objects inheriting from DHTMLSprite to simply add their own setup parameters inside params. Any object using params can ignore parameters not relevant to it. Table 2-1 shows the parameters passed within the params object.

```
var DHTMLSprite = function (params) {
```

Table 2-1. DHTMLSprite object parameters

Parameter	Description
images	Path to the images file
imagesWidth	Pixel width of the images file
width	Pixel width of sprite
height	Pixel height of sprite
$drawTarget	The parent element into which the sprite will append its own div element

Here we make local variable copies of the params properties. Accessing the parameters via local variables is quicker than accessing them as properties of the params object. Local variables defined like this are private and can be accessed only from methods within DHTMLSprite.

```
var width = params.width,
    height = params.height,
    imagesWidth = params.imagesWidth,
```

Next, we append a sprite `div` element to the DOM element specified in `params.$draw Target`. A reference to this sprite `div` is stored in `$element`. The preceding `$` symbol in the variable and property names serves as a reminder that they refer to jQuery objects. A direct reference to the `style` attribute of the sprite `div` is stored in `elemStyle` to optimize the updating of its CSS properties.

```
$element = params.$drawTarget.append('<div/>').find(':last'),
elemStyle = $element[0].style,
// Store a local reference to the Math.floor function for faster access.
mathFloor = Math.floor;
```

Now we set up some initial CSS properties for the sprite `div` element. As we do this only once (when `DHTMLSprite` is initialized), it is reasonable to use the convenient jQuery `css()` function, even though this might not be the fastest way to change the properties.

```
$element.css({
    position: 'absolute',
    width: width,
    height: height,
    backgroundImage: 'url(' + params.images + ')'
});
```

Here we create and store a `DHTMLSprite` object instance in `that`. It contains all the sprite methods. Notice how `that`'s methods refer to the local variables defined earlier. The `that` object has created a closure and has permanent access to variables defined within the context of the outer `DHTMLSprite` function.

```
var that = {
```

The `draw` method simply updates the position of the sprite `div` element:

```
draw: function (x, y) {
    elemStyle.left = x + 'px';
    elemStyle.top = y + 'px';
},
```

The `changeImage()` method changes the sprite image displayed. The calculation to convert an index number to pixel offsets is the same as described earlier, but with some optimizations:

- Instead of `Math.floor()`, the local `mathFloor()` variable reference to the function is called.
- `index` is multiplied only once in the calculation.

```
changeImage: function (index) {
    index *= width;
    var vOffset = -mathFloor(index / imagesWidth) * height;
    var hOffset = -index % imagesWidth;
    elemStyle.backgroundPosition = hOffset + 'px ' + vOffset + 'px';
},
```

Next, we define simple methods to hide, show, and remove the sprite `div` element:

```
show: function () {
    elemStyle.display = 'block';
},
hide: function () {
    elemStyle.display = 'none';
},
destroy: function () {
    $element.remove();
}
};
// Return the instance of DHTMLSprite.
return that;
};
```

A Simple Sprite Application

Here is a basic HTML page that initializes two sprites and draws them:

```
<!DOCTYPE html>
<html>
    <head>
        <title>
            Sprite Demonstration
        </title>
        <script type="text/javascript"
            src="http://ajax.googleapis.com/ajax/libs/jquery/1.4.2/jquery.min.js">
        </script>
        <style type="text/css">
            #draw-target {
                width:480px;
                height:320px;
                background-color: #ccf;
                position:relative;
            }
        </style>
        <script type="text/javascript">
            var DHTMLSprite = function(params) {
                /*** DHTMLSprite code removed for conciseness ***/
            };

            $(document).ready(function() {
```

Here we create an object containing the initialization parameters required to create a sprite:

```
var params = {
    images: '/images/cogs.png',
    imagesWidth: 256,
    width: 64,
    height: 64,
    $drawTarget: $('#draw-target')
};
```

Two sprites are created. Because both sprites are identical in size and use the same drawing area in the DOM, we don't need to change any of the parameters. The first sprite uses the default image index value of 0, while we set the second one's image index to 5.

```
var sprite1 = DHTMLSprite(params),
    sprite2 = DHTMLSprite(params);
sprite2.changeImage(5);
```

Finally, the two sprites are drawn. Figure 2-2 shows the output.

```
        sprite1.draw(64, 64);
        sprite2.draw(352, 192);
    });
  </script>
  </head>
  <body>
    <div id="draw-target">
    </div>
  </body>
</html>
```

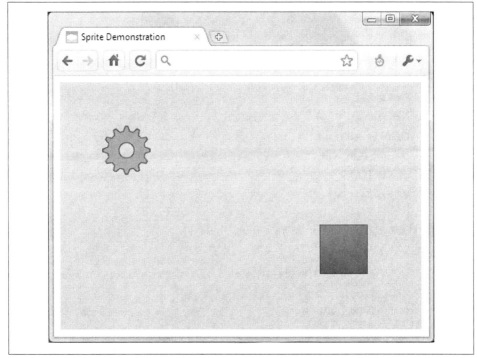

Figure 2-2. Two sprites being drawn

We aren't demanding much of the sprites in this application. Having no movement or animation is rather dull, so let's spice things up a little in the next example.

A More Dynamic Sprite Application

The following application demonstrates a sprite's *raison d'être*: animation and movement. Earlier, we drew two sprites at fixed positions, with no additional means to control their movement. In this example, we'll define a new object: a bouncySprite, which—as its name implies—creates a DHTMLSprite that bounces around the page. One way to achieve this would be for bouncySprite to create a DHTMLSprite and treat it as a separate entity that it controls. A neater solution would be for bouncySprite to inherit all the abilities of DHTMLSprite and augment itself with additional abilities. JavaScript is very comfortable with this kind of inheritance and augmentation:

```
var bouncySprite = function (params) {
```

Setup parameters are stored in local variables for speed. At this point, the params object will also contain parameters for the DHTMLSprite, but these are not relevant to bouncy Sprite. Table 2-2 shows the parameters passed.

```
var x = params.x,
        y = params.y,
        xDir = params.xDir,
        yDir = params.yDir,
        maxX = params.maxX,
        maxY = params.maxY,
```

Table 2-2. bouncySprite object parameters

Parameter	Description
x	Pixel x position
y	Pixel y position
xDir	The x movement direction
yDir	The y movement direction
maxX	Maximum x position
maxY	Maximum y position

animIndex stores the current animation image index:

```
animIndex = 0,
```

We create and reference a DHTMLSprite in that. The params object contains its setup parameters.

```
that = DHTMLSprite(params);
```

Here we augment the DHTMLSprite instance referenced in that with a moveAndDraw method, effectively creating a bouncySprite instance instead:

```
that.moveAndDraw = function () {
```

Move the x and y positions of the sprite by adding the xDir and yDir variables:

```
x += xDir;
y += yDir;
```

The `animIndex` variable is either incremented or decremented depending on the horizontal direction of movement. We then keep it within a range, –4 to +4, using the modulus operator (%). If `animIndex` is negative, it is corrected and given its equivalent positive animation index.

```
animIndex += xDir > 0 ? 1 : -1;
animIndex %= 5;
animIndex += animIndex < 0 ? 5 : 0;
```

Next, we check whether the `bouncySprite` has passed the extents defined by `maxX` and `maxY`. If it has, the direction of movement along the relevant axis is negated, thus causing the `bouncySprite` to "bounce."

```
if ((xDir < 0 && x < 0) || (xDir > 0 && x >= maxX)) {
    xDir = -xDir;
}
if ((yDir < 0 && y < 0) || (yDir > 0 && y >= maxY)) {
    yDir = -yDir;
}
```

The `bouncySprite`'s animation index is updated and drawn at its new position:

```
that.changeImage(animIndex);
that.draw(x, y);
};
```

The `bouncySprite` instance, referenced in `that`, is returned for the application to use:

```
return that;
};
```

Now that we've defined the `bouncySprite` object, we could initialize a handful of them into separate variables and call their `moveAndDraw()` methods individually under the control of a `setInterval()` or `setTimeout()` loop. A better solution, however, is to create another object that can initialize and handle any number of `bouncySprites`. This object will be called `bouncyBoss`. `bouncyBoss` is passed two parameters, as shown in Table 2-3.

```
var bouncyBoss = function (numBouncy, $drawTarget) {
```

Table 2-3. bouncyBoss object parameters

Parameter	Description
numBouncy	The number of bouncySprites to initialize
$drawTarget	The parent element into which the bouncySprites will be appended

The requisite number of `bouncySprite` objects is created and pushed into an array (`bouncys`). Each `bouncySprite` is given a random starting position and movement direction (`xDir` and `yDir`). The maximum extents of `$drawTarget` are also passed.

```
var bouncys = [];
for (var i = 0; i < numBouncy; i++) {
```

```
bouncys.push(bouncySprite({
    images: '/images/cogs.png',
    imagesWidth: 256,
    width: 64,
    height: 64,
    $drawTarget: $drawTarget,
    x: Math.random() * ($drawTarget.width() - 64),
    y: Math.random() * ($drawTarget.height() - 64),
    xDir: Math.random() * 4 - 2,
    yDir: Math.random() * 4 - 2,
    maxX: $drawTarget.width() - 64,
    maxY: $drawTarget.height() - 64
}));
}
```

Now we define a moveAll method, which calls the moveAndDraw method of each bouncy Sprite in the bouncys array. After moving everything, it creates a setTimeout to call itself again, thus creating a continuous loop.

```
var moveAll = function () {
    var len = bouncys.length;
    for (var i = 0; i < len; i++) {
        bouncys[i].moveAndDraw();
    }
    setTimeout(moveAll, 10);
}
// Call the moveAll() function to start.
moveAll();
};
```

The page layout for using the new bouncyBoss object is as follows:

```
<!DOCTYPE html>
<html>
    <head>
        <title>
            Sprite Demonstration
        </title>
        <style type="text/css">
            #draw-target {
                width:480px;
                height:320px;
                background-color:#ccf;
                position:relative;
            }
        </style>
        <script type="text/javascript"
            src="http://ajax.googleapis.com/ajax/libs/jquery/1.4.2/jquery.js">
        </script>
        <script type="text/javascript">
            var DHTMLSprite = function(params) {
                /*** DHTMLSprite code removed for conciseness ***/
            };
            var bouncySprite = function(params) {
                /*** bouncySprite code removed for conciseness ***/
            };
```

```
        var bouncyBoss = function(numBouncy, $drawTarget) {
            /*** bouncyBoss code removed for conciseness ***/
        };
        $(document).ready(function() {
```

A single call to bouncyBoss creates 50 bouncySprite objects and continually calls their moveAndDraw methods. Figure 2-3 shows the output.

```
            bouncyBoss(50, $('#draw-target'));
        });
    </script>
    </head>
    <body>
        <div id="draw-target">
        </div>
    </body>
</html>
```

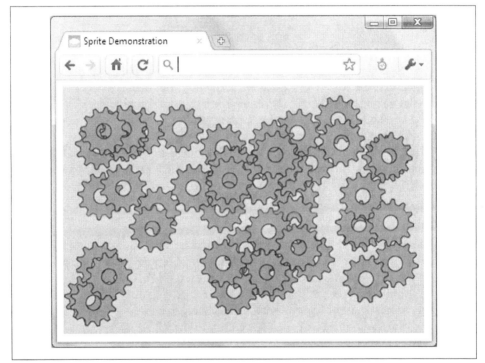

Figure 2-3. Multiple sprite instances being drawn and animated

Converting into a jQuery Plug-in

Converting the bouncy sprite application into a jQuery plug-in adds functionality that takes advantage of jQuery's ability to easily search for DOM elements via CSS selectors and return them as a list for further processing. The plug-in will search for any specified elements and attach multiple `bouncySprite` instances to them via the `bouncyBoss` object. It will also allow you to change the background color of the elements being attached to and the number of `bouncySprite` instances being attached.

Although converting the bouncy sprite application into a flexible jQuery plug-in may sound like a substantial job, there's actually less work involved than you might expect. Because of the modular and self-contained way in which the `DHTMLSprite`, `bouncySprite`, and `bouncyBoss` objects were developed, they will slip unobtrusively into a jQuery plug-in structure.

The initial solitary semicolon may seem odd (it is not a typo), but it protects against problems arising from cases where the code preceding the plug-in does not end with a semicolon as expected. Normally, this is not an issue, as JavaScript will identify the plug-in code after a line break as a new statement. However, if the preceding code and the plug-in were minified, the whitespace—including line breaks—would probably be removed. The plug-in would subsequently fail due to the lack of an identifying break between it and the preceding code.

```
;    // Initial solitary semicolon.
```

Here, we define an anonymous function. This will wrap all the plug-in code into a nice, self-contained context that won't clash with anything outside it. The `$` is simply an argument that will be passed in; in this case, it's the global jQuery object itself (see the last line of the plug-in). Now, instead of calling `jQuery()`, you can use the shorthand method of calling jQuery, `$()`, throughout the plug-in. Passing the jQuery object like this may seem like a waste of time, as it is already defined globally. However, it ensures that any alien code outside the plug-in that redefines the `$` variable (for example, another JavaScript library) will not prevent the plug-in from using the shorthand method of calling jQuery.

```
(function ($) {
```

You augment jQuery's abilities by storing a reference to the plug-in within jQuery's `fn` property. There is a chance that a namespace collision may occur due to another plug-in already being defined with exactly the same name. You can avoid this in most cases by being imaginative with the plug-in name. For instance, "zoom" is probably not a good choice, whereas "cloudZoom" is less likely to clash

```
$.fn.bouncyPlugin = function (option) {
```

We insert the code for `DHTMLSprite`, `bouncySprite`, and `bouncyBoss` here. There is no need to modify them in any way. Because they are stored as local variables, they remain private to the plug-in.

```
var DHTMLSprite = function (params) {
    /*** DHTMLSprite code removed for conciseness ***/
};
var bouncySprite = function (params) {
    /*** bouncySprite code removed for conciseness ***/
};
var bouncyBoss = function (numBouncy, $drawTarget) {
```

```
/*** bouncyBoss code removed for conciseness ***/
};
```

The plug-in can use options defined as properties of the `option` object argument. This is a flexible way of passing options to a plug-in, as it allows all, some, or no options to be passed. The jQuery `extend` function merges the `option` properties with default option properties defined in the `$.fn.bouncyPlugin.defaults` object. The `option` properties have priority where they exist; the default properties are used where they do not. Because default options are public, an application can change them for the plug-in by creating a new `defaults` object in `$.fn.bouncyPlugin.defaults`.

```
option = $.extend({}, $.fn.bouncyPlugin.defaults, option);
```

The plug-in iterates through the list of DOM elements found. For each element, it executes an anonymous function. Within the function, `this` refers to the current element in the list. A jQuery object is created from `this` and stored in `$drawTarget`. The background color defined in `option` is applied to `$drawTarget`, as is a new instance of bouncyBoss:

```
        return this.each(function () {
            var $drawTarget = $(this);
            $drawTarget.css('background-color', option.bgColor);
            bouncyBoss(option.numBouncy, $drawTarget);
        });
    };
    $.fn.bouncyPlugin.defaults = {
        bgColor: '#f00',
        numBouncy: 10
    };
})(jQuery);
```

Here is the plug-in *in situ* in an HTML page. Figure 2-4 shows the output:

```
<!DOCTYPE html>
<html>
    <head>
        <title>
            Sprite Demonstration
        </title>
        <style type="text/css">
            .draw-target {
                width:320px;
                height:256px;
                position:relative;
                float:left;
                margin:5px;
            }
        </style>
        <script type="text/javascript"
            src="http://ajax.googleapis.com/ajax/libs/jquery/1.4.2/jquery.js">
        </script>
        <script type="text/javascript">
```

We insert the plug-in here:

```
                ;(function($) {
                    $.fn.bouncyPlugin = function(option) {
                        /*** bouncyPlugin code removed for conciseness ***/
                    };
                })(jQuery);
```

When the page is ready, the plug-in is called on the desired elements—in this case, anything with a CSS class of draw-target.

```
                $(document).ready(function() {
                    $('.draw-target').bouncyPlugin({
                        numBouncy: 20,
                        bgColor: '#8ff'
                    });
                });
            </script>
        </head>
        <body>
```

Next, we define four div elements with a class of draw-target:

```
            <div class="draw-target">
            </div>
            <div class="draw-target">
            </div>
            <div class="draw-target">
            </div>
            <div class="draw-target">
            </div>
        </body>
    </html>
```

For more in-depth scrutiny of jQuery, including creating plug-ins, see *jQuery Cookbook* by jQuery Community Experts (O'Reilly; *http://oreilly.com/catalog/ 9780596159788*).

Timers, Speed, and Frame Rate

This section deals with programming issues related to throttling graphical updates in JavaScript to give the user an optimal experience. We want graphics that have smooth and fluid movement, and that are neither too quick nor too slow. The performance of the user's computer will influence how fast moving graphics are updated. I'll also discuss a solution for reducing these apparent speed variations on different machines.

Using setInterval and setTimeout

JavaScript's setInterval() and setTimeout() functions allow you to call JavaScript code at regular intervals. Applications that require regular graphical updates, such as arcade games, would be difficult, if not impossible, to write without them.

You can call a function repeatedly by passing it as a *callback* to setInterval():

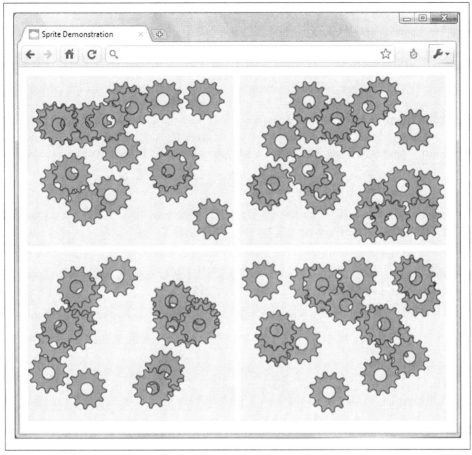

Figure 2-4. Multiple instances of the bouncyBoss object created through a jQuery plug-in

```
// This is a callback function.
var bigFunction = function() {
    // Do something...
    // This code needs to be called regularly.
    // It takes 20ms to execute
};

// setInterval will attempt to call bigFunction() every 50 milliseconds.
setInterval(bigFunction, 50);
```

Notice that `bigFunction()` takes 20 milliseconds (ms) to execute. What happens if a smaller interval is used instead?

```
setInterval(bigFunction, 15);
```

It might seem that the 20ms `bigFunction()` will be called again before the first callback has even returned. In reality, the new callback will be queued until after the first callback has finished.

What happens if the delay is reduced further?

```
setInterval(bigFunction, 5);
```

It would be reasonable to expect each `setInterval()` callback to be queued several times while the first callback executes. In fact, the usual behavior is that only one queued callback to `bigFunction()` will ever be active. Will the queued callback happen immediately after the first callback has finished? Possibly, but not necessarily; other events and code running in the browser can force `setInterval()` callbacks to be delayed or dropped altogether. Callbacks may even occur back to back, at less than the interval specified, if JavaScript sees a window of opportunity to flush the queue.

The important lesson here is that while `setInterval()` works at millisecond resolution, there is no guarantee that callbacks will be executed at the intervals specified.

`setTimeout()` calls a function, once only, after a specified delay. You might think of it as `setInterval()`'s more predictable friend.

```
setTimeout(bigFunction,50);
```

This will call `bigFunction()`, once only, after a delay of 50ms. As with `setInterval()`, the delay should be regarded only as a guide.

You can also use `setTimeout()` to call a function continuously, but with less unpredictable behavior than `setInterval()`:

```
// This is a callback function.
var bigFunction = function() {
    // Do something...
    // This code needs to be called regularly.
    // It takes 20ms to execute
    setTimeout(bigFunction, 10);
};
```

Whenever `bigFunction()` finishes, it sets up another `setTimeout()` with itself as the callback.

In this example, even though the timeout specified is less than the time it takes for bigFunction() to execute, the setTimeout() callback will execute only after bigFunction() has finished. In effect, the frequency of execution will be similar to the following alternative code, which uses `setInterval()`:

```
setInterval(bigFunction, 20+10);
```

Timer Accuracy

Browsers running under Windows have to cope with coarse-grained timers. For example, the underlying operating system timer used in Windows XP offers a 15ms accuracy. This means that JavaScript functions such as `Date()`, `setInterval()`, and `set Timeout()` will not give reliable results when the timings in question are less than 15ms or so. One browser to buck this trend is Google Chrome, which offers 1ms accuracy by switching Windows into an accurate timer mode.

To learn more about the topic of JavaScript timers, read the following online articles:

- *http://ejohn.org/blog/how-javascript-timers-work/*
- *http://ejohn.org/blog/javascript-in-chrome/*

The upshot is that an application should not rely on timings under 15ms, or about 1/64 of a second. Is this a major problem? In most instances, no; it's unlikely that such a time-sensitive application would (or should) be running under JavaScript within a browser. Animations might run a little slower or faster than expected, and applications like games might not give a perfectly consistent frame rate. If one were pedantic enough to scrutinize the cumulative effects of these inaccuracies over a period of time, there would be a noticeable deviation. However, under normal usage conditions, such as playing a game or watching a menu fade in, the deviations would be imperceptible.

One area that you should approach with caution, though, is the use of `Date()` to profile code performance. The following example will yield inaccurate results if the code executed terminates too quickly:

```
var startTime = new Date().getTime();
/*** Execute some code here that takes less than 15 milliseconds ***/
var endTime = new Date().getTime();
var elapsedTime = endTime - startTime;
```

A better solution is to execute the code repeatedly over a longer period of time—say, one second—and then work out the speed of execution from the number of iterations achieved within that time.

Achieving Consistent Speed

One problem with the sprite implementation shown earlier—or, more specifically, the code that moves the sprites—is that different browsers will yield an inconsistent speed of animation and movement, or *frame rate*. For instance, on a 2.8Ghz PC, a fast browser like Opera or Google Chrome will happily move a hundred sprites at 50 frames per second (FPS), whereas Firefox might manage 30 FPS, and Internet Explorer 8 just 25 FPS. Add different hardware into the mix, and you'll see even more frame-rate inconsistencies.

This may not be an issue for cosmetic animations and effects, but for applications like games where a consistent speed of movement is important to playability, these variations are a problem.

To combat this issue, you must modify the calculations used to move and animate the sprites to take into account different frame rates, thus giving an apparently consistent speed in different hardware and software environments. For example, a sprite moving across the screen in two-pixel steps at 30 FPS will appear to move at the same speed as a sprite moving across the screen in one-pixel steps at 60 FPS. The main discernible difference between the two will be that the 30 FPS sprite does not move quite as smoothly as the 60 FPS sprite. However, they will still appear to traverse the screen at the same rate.

A time coefficient must be calculated and used in the movement and animation code. Table 2-4 shows the sort of results required.

Table 2-4. Example time coefficients

Goal FPS	Actual FPS	Time coefficient
60	30	2
60	15	4
30	40	0.75
50	50	1

It's fairly obvious that you calculate the time coefficient by dividing the goal FPS by the actual FPS achieved.

You calculate the actual FPS by making note of the current time in milliseconds, using the JavaScript Date object (the start time). You then execute all the application logic and take the time again (the end time). Here is the code:

```
actualFPS = 1000 / (endTime - startTime);
```

If the demands made on the CPU are too much, the frame rate may become unacceptably slow. A sprite moving across the screen in 10-pixel steps at 6 FPS will look very jerky, which is certainly not suitable for arcade games. As a useful rule of thumb, Table 2-5 gives an idea of frame rates and perceived movement smoothness.

Table 2-5. FPS and perceived movement smoothness

Frames per second	Perceived smoothness
Less than 15	Rather jerky
15–20	Just acceptable
20–30	Reasonably smooth
30–40	Smooth
40+	Very smooth

This is not to say that a low frame rate of 10 FPS is useless. For animated puzzle-style games like *Tetris*, this might be quite acceptable.

Now we create a timeInfo object, which provides all the functionality required to keep animated applications moving at a consistent speed. It is passed a goalFPS parameter, which is the FPS we would like to achieve if possible. If that FPS is not possible, the function adjusts the movement speed so it at least appears that things are running at the goalFPS. The function also returns various other pieces of useful time-related information.

The function returns an object, which contains a getInfo() method. The getInfo() method returns an object containing the useful properties shown in Table 2-6.

```
var timeInfo = function (goalFPS) {
    var oldTime, paused = true,
        interCount = 0,
        totalFPS = 0;
        totalCoeff = 0;
    return {
        getInfo: function () {
```

Table 2-6. Object properties returned from timeInfo.getInfo()

Property	Description
elapsed	The number of milliseconds since the last call to getInfo()
coeff	The coefficient to be used in movement and animation calculations
FPS	The FPS achieved since the last call to getInfo()
averageFPS	The average FPS achieved since the first call to getInfo()
averageCoeff	The average coefficient

The paused variable indicates that getInfo() is being called for the first time, either at the beginning of the application or after a deliberate pause in the application. It ensures that values passed back by getInfo() are benign after a long pause, and will not explode any calculations due to a very large coefficient being returned.

```
if (paused === true) {
    paused = false;
    oldTime = +new Date();
    return {
        elapsed: 0,
        coeff: 0,
        FPS: 0,
        averageFPS: 0,
        averageCoeff: 0
    };
}
```

We calculate the elapsed time by taking the time recorded in oldTime (from the previous call to getInfo()) and subtracting it from the new time. Then, we use the elapsed time to calculate the frame rate. The +new Date() statement is equivalent to new Date().get Time();:

```
var newTime = +new Date();  // get time in milliseconds
var elapsed = newTime - oldTime;
oldTime = newTime;
var FPS = 1000 / elapsed;
iterCount++;
totalFPS += FPS;
```

```
        var coeff = goalFPS / FPS;
        totalCoeff += coeff;
```

An object is returned with useful information properties. Refer back to Table 2-6.

```
        return {
            elapsed: elapsed,
            coeff: goalFPS / FPS,
            FPS: FPS,
            averageFPS: totalFPS / iterCount,
            averageCoeff: totalCoeff / interCount
        };
    },
```

Next, we define a pause() method. This should be called before the application is deliberately paused for any reason.

```
    pause: function () {
        paused = true;
    }
    };
};
```

We can modify the original bouncySprite and bouncyBoss code to use the timeInfo object:

```
var bouncySprite = function (params) {
    var x = params.x,
        y = params.y,
        xDir = params.xDir,
        yDir = params.yDir,
        maxX = params.maxX,
        maxY = params.maxY,
        animIndex = 0,
        that = DHTMLSprite(params);
    that.moveAndDraw = function (tCoeff) {

        x += xDir * tCoeff;
        y += yDir * tCoeff;
        animIndex += xDir > 0 ? 1 * tCoeff : -1 * tCoeff;
        var animIndex2 = (animIndex % 5) >> 0;
        animIndex2 += animIndex2 < 0 ? 5 : 0;

        if ((xDir < 0 && x < 0) || (xDir > 0 && x >= maxX)) {
            xDir = -xDir;
        }
        if ((yDir < 0 && y < 0) || (yDir > 0 && y >= maxY)) {
            yDir = -yDir;
        }
        that.changeImage(animIndex2);
        that.draw(x, y);
    };
    return that;
};
```

The moveAndDraw method now accepts a time coefficient as an argument. The calculations are similar to before, but also use the coefficient. The changeImage() function expects an integer value, but this will not necessarily be the case, as animIndex is affected by the coefficient and may yield noninteger values. To resolve this, we make a copy of animIndex in animIndex2, which is adjusted to be an integer value and then passed to changeImage():

```
var bouncyBoss = function (numBouncy, $drawTarget) {
    var bouncys = [],
        timer = timeInfo(40);
    for (var i = 0; i < numBouncy; i++) {
        bouncys.push(bouncySprite({
            images: '/images/cogs.png',
            imagesWidth: 256,
            width: 64,
            height: 64,
            $drawTarget: $drawTarget,
            x: Math.random() * ($drawTarget.width() - 64),
            y: Math.random() * ($drawTarget.height() - 64),
            xDir: Math.random() * 4 - 2,
            yDir: Math.random() * 4 - 2,
            maxX: $drawTarget.width() - 64,
            maxY: $drawTarget.height() - 64
        }));
    }
    var moveAll = function () {
        var timeData = timer.getInfo();
        var len = bouncys.length;
        for (var i = 0; i < len; i++) {
            bouncys[i].moveAndDraw(timeData.coeff);
        }
        setTimeout(moveAll, 10);
    }
    moveAll();
};
```

The bouncyBoss object now creates an instance of timeInfo (stored in timer) with a 40 FPS goal. moveAll() calls timeInfo.getInfo() at every iteration to get the time coefficient and passes this to the moveAndDraw() method of each bouncySprite instance. Notice how only one instance of timeInfo is required, as it makes sense for each instance of bouncySprite to use the same coefficient for any particular iteration.

Internet Explorer 6 Background Image Caching

Still acting like the cantankerous old relative who won't go away, Internet Explorer 6 (IE6) doesn't always deal well with perfectly valid cross-browser code. Specifically, IE6 has issues with background images whereby they are not cached as they should be. This means that every time a background image is accessed multiple times, rather than reading a locally cached copy of the image from memory, IE6 retrieves it from the server again. This obviously hampers performance significantly if background images are being used for animation. If IE6 compatibility is important to you, use this simple workaround for the problem:

```
// IE6 background image caching fix.
// Include this JavaScript at the top of your page.
try {
    document.execCommand("BackgroundImageCache", false, true);
} catch(e) {}
```

CHAPTER 3

Scrolling

Browser *scrolling* is the typically mundane action of moving scroll bars up and down or left and right. You use scrolling to move a *viewport* over content that is too long to view in its entirety within the confines of the browser window or designated browser element. In this chapter, we will examine more graphically creative uses of scrolling, initially from a purely CSS perspective, and then move on to more advanced scrolling effects that JavaScript makes possible.

Why even bother covering CSS scrolling in a book about JavaScript graphics? One reason is to highlight the limitations of using just CSS versus programmed effects in JavaScript. In addition, you can add some nice touches with just CSS, and those are worth investigating.

CSS-Only Scrolling Effects

CSS can provide some basic control of scrolling content, which you can use to good effect. In the atmospheric Retro Theater sample on the CSS Zen Garden website (Figure 3-1), the main website content within the cinema screen is surrounded by div elements that contain the cinema architecture images. As the user moves the browser's vertical scroll bar, the main website content within the cinema screen (the viewport) is transformed into what appears to be black-and-white movie credits that move vertically.

How is this effect created? Using the bottom part of the theater with the seats as an example, the CSS reads as follows:

```
#extraDiv3
{
    position:fixed !important;
    position:absolute;
    bottom:0;
    left:0;
    width:100%;
    height:30% !important;
    height:110px;
```

Figure 3-1. This simple but effective use of CSS in Retro Theater by Eric Rogé creates a convincing scrolling cinema screen effect (http://www.csszengarden.com/?cssfile=202/202.css)

```
    min-height:110px;
    max-height:318px;
    background:url('bas.png') no-repeat 50% 0%;
    z-index:4;
}
```

The key to the effect lies in the `position:fixed` CSS rule, which ensures that the `div` element stays at the same place relative to the window. In this case, the `div` is positioned to remain at the bottom of the window. There are a few additional rules to ensure that the element stays within a height range.

Figure 3-2 shows a more elaborate example of CSS-only scrolling. In the Silverback website, you will notice three overlaid layers of twigs and leaves that hang from the top of the page. When the user resizes the browser window, these layers move at different speeds to give a three-dimensional effect, with the layer in the foreground moving the quickest and the farthest layer moving the slowest. This kind of effect is called *parallax scrolling* and is often used in two-dimensional video games and cartoon animation. In this instance, the entire width of the browser window is used as the viewport.

The code in Example 3-1 uses a similar technique, creating the parallax effect shown in Figure 3-3. The effect uses three images in 256-color PNG format (Figure 3-4). Notice how a blurred effect has been used on the frontmost grass image to further enhance the illusion of depth.

Figure 3-2. Parallax scrolling effect in the twigs and leaves at the top of the page (http://silverbackapp .com/)

 The images used in Figure 3-4 are 8-bit (256-color) PNG images with alpha. As well as having a smaller memory footprint than 32-bit images, they will also display (albeit without their alpha pixels) on browsers that don't support transparent PNG images, such as IE6.

Example 3-1. CSS parallax scrolling

```
<!DOCTYPE html>
<html>
<head>
    <meta http-equiv="Content-Type" content="text/html; charset=utf-8">
    <title>CSS Parallax</title>
    <style type="text/css">
        body {
            padding:0px;
            margin:0px;
        }

        .layer {
            position:absolute;
            width:100%;
            height:256px;
        }
```

```
#back {
    background: #3BB9FF url(back1.png) 20% 0px;

}
#middle{
    background: transparent url(back2.png) 30% 0px ;

}
#front{
    background: transparent url(back3.png) 40% 0px;

}
    </style>
</head>
<body>
    <div id = "back" class = "layer"></div>
    <div id = "middle" class = "layer"></div>
    <div id = "front" class = "layer"></div>
</body>
</html>
```

Figure 3-3. Parallax CSS effect with three layers

Figure 3-4. The component images of the parallax effect

The CSS in Example 3-1 defines three unique layer styles: `back`, `middle`, and `front`. The key to the parallax effect is the percentage set for the horizontal background positions for each layer. As the window changes size, the layers keep their horizontal background position percentage relative to the window width, and hence appear to move at different speeds. The width of the layers will expand to the full width of the window, with the image being repeated along the layer's length. The layers use `position:absolute` so they appear one on top of the other.

Scrolling with JavaScript

Although the CSS scrolling techniques described earlier can give some nice effects, the lack of control is frustrating: the parallax effects work only when the browser window is resized, so there is no guarantee that the user will even see the effect. However, with JavaScript, there are no limitations as to how and when scrolling effects can occur. In this section, we will examine two types of JavaScript scrolling techniques: background image scrolling and the more sophisticated tile-based image scrolling.

Background Image Scrolling

The following section recreates the CSS effect in Figure 3-3, but this time, the movement of the mouse over the page controls the direction and speed of scrolling via JavaScript. As the mouse moves to either the left or right of the page, the scrolling will accelerate in the same direction, slowing to a stop as the mouse moves into the middle of the page, or stopping completely when the mouse leaves the page altogether.

With the CSS scrolling code shown earlier in Example 3-1, the background image positions were specified as a percentage of the browser window size. In Example 3-2, the background image positions are manipulated as pixel positions.

 For convenience, jQuery is used in the example code.

Example 3-2. Simple JavaScript scrolling

```
<!DOCTYPE html>
<html>
<head>
    <meta http-equiv="Content-Type" content="text/html; charset=utf-8">
    <title>CSS Parallax</title>
    <style type="text/css">
        body {
            padding:0px;
            margin:0px;
        }
```

```
            .layer {
                position:absolute;
                height:256px;
                width:100%;
            }

            #back {
                background: #3BB9FF url(back1.png);
            }

            #middle{
                background: transparent url(back2.png);
            }

            #front{
                background: transparent url(back3.png);
            }
        </style>
        <script type="text/javascript"
            src="http://ajax.googleapis.com/ajax/libs/jquery/1.5.0/jquery.min.js">
        </script>

        <script type="text/javascript">
            $(function () {
                var speed = 0,
                    $back = $('#back'),      // Initial speed.
                    $middle = $('#middle'),  // Cache layers as jQuery objects.
                    $front = $('#front'),
                    xPos = 0,                // Initial x position of background images.
                    $win = $(window);        // Cache jQuery reference to window.


                // Respond to mousemove events.
                $(document).mousemove(function (e) {
                    var halfWidth = $win.width()/2;
                    // Calculate speed based on mouse position.
                    // 0 (center of screen) to 1 at edges.
                    speed = e.pageX - halfWidth;
                    speed /= halfWidth;
                });

                // Kill speed on mouseout.
                $(document).mouseout(function (e) {
                    speed = 0;
                });

                // Every 30ms, update each layer's background image position.
                // The two front layers use a scaled-up x position to
                // create the parallax effect.
                setInterval(function () {

                    // Update the background position variable.
                    xPos += speed;
```

```
            // Apply it to the layers' background image positions,
            // scaled up for the front two layers so they move quicker
            // than the farthest layer.
            $back.css({
                backgroundPosition: xPos + 'px 0px'
            });
            $middle.css({
                backgroundPosition: (xPos * 2) + 'px 0px'
            });
            $front.css({
                backgroundPosition: (xPos * 3) + 'px 0px'
            });


        }, 30);

    });
    </script>

</head>
<body>
    <div id = "back" class = "layer"></div>
    <div id = "middle" class = "layer"></div>
    <div id = "front" class = "layer"></div>
</body>
</html>
```

The JavaScript scrolling code in Example 3-2 works as follows:

- When a mousemove event occurs, calculate a speed based on the position of the mouse.
- When a mouseout event occurs, set the speed to 0.
- Every 30 milliseconds, take the calculated speed and add it to an x-position variable (xPos). Apply a scaled xPos to the horizontal background image position of each layer. The following scales are applied to each layer's x position: ×1, ×2, and ×3.

Tile-Based Image Scrolling

One drawback of the previous scrolling example is the use of large repeating images that are tiled across the browser window. As the background images scroll by, their lack of variety soon becomes apparent. One solution is to use much larger images, which must scroll a lot further before they repeat. This creates another problem, however, whereby the image size can soon get out of hand if the content is large. For example, say the required content area was 2,048 pixels square (roughly twice the size of a typical netbook screen). This would require a four-megapixel image—and just for a single layer. What if we want content that is 100,000 pixels square with three parallax layers? Obviously, this large-image–based approach is not practical when you require large areas of scrolling graphical content.

A more effective solution is to use *tile-based image scrolling*. A set of image tiles of uniform size (say, 64 pixels square) is reused many times over the content area. The content area effectively becomes a uniform grid of tiles, or a "map." The tiles are drawn and arranged within the map in such a way that they give the illusion of a massive, single bitmap being used. Each tile is simply referenced by an index number, and the definition of the map is just an array of these index numbers. So, a 2,048-pixel-square map using 64-pixel–square tiles would require 32 × 32, or 1,024, tile indexes to be stored. In many ways, the concept of using small repeating elements to create a much larger whole is analogous to how a simple text file works: the text file is stored as character indexes (ASCII code), not as a huge bitmap.

One brute-force approach to getting this technique working is to create a `div` element as a "handle" and attach `image` elements to it, with each `image` element representing a tile in the map. By moving the handle element around within a smaller viewport `div`, you achieve the scrolling effect. This does actually work, but there are a couple of issues that spoil this technique:

- You have to insert lots of tile elements (image elements) into the DOM. A large map might need many thousands of tiles. Big DOMs can mean poor performance and increased memory consumption as the browser struggles to handle all of the image elements, even though they might not all be visible at once.

- Each unique `image` element tile requires its own bitmap to be loaded over the network. For a handful of unique tiles, this isn't a problem; for hundreds of tiles, it can cause the page to load slowly.

The second issue is easily solved. As with the DHTML sprites covered in Chapter 2, we can use `div` elements instead of `image` elements. `div`s can reference smaller portions of a single large bitmap (or *tileset*) as their background image. This means fewer images to load over the network, and the ability to easily change the image within a tile just by changing its CSS background position.

We can significantly reduce the number of tiles required in the DOM by using the snapping technique described in the following section.

Snapping...

We can solve the problem of having a large number of tiles in the DOM by ensuring that only the minimum number of tiles required to fill the viewport is ever used. Figure 3-5 illustrates a viewport window that is 640 × 384 pixels in size. The grid behind represents the visible area of the map, composed of 64-pixel-square tiles. There is a maximum of 11 horizontal tiles and 7 vertical tiles that can possibly be displayed within a viewport of this size—77 tiles in total. This is irrespective of the size of the map, which can be huge. The calculation for determining the maximum number of tiles that can be displayed along a viewport axis is as follows (`axisSize` and `tileWidth` are measured in pixels):

```
numTilesAxis = Math.ceil((axisSize + tileWidth) / tileWidth);
```

We need a method whereby only this calculated maximum number of tiles is ever created and manipulated, regardless of the map size.

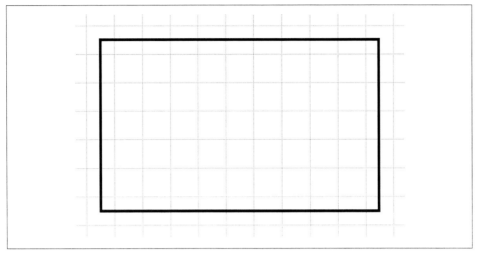

Figure 3-5. The maximum number of 64-pixel tiles displayed on a 640 × 384 pixel viewport is 77

Imagine the scroll position is increasing rightward through the map, and hence the 77 tiles are scrolling to the left. What happens when the leftmost tiles are totally outside the viewport? There are no more tile elements to the right of the viewport (even though the map extends to the right), so a blank area will be displayed—this is not what we want. The solution is to "snap" all the tiles to the right again, so that the maximum amount of scrolling is never more than one tile in size. We can employ the same method for all scrolling directions.

 What is the map scroll position? Imagine the entire map is a single huge bitmap. The map scroll position refers to the "pixel" in this virtual bitmap that appears in the top-left corner of the viewport.

How is the snap position calculated? Divide the current map scroll position by the tile width and take the negative of the remainder, as follows:

```
snapPos =  -(scrollPosition % tileWidth);
```

If the tile width was 64 pixels and the horizontal scroll position increases by 8 pixels each time (starting at 0), the snap positions would repeat as follows:

0, –8, –16, –24, –32, –40, –48, –56, 0, –8, –16, –24, –32, –40, –48, –56, etc.

The snap position is then used as either the `left` or `top` position (depending on vertical or horizontal scrolling) of the handle element that contains all the tiles. The same calculation will work for left and right or up and down movement. Snap positions are calculated separately for the horizontal and vertical axes.

You may have realized that merely snapping all the tiles to the right again will display the same part of the map again and again, with a jerking motion as the scroll position increases; you also need to change the tile bitmaps depending on the scroll position. To select the correct bitmap, you must extract the appropriate tile index number from the map. You calculate this as follows (remember, the map is just an array of tile index numbers), assuming positions and sizes are specified as whole tile units (as opposed to pixels):

```
index = map[(yPos * mapWidth) + xPos];
```

...and Wrapping

One very useful feature that you can add to tile scrolling is the ability to "wrap" a map infinitely. Without wrapping, when the map scrolls in a particular direction across the viewport, at some point the extreme edge of the map will come into view. There is nothing further to be displayed in that direction, so empty space appears; in other words, we have reached the end of the map.

With wrapping, where the extreme edge of the map is visible and the map ends, we display the tiles from the opposite extreme edge of the map again. This allows the scrolling to continue infinitely in any direction, giving the illusion of a map that stretches forever. As long as the extreme edges of the map line up with each other when displayed side by side, it all looks perfectly natural and there is no "end" to the map.

Map wrapping is perfect for situations where you need a continuous moving background effect—for example, a sky with clouds, a space background with stars and planets, or rolling hills.

Keeping things fast

Even though we've drastically reduced the number of tiles using the snapping method, a three-layer parallax scroll within a viewport of 640 × 384 pixels would still have 3 × 77, or 231, tiles. We could reduce this number by using a larger tile size. For example, if one of the parallax layers is a basic sky with a few clouds, we could probably use 128-pixel tiles, thus reducing the number of tiles for that layer from 77 to 24.

Manipulating the tiles should be kept to an absolute minimum while scrolling to ensure a rapid frame rate: precalculate as much as you can, and leave the actual scrolling code to do as little as possible. The optimizations within the scrolling code loop include:

- No function calls, especially jQuery, as the innocuous $ function can be doing a lot behind the scenes.
- Just basic loops and arithmetic.

- A reference to the style property of each tile is stored in an array, enabling you to quickly change properties such as background position.
- The background position of each tile index is stored as a string in an array in the following format: `'0px 0px'`, `'0px 64px'`, etc. You can then push these strings straight into the background position property in one go instead of updating the `left` and `top` properties separately.
- Because you only ever add the visible tiles to the DOM once during viewport setup, the browser will not try to reflow the page content or perform any other time-consuming actions during scrolling.

Browser *reflow* is the action that recalculates the positions and sizes of all of the DOM elements when something within the page flow changes. Absolute or fixed-position elements are taken out of the flow, and you can manipulate them with impunity without triggering a reflow.

Tile scrolling code

The tile scrolling code is split into two main parts:

- Initialization and precalculation
- Drawing

A single instance of `tileScroller` handles the scrolling within a single viewport. The setup parameters are passed in as an object with the properties shown in Table 3-1.

Table 3-1. Parameters passed to tileScroller

Property	Description
`$viewport`	Viewport element in DOM
`tileWidth`	Width of tiles, in pixels
`tileHeight`	Height of tiles, in pixels
`wrapX`	Whether to wrap map horizontally
`wrapY`	Whether to wrap map vertically
`mapWidth`	Width of map, in tiles
`mapHeight`	Height of map, in tiles
`image`	URL of single tileset image that contains individual tile images
`imageWidth`	Width of the tileset image, in pixels
`imageHeight`	Height of tileset image, in pixels
`map`	An array of tile index numbers

Figure 3-6 shows the scrolling code in Example 3-3 in action with three layers.

Example 3-3. Three-layer tile-based scrolling

```
// One instance of tileScroller is required for each viewport.
var tileScroller = function (params) {

    var that = {},
        $viewport = params.$viewport,
        // Calculate maximum number of tiles that can be displayed in viewport.
        tilesAcross = Math.ceil(($viewport.innerWidth()
            + params.tileWidth) / params.tileWidth),
        tilesDown = Math.ceil(($viewport.innerHeight()
            + params.tileHeight) / params.tileHeight),

        // Create a handle element that all tiles will be attached to.
        // If this element is moved, so all the attached tiles will move.
        html = '<div class="handle" style="position:absolute;">',
        left = 0,      // General counters.
        top = 0,
        tiles = [],     // Stores a reference to each tile's style property.
        tileBackPos = [], // Stores the background position offset for each tile.

        mapWidthPixels = params.mapWidth * params.tileWidth,
        mapHeightPixels = params.mapHeight * params.tileHeight,
        handle, i; // General counter.

    // Attach all the tiles to the handle. This is done by creating
    // a big DOM string containing all the tiles and attaching it
    // in one jQuery call. This is faster than attaching each one individually.
    for (top = 0; top < tilesDown; top++) {
        for (left = 0; left < tilesAcross; left++) {
            html += '<div class="tile" style="position:absolute;' +
            'background-image:url(\'' + params.image + '\');' +
            'width:' + params.tileWidth + 'px;' +
            'height:' + params.tileHeight + 'px;' +
            'background-position: 0px 0px;' +
            'left:' + (left * params.tileWidth) + 'px;' +
            'top:' + (top * params.tileHeight) + 'px;' + '"/>';
        }
    }
    html += '</div>';
    // Put the whole lot in the viewport.
    $viewport.html(html);

    // Get a reference to the handle DOM element.
    handle = $('.handle', $viewport)[0];

    // For each tile in the viewport, store a reference to its
    // css style attribute for speed.
    // This will be updated with the tile's visibility status
    // when scrolling later on.
    for (i = 0; i < tilesAcross * tilesDown; i++) {
        tiles.push($('.tile', $viewport)[i].style);
    }

    // For each tile image in the large bitmap, calculate and store the
    // the pixel offsets to be used for the tiles' background image.
```

```
// This is quicker than calculating when updating later.
tileBackPos.push('Opx Opx'); // Tile zero - special 'hidden' tile.
for (top = 0; top < params.imageHeight; top += params.tileHeight) {
    for (left = 0; left < params.imageWidth; left += params.tileWidth) {
        tileBackPos.push(-left + 'px ' + -top + 'px');
    }
}


// Useful public variables.
that.mapWidthPixels = mapWidthPixels;
that.mapHeightPixels = mapHeightPixels;


// The 'draw' function.
that.draw = function (scrollX, scrollY) {
    // If wrapping, transform start positions to valid positive
    // positions within the dimensions of the map.
    // This makes the wrapping code simpler later on.
    var wrapX = params.wrapX,
        wrapY = params.wrapY;
    if (wrapX) {
        scrollX = (scrollX % mapWidthPixels);
        if (scrollX < 0) {
            scrollX += mapWidthPixels;
        }
    }
    if (wrapY) {
        scrollY = (scrollY % mapHeightPixels);
        if (scrollY < 0) {
            scrollY += mapHeightPixels;
        }
    }

    var xoff = -(scrollX % params.tileWidth),
        yoff = -(scrollY % params.tileHeight);
    // >> 0 alternative to math.floor. Number changes from a float to an int.
    handle.style.left = (xoff >> 0) + 'px';
    handle.style.top = (yoff >> 0) + 'px';

    // Convert pixel scroll positions to tile units.
    scrollX = (scrollX / params.tileWidth) >> 0;
    scrollY = (scrollY / params.tileHeight) >> 0;


    var map = params.map,
        sx, sy = scrollY,        // Copies of scrollX & Y positions (tile units).
        countAcross, countDown, // Loop counts for drawing tiles.
        mapWidth = params.mapWidth,     // Copy of map width (tile units).
        mapHeight = params.mapHeight,   // Copy of map height (tile units).
        i,                 // General counter.
        tileInView = 0, // Start with top-left tile in viewport.

        tileIndex, // Tile index number taken from map.
        mapRow;
    // Main drawing loop.
```

```
        for (countDown = tilesDown; countDown; countDown--) {
            // Wrap vertically?
            if (wrapY) {
                if (sy >= mapHeight) {
                    sy -= mapHeight;
                }
            } else
            // Otherwise, clip vertically (just make the whole row blank).
            if (sy < 0 || sy >= mapHeight) {
                for (i = tilesW; i; i--) {
                    tiles[tileInView++].visibility = 'hidden';
                }
                sy++;
                continue;
            }
            // Draw a row.
            sx = scrollX,
            mapRow = sy * mapWidth;
            for (countAcross = tilesAcross; countAcross; countAcross--) {
                // Wrap horizontally?
                if (wrapX) {
                    if (sx >= mapWidth) {
                        sx -= mapWidth;
                    }
                } else
                // Or clipping horizontally?
                if (sx < 0 || sx >= mapWidth) {
                    tiles[tileInView++].visibility = 'hidden';
                    sx++;
                    continue;
                }
                // Get tile index no.
                tileIndex = map[mapRows + sx];
                sx++;
                // If tile index nonzero, then 'draw' it;
                if (tileIndex) {
                    tiles[tileInView].visibility = 'visible';
                    tiles[tileInView++].backgroundPosition = tileBackPos[tileIndex];
                }
                // otherwise, hide it.
                else {
                    tiles[tileInView++].visibility = 'hidden';
                }
            }
            sy++;
        }
    };
    return that;
};
```

Figure 3-6. Tile scroller in action

Creating tile maps with Tiled

Manually entering all the tile indexes for a map would be laborious and error prone for anything but the most trivial case. Luckily, there are various tile map editors available that can make the process of designing tile maps significantly quicker. Arguably, the best of the bunch is Tiled (*http://www.mapeditor.org/*; shown in Figure 3-7), an excellent open source editor by Thorbjørn Lindeijer and other contributors. It is available for various operating systems, including Windows, Mac, and Linux.

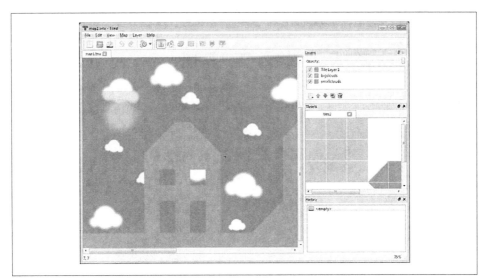

Figure 3-7. The Tiled tile map editor

The Tiled wiki offers a useful introduction to creating a map with Tiled, at *http://sour ceforge.net/apps/mediawiki/tiled/index.php?title=Creating_a_simple_map_with_Tiled.*

Tiled allows you to create multilayered maps, and in the following examples, the layers are used to create the parallax scrolling effect shown in Figure 3-6. The layers used are:

- Small clouds
- Big clouds
- Foreground

Only one tileset image is used in the examples that follow, although Tiled allows you to manage multiple tileset images. Not only does this feature help you better organize tileset images, but you could also use it to group like-colored tiles together and then save the images as smaller 8-bit (256-color) PNGs instead of 32-bit PNGs (millions of colors). This would reduce bandwidth, and you would hardly notice the lower color resolution due to the shared colors among the tiles.

Tiled allows you to create orthogonal (regular rectangular grid) maps, as shown previously in Figure 3-7, or isometric maps, as shown in Figure 3-8. To create a new map for the tile scroller, select New, and the dialog in Figure 3-9 will appear. Set the type of map required (orthogonal), the width and height of the map (in tile units), and the width and height of the tiles (in pixels).

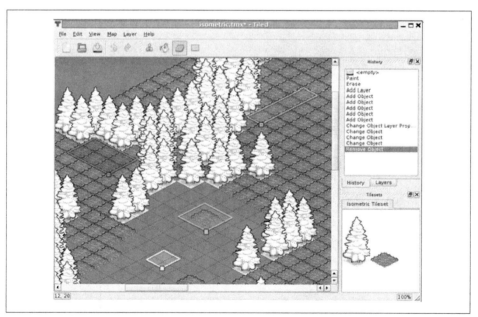

Figure 3-8. Isometric map in Tiled

Figure 3-9. Map setup dialog

Click OK, and Tiled will automatically create a map layer called "Tile Layer 1." You can rename this layer by double-clicking its name in the Layers panel. You can add more layers by selecting Layer→Add Tile Layer.

You can't do anything useful with these layers yet, because you have no tileset images to use. Select Map→New Tile Set, and the dialog in Figure 3-10 will appear. Choose a name for the tileset and browse your computer's folders for a tileset image. You can leave the "Use transparent color" checkbox unchecked if you are not using any special color to represent transparent areas in your tileset images.

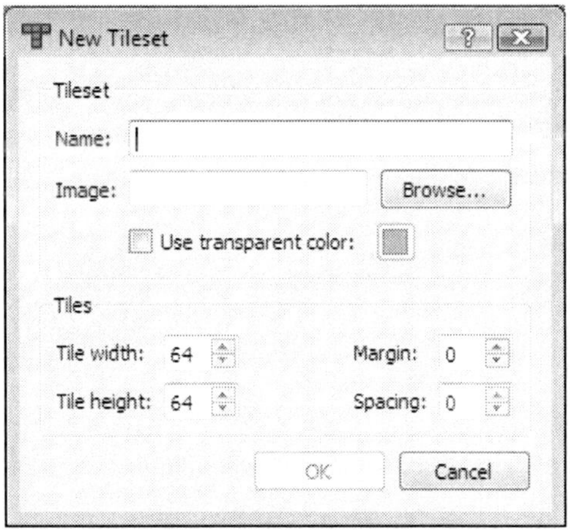

Figure 3-10. Tileset setup dialog

When the tileset image has loaded, you can select tile-sized portions of the tileset image and use them as a brush to place tiles in the main mapping area. By clicking and dragging the mouse on the tileset, you can select multiple tiles in a rectangular pattern as the brush, speeding up the mapping process where multiple tiles make up a single element in the map. For example, a building may be composed of eight tiles, and you can select all eight at once from the tileset.

Once you've created the map, all that remains is to save the Tiled map file and copy it onto the server along with the tileset image. The next section explains how the Tiled map file can be parsed and used with the tile scroller code.

Tiled file format. The Tiled file —format is XML (see Example 3-4), although the file extension used is *.tmx*. XML format files have a number of benefits:

- They are human readable, making it easy to study the data.
- They are easy to edit with a simple text editor.
- Most programming languages and libraries have XML parsing utilities.

Example 3-4. Tiled file format

```
<?xml version="1.0" encoding="UTF-8" ?>
<map version="1.0" orientation="orthogonal" width="32" height="16" tilewidth="64"
tileheight="64">
    <tileset firstgid="1" name="tiles2" tilewidth="64" tileheight="64">
        <image source="tiles2.png" width="512" height="320" />
    </tileset>
    <layer name="smallclouds" width="32" height="16">
        <data encoding="csv">
            0,1,2,3,0,0,0,0,0,0,0,0,0,0,0,0,0,0,0,0,0,15,16,0,0,0,0,0,0,0,7,8,0, ...
            <!-- Rest of data deliberately omitted -->
        </data>
    </layer>
    <layer name="bigclouds" width="32" height="16">
        <data encoding="csv">
            0,0,0,0,0,0,0,0,4,5,6,0,0,0,0,0,0,0,0,0,0,0,0,0,0,0,0,0,0,0,0,0, ...
            <!-- Rest of data deliberately omitted -->
        </data>
    </layer>
    <layer name="foreground" width="32" height="16">
        <data encoding="csv">
            0,0,0,0,0,0,0,0,0,0,0,0,0,0,0,20,22,0,0,0,0,0,0,0,0,0,0,0,0,0,0,0, ...
            <!-- Rest of data deliberately omitted -->
        </data>
    </layer>
</map>
```

Tiled can save the map data (<data> tag in the XML file) in the following formats:

- Base64 encoded
- Base64 gzip (compressed)
- Base64 zlib (compressed)
- CSV (comma-separated values)

jQuery allows you to effortlessly parse XML data, a process that takes place in the loadMap() function (Example 3-5) via the jQuery ajax() command.

For JavaScript, it's simplest to use CSV, as you can put the values directly into a Java-Script array by using the split() function on the data. Using any of the other formats would require you to add code to decompress the data and base64-decode it. However, compression may be desirable if the maps are very large—CSV data is not particularly compact but will suffice for these examples.

To save the map data as CSV, set the following preferences in Tiled:

Edit→Preferences→Saving and Loading→Store the tile layer data as→CSV

One thing to look out for when you're parsing XML files in JavaScript is that the raw data is treated as strings, not numerical values. This means that pulling out two apparently numeric values and adding them together would produce the results shown here:

```
var val1 = '64', val2 = '64';// String values as stored in XML file.
var total = val1 + val2;      // = string '6464', not number 128.
```

In other words, we end up with string concatenation, not numeric addition.

To ensure that values taken from the XML file are treated as numerical values instead of strings, place a plus sign (+) in front of them:

```
var val1 = '64', val2 = '64';// Values as stored in XML file.
var total = +val1 + +val2;    // = number 128 as desired.
```

This is a shorthand way of doing the following:

```
var val1 = '64', val2 = '64';// Values as stored in XML file.
var total = parseInt(val1) + parseInt(val2);    // = number 128 as desired.
```

In the following loadMap() function (Example 3-5), a Tiled map file with multiple layers is loaded via ajax() and parsed. After working out the required parameters from the Tiled file, it initializes tileScroller objects for each layer and creates the required viewports in the DOM. Once all the map layers and viewports have been set up, a callback is executed. Typically, this callback contains code to control the scrolling in each viewport.

Example 3-5. Loading a Tiled map via ajax()

```
var loadMap = function(xmlFile,$viewports,callback) {
    var tileScrollers = []; // Array of tileScroller instances for each viewport.
    $.ajax({
        type: "GET",
        url: xmlFile,
        dataType: "xml",
        // Success function called when map has loaded.
        success: function(xml) {
            // Get references to image and map information.
            var $imageInfo = $(xml).find('image'),
                $mapInfo = $(xml).find('map'),
                i;
            // For each layer, create a tileScroller object.
```

```
$(xml).find('layer').each(function() {
    // Setup parameters to pass to tileScroller.
    // The + operator before some values is to ensure
    // they are treated as numerics instead of strings.
    var params = {
        tileWidth: +$mapInfo.attr('tilewidth'),
        tileHeight:+$mapInfo.attr('tileheight'),
        wrapX:true,
        wrapY:true,
        mapWidth:+$mapInfo.attr('width'),
        mapHeight:+$mapInfo.attr('height'),
        image:$imageInfo.attr('source'),
        imageWidth: +$imageInfo.attr('width'),
        imageHeight: +$imageInfo.attr('height')
    },
        // Get the actual map data as an array of strings.
        mapText = $(this).find('data').text().split(','),
        // Create a viewport.
        $viewport = $('<div>');
        $viewport.attr({
            'id':$(this).attr('name')
        }).css({
            'width':'100%',
            'height':'100%',
            'position':'absolute',
            'overflow':'hidden'
        });
        // Attach viewport to viewports wrapper.
        $viewports.append($viewport);
        // Store viewport in parameters.
        params.$viewport = $viewport;
        // Create a map array and store in parameters.
        params.map = [];
        // Convert previous text array map into numeric array.
        for(i=0;i<mapText.length;i++) {
            params.map.push(+mapText[i]);
        }
        // Create a tileScroller and save reference.
        tileScrollers.push( tileScroller(params) );
    });
    // Call callback when map loaded, passing array
    // of tileScrollers as parameter.
    callback(tileScrollers);
    }
});
};
```

Tile scroller page layout

The actual HTML page for the tile scrolling (Example 3-6) contains a call to load
Map(), which initializes all the viewports and contains code for moving each scrolling
layer at different speeds (parallax effect) when the mouse moves. We accomplish this
via a setInterval call of 30 milliseconds. Notice the viewports div CSS at the top of the

page, which defines the size of the viewports, and the div itself at the end of the page. This is where all the viewports created in loadMap() will be inserted.

Example 3-6. Tile-scrolling page code

```
<!DOCTYPE html>
<html>
<head>
    <meta http-equiv="Content-Type" content="text/html; charset=utf-8">
    <title>JavaScript Tile Map Scrolling</title>
    <style type="text/css">
        body {
            padding:0px;
            margin:0px;
        }
        #viewports {
            position:absolute;
            border:4px solid #000;
            background-color:#3090C7;
            width:640px;
            height:384px;
        }

    </style>
    <script type="text/javascript"
        src="http://ajax.googleapis.com/ajax/libs/jquery/1.5.0/jquery.min.js">
    </script>

    <script type="text/javascript">
        $(function () {

            var tileScroller = function (params) {
                /*** CODE REMOVED FOR CONCISENESS ***/
            };

            var loadMap = function(xmlFile,$viewports,callback) {
                /*** CODE REMOVED FOR CONCISENESS ***/
            };

        // Call the loadMap function. The callback passed
        // is a function that scrolls each viewport at different speeds according
        // to mouse movement.
        loadMap("map1.tmx", $('#viewports'), function (tileScrollers) {

            var ts1 = tileScrollers[0],   // Get the three tileScrollers.
                ts2 = tileScrollers[1],
                ts3 = tileScrollers[2],
                scrollX = 0,              // Current scroll position.
                scrollY = 0,
                xSpeed = 0,              // Current scroll speed.
                ySpeed = 0,
                // Width and height of viewports.
                viewWidth = $('#viewports').innerWidth(),
                viewHeight = $('#viewports').innerHeight();
```

```
            // As mouse is moved around viewports,
            // calculate a speed to scroll by.
            $('#viewports').mousemove(function (ev) {
                xSpeed = ev.clientX - (viewWidth / 2);
                xSpeed /= (viewWidth / 2);
                xSpeed *= 10;
                ySpeed = ev.clientY - (viewHeight / 2);
                ySpeed /= (viewHeight / 2);
                ySpeed *= 10;
            });
            // Every 30 milliseconds, update the scroll positions
            // for the three tileScrollers.
            setInterval(function () {
                // Each tileScroller is given a different scroll position
                // for a parralax effect.
                ts1.draw(scrollX / 3, scrollY / 3);
                ts2.draw(scrollX / 2, scrollY / 2);
                ts3.draw(scrollX, scrollY);
                // Update scroll position.
                scrollX += xSpeed;
                scrollY += ySpeed;
                // Stop scrolling at edges of map.
                // This code can be removed to test the wrapping.
                if (scrollX < 0) {
                    scrollX = 0;
                }
                if (scrollX > ts3.mapWidthPixels - viewWidth) {
                    scrollX = ts3.mapWidthPixels - viewWidth;
                }
                if (scrollY < 0) {
                    scrollY = 0;
                }
                if (scrollY > ts3.mapHeightPixels - viewHeight) {
                    scrollY = ts3.mapHeightPixels - viewHeight;
                }
            }, 30);
        });

    });
    </script>

</head>
<body>
    <!-- This div will contain the three viewports -->
    <div id="viewports"></div>
</body>
</html>
```

CHAPTER 4

Advanced UI

Graphics aren't just about pretty pictures. By giving users more attractive and interesting interface elements, you enable them to interact with your pages more effectively. In this chapter, we'll discover how to mitigate the limitations of HTML form elements by using libraries or custom-coded elements to improve the user experience in your applications.

HTML5 Forms

HTML5 introduces a number of new form elements that offer increased functionality, taking some of the load off the web designer in terms of form validation and specialized widget rendering. These features enable a richer browsing experience with (in theory) no additional client-side programming required.

 Of course, while having validation on the client side is convenient, it's easy to create a spoof form that sends invalid data to a server. All form inputs should also be validated on the server side to avoid the security ramifications of malicious or junk data being processed.

The new HTML5 inputs include the following types:

- email
- tel
- url
- number
- range
- search
- color
- date
- week

- month
- time
- datetime
- datetime-local

Implementing these new input types is no different than implementing existing input types like hidden, text, or password:

```
<input type='date'>
```

Although these HTML5 facilities are a step in the right direction for cross-browser rich form elements, there are some limitations:

- Browser support is patchy, to say the least, with unsupported elements being replaced by regular <input> tags.
- Appearance and behavior will vary from browser to browser. This is important if you require a consistent look and feel for a website.

Figure 4-1 shows how an HTML5 date input element looks in Opera, Chrome, and Firefox. Opera shows a full calendar with various bells and whistles, whereas Chrome keeps things basic with just up and down buttons to increase or decrease the date. Firefox shows nothing but a regular input.

Figure 4-1. From top to bottom, HTML5 date selector inputs in Opera, Chrome, and Firefox

Opera's is obviously the best attempt at a date input (although the presentation is less than inspiring), while Chrome's looks like an afterthought. This kind of inconsistency is frustrating, and until these new HTML5 inputs produce reasonably consistent results on a cross-browser basis, we have to rely on JavaScript to create the results we want. In reality, this is not a bad thing, as JavaScript offers more exciting possibilities than the standard browser offerings.

The next section investigates popular JavaScript user interface libraries, which you can use to create highly functional web applications that look just like (or even better than!) traditional native desktop applications. Even if it is not possible to store a user's application data on a remote server, some modern browsers such as Google Chrome offer local database storage facilities as a viable alternative. You will need to keep an eye on the latest developments in this area, as support for local storage is not standardized and will be patchy.

Using JavaScript UI Libraries

While HTML5 rich input elements might currently be a little too raw to use reliably, we can use JavaScript to provide attractive and consistent results across browsers. There are two approaches to doing this: use an existing JavaScript user interface library, or create user interface widgets from scratch.

In this section, I will give you a brief overview of two of the most popular JavaScript user interface libraries, jQuery UI and Ext JS. Some people may see these two libraries as competing products (and there is invariably some overlap), but take a closer look and you'll see that they are (arguably) quite different in their intended uses. For example, if you were developing an ecommerce web application, you might find the lighter jQuery UI suitable for the frontend, customer-facing side, and Ext JS suitable for the complex backend, administration side. One big difference between the two, and an indicator of where these projects are going, is the size of the full zipped downloads (including samples and documentation): jQuery UI weighs in at a lightweight 1 MB, whereas Ext JS is a meaty 13 MB.

Using jQuery UI for Enhanced Web Interfaces

The jQuery UI library is built on top of jQuery to provide additional user interface elements. Certainly, anyone using jQuery is well advised to investigate jQuery UI, as a large chunk of the code—jQuery itself—will already be loaded on the page. You can find jQuery UI at *http://www.jqueryui.com*.

Figure 4-2 shows various jQuery UI elements styled with one of the attractive 24 themes available. In this example, we are using the Start theme. With a few minor variations, all of these elements will display correctly and consistently on virtually all browsers.

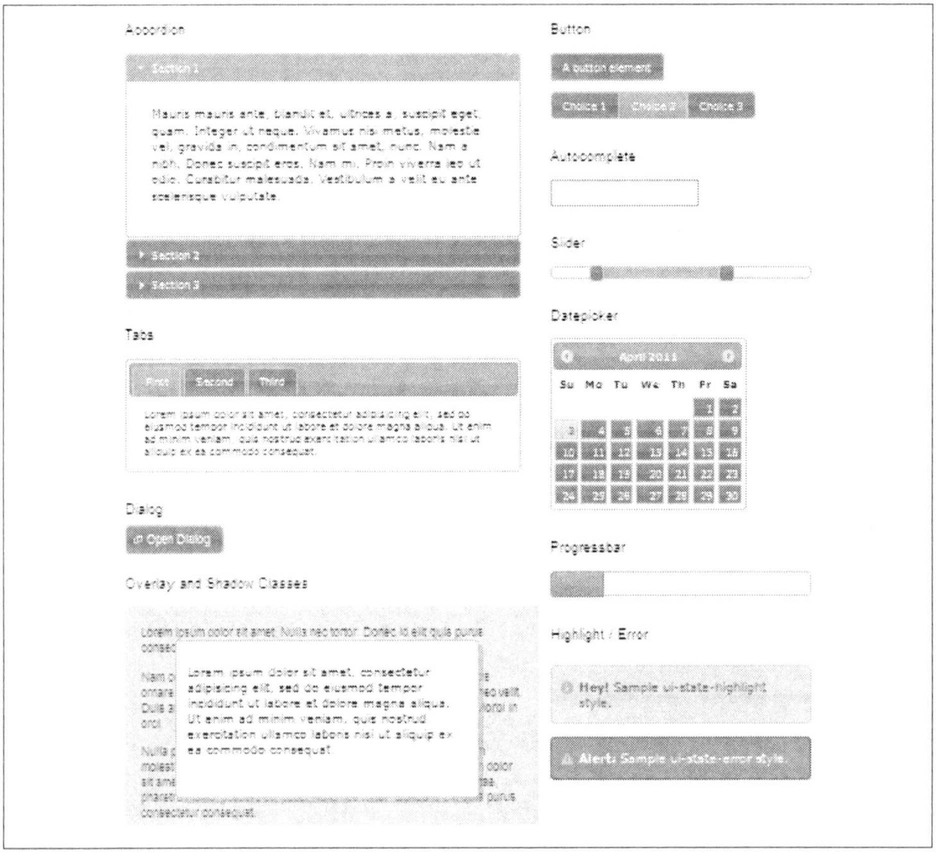

Figure 4-2. jQuery UI elements

jQuery UI currently features the following user interface elements:

- Accordion
- Autocomplete
- Button
- Datepicker
- Dialog
- Progressbar
- Slider
- Tabs

This is not a vast selection, but the widgets are attractive and stable, and additional widgets are in the pipeline. The library is easy to use, relatively lightweight, and suitable for most basic form-related and page layout tasks. To gain a realistic expectation of the library, think about it as offering an enhanced website experience rather than a heavy-duty application experience.

As well as user interface widgets, jQuery UI provides useful lower-level interactions that you can apply to arbitrary DOM elements:

Draggable
> Move elements around with the mouse.

Droppable
> Generate an event when one element is dropped on another.

Resizable
> Resize elements by dragging the edges and corners.

Selectable
> Click to highlight single or multiple elements.

Sortable
> Reorder elements by dragging them.

You can use these to create your own specialized widgets.

Loading and using jQuery UI

Installing and using jQuery UI is straightforward, with a just few JavaScript and CSS includes at the top of the page. All of the required files—jQuery, jQuery UI, and CSS themes with related imagery—can be conveniently loaded from the Google content delivery network (CDN), although you can install everything on your own web server if desired.

Example 4-1 shows how to set up a basic jQuery UI page with a single date picker widget. Figure 4-3 shows the output.

Example 4-1. Basic jQuery UI setup

```
<!DOCTYPE html>
<html>
<head>
    <title>jQuery UI</title>
    <meta http-equiv="Content-Type" content="text/html; charset=utf-8">

    <!--    jQuery UI font sizes are relative to document's,
            so set a base size here. -->
    <style type="text/css">
        body {
            font-size: 12px;
            font-family: sans-serif
        }
    </style>

    <!-- Load the jQuery UI style sheet. -->
    <link rel="stylesheet" href="
        http://ajax.googleapis.com/ajax/libs/jqueryui/1.8.11/themes/start/jquery-ui.css"
```

```
            type="text/css" media="all" />

    <!-- Load jQuery. -->
    <script src="http://ajax.googleapis.com/ajax/libs/jquery/1.5.1/jquery.min.js"
        type="text/javascript"></script>

    <!-- Load jQuery UI. -->
    <script src="http://ajax.googleapis.com/ajax/libs/jqueryui/1.8.11/jquery-ui.min.js"
        type="text/javascript"></script>


    <script>
        // On DOM loaded, initialize a date picker widget on the input element
        // with id of 'datepicker'.
        $(function() {
            $("#datepicker").datepicker();
        });
    </script>
</head>
<body>
    <!-- The following input element will be turned into a date picker. -->
    <p>Enter Date: <input type="text" id="datepicker"></p>
</body>
</html>
```

Figure 4-3. jQuery UI date input

Theming jQuery UI

It's easy to use one of the other jQuery UI themes if the Start theme doesn't suit your needs. On the line that loads the jQuery UI CSS style sheet file, change the *start/* part of the path to one of the other theme names; for example:

> *...ajax/libs/jqueryui/1.8.11/themes/ui-lightness/jquery-ui.css*

or:

> *...ajax/libs/jqueryui/1.8.11/themes/le-frog/jquery-ui.css*

Where a theme name contains a space—for example, UI Lightness—substitute a hyphen instead and convert the name to lowercase: *ui-lightness*.

For a full list of the 24 available standard themes, visit *http://jqueryui.com/themeroller/*.

As mentioned previously, in addition to linking directly to the themes via Google's CDN, you can download the themes and store them on your own server if desired.

As well as the standard themes, the Page Themes page also contains a ThemeRoller application (Figure 4-4), which allows you to modify existing themes or create new ones from scratch. You can then download and use these custom themes instead of the standard ones. Note that the jQuery UI font sizes are relative to the page's base font size, so it's worth setting up a default font size for the page; otherwise, fonts may appear too large.

Figure 4-4. jQuery UI ThemeRoller

Heavy Duty UI with Ext JS

In contrast to jQuery UI, Ext JS offers a full-on, heavy-duty user interface system. It offers a seemingly endless array of user interface functionality built into a more rigidly defined application framework. Ext JS enables the development of web applications that are virtually indistinguishable from native operating system GUI applications. It's suitable for complex backend administration interfaces (e.g., ecommerce administration) or elaborate frontend web applications (e.g., an art package). The flip side is that using Ext JS might be like cracking a nut with a sledgehammer if all you want is a couple of extra widgets and some tabbed content. Take a look at jQuery UI if your requirements are lighter.

You can find Ext JS on the Sencha website: *http://www.sencha.com*.

It is almost pointless to list the full functionality of Ext JS, as there is very little it doesn't do. Some examples on the Sencha website go way beyond basic widgets and include applications such as entire web desktops, complex data grids, and forum browsers. There are layout managers to split up and organize UI page content, as well as facilities to bind various widgets to remote data sources. Some unexpected Ext JS features include Google Maps and chart windows (Figure 4-5 and Figure 4-6).

Figure 4-5. Ext JS maps

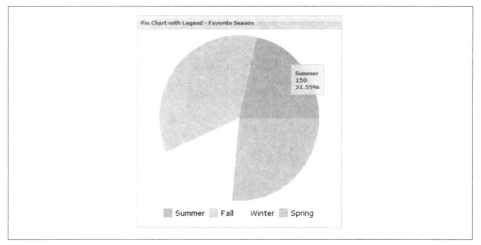

Figure 4-6. Ext JS charts

Loading and using Ext JS

Like the jQuery UI, loading the resources for Ext JS is straightforward, with the convenience of a content delivery network version of the required CSS and JavaScript files. These files are hosted on the Cachefly network, but you can install them on your own server if desired.

Although you can use Ext JS to manipulate DOM elements directly like jQuery, the Ext JS "way" is naturally more biased toward creating objects and having them magically appear on the page. In many regards, working with Ext JS is more akin to traditional, non-DOM-based application development. This method of working may have some benefits in terms of readability in larger projects. Ultimately, whether you prefer the Ext JS or jQuery way is largely a matter of personal taste.

Example 4-2 creates a window object (not to be confused with the standard DOM window) and attaches a date widget, a spacer object, and a slider widget (Figure 4-7).

Example 4-2. Basic Ext JS setup

```
<!DOCTYPE html>
<html>
<head>
    <title>Ext JS</title>
    <meta http-equiv="Content-Type" content="text/html; charset=utf-8">

    <!-- Load the Ext JS CSS. -->
    <link rel="stylesheet" type="text/css"
        href="http://extjs.cachefly.net/ext-3.3.1/resources/css/ext-all.css" />

    <!-- Load the Ext JS base JavaScript. -->
    <script type="text/javascript"
        src="http://extjs.cachefly.net/ext-3.3.1/adapter/ext/ext-base.js">
    </script>

    <!-- Load the rest of Ext JS.  -->
    <script type="text/javascript"
        src="http://extjs.cachefly.net/ext-3.3.1/ext-all.js">
    </script>

    <script type="text/javascript">

    // Tell Ext JS where to find a transparent gif image
    // (used for rendering various elements).

    Ext.BLANK_IMAGE_URL =
        'http://extjs.cachefly.net/ext-3.0.0/resources/images/default/s.gif';

    // Ext JS onReady is called when the DOM has loaded,
    // similar to jQuery's $(function(){}).
    Ext.onReady(
        function(){

            // Create a DateField object.
            var dateField = new Ext.form.DateField({
```

```
                    fieldLabel: 'Date Widget',
                    emptyText:'Enter date...',
                    format:'Y-m-d',
                    width: 128
                }),

                // Create a Slider object.
                slider = new Ext.Slider({
                    width: 280,
                    minValue: 0,
                    maxValue: 100,
                    plugins: new Ext.slider.Tip()
                }),

                // Create a Spacer object.
                space = new Ext.Spacer({
                    height:64
                }),

                // Create a Window object to attach all of the above.
                win = new Ext.Window({
                    title: 'Ext JS Demo',
                    bodyStyle:'padding: 10px',
                    width:320,
                    height:280,
                    items:[dateField, space, slider],
                    layout:'form'
                });

                // Show the window.
                win.show();
            }
    );
    </script>
</head>
    <body>
    </body>
</html>
```

Creating UI Elements from Scratch

Using existing UI libraries makes perfect sense in many applications, but there are times
when only a completely custom-coded widget will do. Frameworks like jQuery make
this sort of thing a lot easier to develop, and you can tweak the element's appearance
and behavior in a completely free manner without having to worry about it "fitting in"
with a UI framework.

Figure 4-7. Ext JS window object, date picker, and slider (partially obscured)

You can also employ some of the techniques used in the sprites and games sections of this book to create dynamic widgets; for example:

- Absolutely positioned DOM elements (position: absolute) for free-roaming widget elements
- Timers for animation (setInterval(), setTimeout())
- Background image position manipulation to reveal limited portions of a larger bitmap image

jQuery does have some animation facilities, as you'll see in the *TilePic* game in Chapter 9, but writing customized animation code gives you the flexibility to apply more interesting effects. The following section describes how to create a 3D carousel widget that uses custom animation to scale and move elements in elliptical paths.

Creating a 3D Carousel

In this section, we will develop a carousel widget plug-in from scratch using jQuery. It takes a bunch of regular HTML images on a page (Figure 4-8) and transforms them into a spinning carousel widget with a 3D scaling effect (Figure 4-9).

Figure 4-8. Regular images, ripe for converting into a carousel

Figure 4-9. Regular images converted into a 3D spinning carousel

Why would we want to do this?

- It looks nice and adds visual interest.
- Groups of images can take up less space.
- It allows a varying number of images to occupy the same space.

Carousel specifications

When developing a user interface element like this, we need to take into account the diversity of target browsers and circumstances under which the page may be viewed. For example:

- What happens if JavaScript is turned off?
- What happens if a text-only screen reader is being used?
- What happens on older browsers like IE6?

The user should be presented with the regular images (or text equivalents from `alt` tags) if the carousel cannot be initialized. It is up to the carousel plug-in to take these normal images and turn them into something more interesting if the browser environment facilitates this. It's unacceptable for the images to simply disappear in their entirety if the carousel cannot be initialized. Also, the page's HTML should not have to be compromised in terms of WC3 validation or semantics in order to use the carousel.

Although it's not one of our deliberate goals, the carousel should work with older browsers such as IE6/7. Although the popularity of these insecure browsers is (thankfully) declining, there is still a substantial minority of people using them. According to Microsoft's IE6 Countdown website (*http://www.theie6countdown.com*), a site designed to discourage use of IE6, 11.4% of Internet users were using IE6 as of April 2011.

 Although the carousel works with IE6, the PNG images used in the following example do not render correctly. If this is an issue, the simple fix is to instead use JPEG images, which render correctly on all browsers.

There should be no limit to the number of carousels that can be visible on the page. This means that we'll need to develop the widget with nice encapsulated code that can be instanced an unlimited number of times. Implementing the carousel as a jQuery plug-in makes it easy to initialize multiple carousels. We just need to wrap the carousel images in elements that jQuery can identify, and apply the plug-in call to them. For example, the following code initializes a carousel on all wrapping elements with a CSS class of `carousel3d`:

```
$('.carousel3d').Carousel();
```

These additional specifications will also improve the look and feel of the carousel:

- All images should retain their attributes and any event-based functionality attached to them.
- Links surrounding the images should not be affected by the carousel.
- The appearance of the carousel should be flexible in terms of the overall dimensions and scaling of the carousel items.
- The carousel will automatically evenly space a variable number of elements.
- The carousel elements should neatly fade in when their images load, avoiding any flickering or jerking effects as the DOM is changed.
- When the user hovers his mouse over carousel items, the carousel will stop spinning, and start again when he moves the mouse away. This will make it easier to select items.

Carousel image loading

For the carousel to be initialized correctly, we must know the width and height of the image items in order to perform all the calculations related to carousel item positions and scaling. In an ideal world, we'd know the sizes of all images being used in the carousel before they're loaded. In practice, this won't necessarily be the case, but we can find the size of an image once it has loaded by reading its width and height properties.

However, detecting *when* an image has loaded is a more frustrating task than you might expect. It is not as simple as attaching a load event to an image and acting when the event occurs. Unfortunately, image load events are inconsistent across different browsers. Browsers may or may not trigger the load event for image loading, and if they do, they may not trigger the event when the image is loaded from the browser cache instead of the network. One fail-safe way of ensuring that images have been loaded is to listen for the window load event. When this event is fired, it means that all the page assets have been loaded. The drawback of this method is that the entire page must be loaded before the user can start interacting with the contents.

It might seem wasteful to trigger the loading of images that are already specified within image elements in the DOM. In fact, there is very little overhead involved, as the images will be obtained from the browser cache if they have been loaded previously.

The following loadImage() function facilitates image-loading initialization and detection. It takes into account the various browser idiosyncrasies, enabling image loading to be initialized and executing a callback function when the image has arrived either from the network or browser cache. The function works with existing image elements already in the DOM, or with image elements created with new Image(). loadImage() expects an image element, the source URL of the image, and a callback function as arguments.

```
// Function to execute a callback when an image has been loaded,
// either from the network or from the browser cache.

var loadImage = function ($image, src, callback) {

    // Bind the load event BEFORE setting the src.
    $image.bind("load", function (evt) {

        // Image has loaded, so unbind event and call callback.
        $image.unbind("load");
        callback($image);

    }).each(function () {
        // For Gecko-based browsers, check the complete property,
        // and trigger the event manually if image loaded.
        if ($image[0].complete) {
            $image.trigger("load");
        }
    });
    // For Webkit browsers, the following line ensures load event fires if
    // image src is the same as last image src. This is done by setting
    // the src to an empty string initially.
    if ($.browser.webkit) {
        $image.attr('src', '');
    }
    $image.attr('src', src);
};
```

Notice how the event is bound *before* the image source is set. This prevents a load event from being triggered for instantly loaded cached images before the event handler has been set up.

Carousel item objects

The carousel is composed of several carousel items that spin around a central point, shrinking into the distance to create a 3D effect. Each carousel item is treated as an individual object instance, created via the createItem() function. This function performs various tasks related to handling a single carousel item:

- It triggers the initial image loading (via loadImage()) for the item (the image may already be in the browser cache).

- Once the image has loaded, it fades in, and saves the width and height (orgWidth, orgHeight) for the scaling calculations in the update() function.

- The update() function alters the item's position, scale, and z depth according to the item's rotation angle.

```
// Create a single carousel item.
var createItem = function ($image, angle, options) {
    var loaded = false, // Flag to indicate image has loaded.
        orgWidth,       // Original, unscaled width of image.
        orgHeight,      // Original, unscaled height of image.
        $originDiv,     // Image is attached to this div.
```

```
    // A range used in the scale calculation to ensure
    // the frontmost item has a scale of 1,
    // and the farthest item has a scale as defined
    // in options.minScale.
    sizeRange = (1 - options.minScale) * 0.5,

    // An object to store the public update function.
    that;

// Make image invisible and
// set its positioning to absolute.
$image.css({
    opacity: 0,
    position: 'absolute'
});
// Create a div element ($originDiv). The image
// will be attached to it.
$originDiv = $image.wrap('<div style="position:absolute;">').parent();

that = {
    update: function (ang) {
        var sinVal, scale, x, y;

        // Rotate the item.
        ang += angle;

        // Calculate scale.
        sinVal = Math.sin(ang);
        scale = ((sinVal + 1) * sizeRange) + options.minScale;

        // Calculate position and zIndex of origin div.
        x = ((Math.cos(ang) * options.radiusX) * scale) + options.width / 2;
        y = ((sinVal * options.radiusY) * scale) + options.height / 2;
        $originDiv.css({
            left: (x >> 0) + 'px',
            top: (y >> 0) + 'px',
            zIndex: (scale * 100) >> 0
        });
        // If image has loaded, update its dimensions according to
        // the calculated scale.
        // Position it relative to the origin div, so the
        // origin div is in the center.
        if (loaded) {
            $image.css({
                width: (orgWidth * scale) + 'px',
                height: (orgHeight * scale) + 'px',
                top: ((-orgHeight * scale) / 2) + 'px',
                left: ((-orgWidth * scale) / 2) + 'px'
            });
        }
    }
};

// Load the image and set the callback function.
```

```
loadImage($image, $image.attr('src'), function ($image) {
    loaded = true;
    // Save the image width and height for the scaling calculations.
    orgWidth = $image.width();
    orgHeight = $image.height();
    // Make the item fade-in.
    $image.animate({
        opacity: 1
    }, 1000);

});
return that;
};
```

The image element passed to the `createItem()` function is the original one from the DOM. Apart from some minor CSS changes and being attached to a "handle" `div` element, the image element retains any events attached to it, and any wrapping anchor elements will still work.

The carousel object

The carousel object is the "brains" of the carousel, performing various initialization and processing tasks to handle the individual carousel items:

- It iterates through all the image children of a wrapping element, initializing a carousel item for each image. It stores a reference to each carousel item in the `items[]` array.
- It listens for `mouseover` and `mouseout` events that bubble up from the carousel items. When it detects a `mouseover` event on an image, the carousel pauses. When it detects a `mouseout` event, the carousel restarts after a small delay; the delay prevents sudden stop-start behavior as the user moves her mouse over the gaps between carousel items.

Finally, we create a `setInterval()` loop that updates a carousel rotation value and passes this to each carousel item by calling its `update()` function. The carousel performs this action every 30ms (or as specified in the options in the `frameRate` property). The default value of 30ms ensures smooth animation. Larger values will be less smooth but tax the CPU less; they may be suitable if the page contains several carousels.

```
// Create a carousel.
var createCarousel = function ($wrap, options) {
    var items = [],
        rot = 0,
        pause = false,
        unpauseTimeout = 0,
        // Now calculate the amount to rotate per frameRate tick.
        rotAmount = ( Math.PI * 2) * (options.frameRate/options.rotRate),
        $images = $('img', $wrap),
        // Calculate the angular spacing between items.
        spacing = (Math.PI / $images.length) * 2,
        // This is the angle of the first item at
```

```
        // the front of the carousel.
        angle = Math.PI / 2,
        i;

    // Create a function that is called when the mouse moves over
    // or out of an item.
    $wrap.bind('mouseover mouseout', function (evt) {
        // Has the event been triggered on an image? Return if not.
        if (!$(evt.target).is('img')) {
            return;
        }

        // If mouseover, then pause the carousel.
        if (evt.type === 'mouseover') {
            // Stop the unpause timeout if it's running.
            clearTimeout(unpauseTimeout);
            // Indicate carousel is paused.
            pause = true;
        } else {
            // If mouseout, restart carousel, but after a small
            // delay to avoid jerking movements as the mouse moves
            // between items.
            unpauseTimeout = setTimeout(function () {
                pause = false;
            }, 200);
        }

    });

    // This loop runs through the list of images and creates
    // a carousel item for each one.
    for (i = 0; i < $images.length; i++) {
        var image = $images[i];
        var item = createItem($(image), angle, options);
        items.push(item);
        angle += spacing;
    }

    // The setInterval will rotate all items in the carousel
    // every 30ms, unless the carousel is paused.
    setInterval(function () {
        if (!pause) {
            rot += rotAmount;
        }
        for (i = 0; i < items.length; i++) {
            items[i].update(rot);
        }
    }, options.frameRate);
};
```

The jQuery plug-in part

We initialize carousels via a standard jQuery plug-in function. This allows carousels to be initialized on any selector in the usual way. We could define the HTML layout of a five-element carousel and three-element carousel like this:

```
<div class="carousel" ><!-- This is the wrapping element -->
    <img src="pic1.png" alt="Pic 1"/>
    <img src="pic2.png" alt="Pic 2"/>
    <img src="pic3.png" alt="Pic 3"/>
    <img src="pic4.png" alt="Pic 4"/>
    <img src="pic5.png" alt="Pic 5"/>
</div>

<div class="carousel" ><!-- This is the wrapping element -->
    <img src="pic1.png" alt="Pic 1"/>
    <img src="pic2.png" alt="Pic 2"/>
    <img src="pic3.png" alt="Pic 3"/>
</div>
```

Notice the use of a wrapping div to define which elements are actually part of the carousel. In this example, we've applied the CSS class carousel to identify the wrapping elements, but you could use any other combination of selectors. You could wrap the individual image elements with link anchor elements, or bind events to them. Links and events will continue to work when the images become part of a carousel.

To initialize the two carousels, we make a standard jQuery plug-in call:

```
$('.carousel').Carousel();
```

Or with options:

```
$('.carousel').Carousel({option1:value1, option2:value2...});
```

Here is the plug-in code:

```
// This is the jQuery plug-in part. It iterates through
// the list of DOM elements that wrap groups of images.
// These groups of images are turned into carousels.
$.fn.Carousel = function(options) {
    this.each( function() {
        // User options are merged with default options.
        options = $.extend({}, $.fn.Carousel.defaults, options);
        // Each wrapping element is given relative positioning
        // (so the absolute positioning of the carousel items works),
        // and the width and height are set as specified in the options.
        $(this).css({
            position:'relative',
            width: options.width+'px',
            height: options.height +'px'
        });
        createCarousel($(this),options);
    });
};
```

We also define a set of default options. You can override these when initializing the carousel.

```
// These are the default options.
$.fn.Carousel.defaults = {
    radiusX:230,    // Horizontal radius.
    radiusY:80,     // Vertical radius.
    width:512,      // Width of wrapping element.
    height:300,     // Height of wrapping element.
    frameRate: 30,  // Frame rate in milliseconds.
    rotRate: 5000,  // Time it takes for carousel to make one complete rotation.
    minScale:0.60   // This is the smallest scale applied to the farthest item.
};
```

Carousel page layout

The following page layout (Example 4-3) defines a single carousel with nine carousel items. For demonstration purposes, one of the items is a link (the Leonardo da Vinci self-portrait), and one has a click event bound to it (the *Mona Lisa*).

Example 4-3. Two carousels set up on a page

```
<!DOCTYPE html>
<html>
<head>
    <meta http-equiv="Content-Type" content="text/html; charset=utf-8">
    <title>Carousel</title>
    <style type="text/css">
        img { border:none;}
    </style>
    <script
        src="http://ajax.googleapis.com/ajax/libs/jquery/1.5.1/jquery.min.js">
    </script>

    <script type="text/javascript">

    // Start of jQuery carousel plug-in.
    (function($) {

        // Function to execute a callback when an image has been loaded,
        // either from the network or from the browser cache.
        var loadImage = function ($image, src, callback) {
            /*** CODE REMOVED FOR CONCISENESS ***/
        };

        // Create a single carousel item.
        var createItem = function ($image, angle, options) {
            /*** CODE REMOVED FOR CONCISENESS ***/
        };
        // Create a carousel.
        var createCarousel = function ($wrap, options) {
            /*** CODE REMOVED FOR CONCISENESS ***/
        };

        // This is the jQuery plug-in part. It iterates through
```

```
            // the list of DOM elements that wrap groups of images.
            // These groups of images are turned into carousels.
            $.fn.Carousel = function(options) {
                /*** CODE REMOVED FOR CONCISENESS ***/
            };

            // These are the default options.
            $.fn.Carousel.defaults = {
                /*** CODE REMOVED FOR CONCISENESS ***/
            };
    })(jQuery);
    // End of jQuery carousel plug-in.

    $(function(){
            // Create a carousel on all wrapping elements
            // with a class of .carousel.
            $('.carousel').Carousel({
                width:512, height:300,   // Set wrapping element size.
                radiusX:220,radiusY:70, // Set carousel radii.
                minScale:0.6            // Set min scale of rearmost item.

            });

            // Bind a click event to one of the pictures (Mona Lisa)
            // to show events are preserved after images become
            // carousel items.
            $('#pic2').bind('click', function() {
                alert('Pic 2 clicked!');
            });
    });
    </script>

</head>
<body>

    <div class="carousel" ><!-- This is the wrapping element -->
        <a href="http://en.wikipedia.org/wiki/Self-portrait_(Leonardo_da_Vinci)"
            target="_blank">
            <img src="pic1.png" alt="Pic 1"/>
        </a>
        <img id="pic2" src="pic2.png" alt="Pic 2"/>
        <img src="pic3.png" alt="Pic 3"/>
        <img src="pic4.png" alt="Pic 4"/>
        <img src="pic5.png" alt="Pic 5"/>
        <img src="pic6.png" alt="Pic 6"/>
        <img src="pic7.png" alt="Pic 7"/>
        <img src="pic8.png" alt="Pic 8"/>
        <img src="pic9.png" alt="Pic 9"/>
    </div>

</body>
</html>
```

Try adjusting the code to include additional carousels with varying numbers of elements. Add more click functionality to some of the other images, or create links out of them.

The days of web applications looking like an inadequate homage to fancy native desktop applications is long gone. With all the tools currently available, there is no reason why a modern web application cannot look even better than its desktop equivalent. Indeed, with ever-improving browsers, JavaScript performance, and libraries, cloud-based web applications are a viable alternative to traditional native applications in many situations. And with the web-based approach, users get the added benefit of being able to keep their software up to date without any client installation and update hassles.

CHAPTER 5

Introduction to JavaScript Games

On May 22, 2010, Google released its own version of the retro-classic, dot-chomping game *Pac-Man*. The game, developed to celebrate *Pac-Man*'s 30th anniversary, appeared in place of the usual Google logo on the search engine's home page (Figure 5-1). Many people initially assumed that this fun remake was created with HTML5, but a closer inspection revealed that it used nothing more than regular DHTML (excluding the sound). Continuing with the retro-classic theme, in this chapter we will develop our own DHTML game: *Orbit Assault*, a variation of the legendary *Space Invaders* (Figure 5-2).

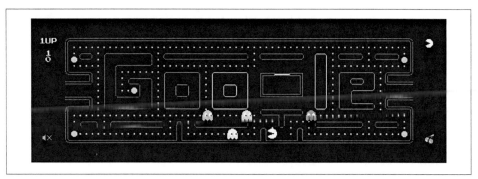

Figure 5-1. Pac-Man was a surprise addition to Google's home page

Actually creating an entire game from scratch might seem like heavy going, but it's the best way to introduce many of the concepts involved in game development.

But why limit ourselves to DHTML? Why not jump straight into using something more powerful, like HTML5 Canvas? Think of it as high-altitude training: if we can create something good with just DHTML, we are equipped to create something even better using Canvas.

Space Invaders was released in 1978 by the Japanese Taito Corporation, and was developed by Tomohiro Nishikado. He not only designed and programmed the game,

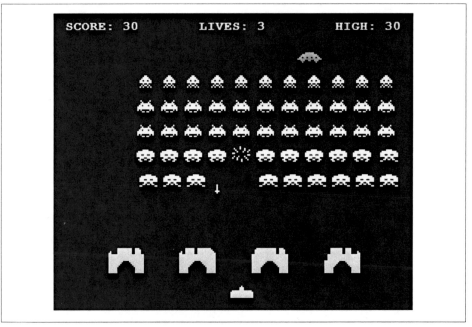

Figure 5-2. Orbit Assault, an arcade game—DHTML style

but also created the hardware on which it ran. Regarded as an icon of the video games industry, the compulsive and addictive game is still fun today.

To ensure that our DHTML *Orbit Assault* game is equally fun to play for a good proportion of Internet users, we'll set the following requirements:

- It should work on popular browsers on different hardware.
- Within reason, we should aim for a consistent speed, regardless of browser or hardware.
- We should preserve the best characteristics of the original *Space Invaders* game, including trickier elements like destructible shields.

We've done some of the work already: we will use the DHTMLSprite and timeInfo objects developed in Chapter 2.

Game Objects Overview

Orbit Assault uses six key game objects to create its addictive gameplay. The following descriptions offer some insight into the behavioral characteristics of these objects and how they interact. Figure 5-3 shows the sprite images used by the objects.

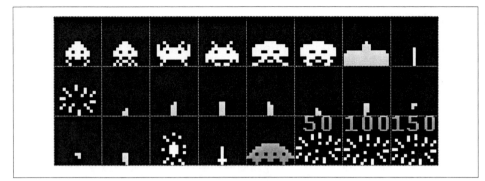

Figure 5-3. Orbit Assault uses 32-pixel-square sprites arranged in a single bitmap

Alien invaders

Probably the most memorable characteristic of the original *Space Invaders* is the hypnotic choreography of the aliens as they traverse the screen. Arranged in a grid of 5 rows and 11 columns, the aliens move horizontally until one of them touches the edge of the play area. At this point, they all descend slightly and reverse their horizontal direction. If any of the aliens reaches the bottom of the play area, the game ends.

To destroy the aliens, the player fires laser bolts from his tank. The lowest alien in each column can drop bombs, which the player must dodge while trying to eliminate each row of aliens. The topmost aliens are the smallest and award 40 points when hit. The next two rows are slightly wider and award 20 points, while the largest aliens on the bottom two rows award 10 points.

As the player eliminates each wave of 55 aliens, the next wave begins lower than the one previous. One gameplay tip is to destroy the aliens on the extreme edges first, as this extends the time before an alien reaches the extents of the play area, making all the aliens descend.

The original *Space Invaders* hardware was too slow to move all 55 aliens simultaneously, so each alien was moved in turn every game cycle (about 1/60 of a second). This is the reason for the characteristic shimmering effect of the alien group's movement, and it also produces an ingenious gameplay mechanic: the fewer aliens there are, the faster they move. This is merely a side effect of each alien's turn to move becoming more frequent as other aliens are gradually eliminated. The final solitary alien moves very quickly, as it does not have to wait for its turn at all.

One common mistake in *Space Invaders* remakes is having all the aliens move simultaneously as a solid group. This requires additional code to speed up the aliens depending on how many remain, and it also loses one of the most recognizable aspects of the original game.

Alien bombs

The lowest alien in each column can drop bombs on the player, although in practice only one alien bomb is usually visible at a time. The alien bombs can be destroyed by laser bolts fired from the player's tank. Alien bombs will damage the player's protective shields piece by piece.

Shields

The player's tank is protected by four shields, although these gradually erode as they are damaged by both alien bombs and the tank's laser. The shields are a double-edged sword: while they provide cover, they can also prevent the player's laser from hitting the aliens. One gameplay tip is to blast a narrow hole through the shields that will allow the tank's laser to pass through but still offer protection.

The shields in the original game were destroyed in small and irregular pixel stages, and this can be tricky to emulate using DHTML. In our version of the game, each shield is split into 48 separate elements, which provides a fine enough destruction resolution to provide an authentic feel, but is still sensible in terms of CPU utilization.

Player's tank

The tank moves horizontally under the player's control and can be destroyed by a single hit from an alien bomb. It can fire single laser bolts at the aliens, and its movement extents are limited to just beyond the left and right shields. The player starts with four available tanks, and an additional one is awarded every 5,000 points.

Tank's laser

The tank shoots vertical laser bolts that will damage the protective shields, destroy aliens, and intercept alien bombs. Only one laser bolt can be deployed at a time, which makes the game more challenging: a missed shot that travels to the top of the play area results in a costly delay before the player can fire another.

Mystery saucer

At random intervals, a flying saucer appears above the aliens and moves horizontally across the play area. Should the tank's laser manage to hit the saucer, the player is awarded a random bonus score of 50, 100, or 150 points.

The Game Code

This section examines the entire code for the game, deconstructing all the game elements and covering them in detail.

Game-Wide Variables

Here, the various game variables are defined; for clarity and convenience, the unchanging constants appear in all uppercase. $drawTarget refers to the play area, which is defined as a div element within the page:

```
var PLAYER = 1,
    LASER = 2,
    ALIEN = 4,
    ALIEN_BOMB = 8,
    SHIELD = 16,
    SAUCER = 32,
    TOP_OF_SCREEN = 64,
    TANK_Y = 352 - 16,
    SHIELD_Y = TANK_Y - 56,
    SCREEN_WIDTH = 480,
    SCREEN_HEIGHT = 384,
    ALIEN_COLUMNS = 11,
    ALIEN_ROWS = 5,
    SYS_process,
    SYS_collisionManager,
    SYS_timeInfo,
    SYS_spriteParams = {
        width: 32,
        height: 32,
        imagesWidth: 256,
        images: '/images/invaders.png',
        $drawTarget: $('#draw-target')
    };
```

Reading Keys

jQuery makes reading keyboard input in JavaScript relatively easy. By listening for keydown and keyup events bound to the page (document), and reading the which property of the passed event{} object after the keyboard event is triggered, we can determine which keys have been pressed or released. *Orbit Assault* requires checking for three keys—left, right, and fire:

```
var keys = function () {
```

The keyMap{} object maps event key codes to the name of the game button we are interested in. In this case, key Z is the left button, key X is the right button, and key M is the fire button. We can change these to any other desired keys (see Table 5-1):

```
var keyMap = {
    '90': 'left',
    '88': 'right',
    '77': 'fire'
},
```

Table 5-1. JavaScript key codes

Button	Code	Button	Code	Button	Code
Backspace	8	Tab	9	Enter	13
Shift	16	Ctrl	17	Old	18
Pause/Break	19	Caps Lock	20	Escape	27
Page Up	33	Page Down	34	End	35

Button	Code	Button	Code	Button	Code
Home	36	Left arrow	37	Up arrow	38
Right arrow	39	Down arrow	40	Insert	45
Delete	46	0	48	1	49
2	50	3	51	4	52
5	53	6	54	7	55
8	56	9	57	a	65
b	66	c	67	d	68
e	69	f	70	g	71
h	72	i	73	j	74
k	75	l	76	m	77
n	78	o	79	p	80
q	81	r	82	s	83
t	84	u	85	v	86
w	87	x	88	y	89
z	90	Left window	91	Right window	92
Select	93	Numeric pad 0	96	Numeric pad 1	97
Numeric pad 2	98	Numeric pad 3	99	Numeric pad 4	100
Numeric pad 5	101	Numeric pad 6	102	Numeric pad 7	103
Numeric pad 8	104	Numeric pad 9	105	Multiply	106
Add	107	Subtract	109	Decimal point	110
Divide	111	F1	112	F2	113
F3	114	F4	115	F5	116
F6	117	F7	118	F8	119
F9	120	F10	121	F11	122
F12	123	Num Lock	144	Scroll Lock	145
Semicolon	186	Equals sign	187	Comma	188
Dash	189	Period	190	Forward slash	191
Grave accent	192	Open bracket	219	Backslash	220
Close bracket	221	Single quote	222		

The kInfo{} object contains the three game button states, stored as 1 for pressed and 0 for released. You can check the returned kInfo{} object (referenced in the game-wide SYS_keys variable) at any time for the game button status:

```
kInfo = {
    'left': 0,
    'right': 0,
```

```
        'fire': 0
    },
    key;
```

The keydown and keyup events are bound to the page (document). When a keyboard event is triggered, we perform a check to see whether the key pressed is in keyMap{}. If it is, the appropriate game button state is set in kInfo{}. The return false statement prevents the keyboard events from bubbling up to the browser itself (for the keys defined in keyMap{} only) and doing annoying things like scrolling the page (if cursor keys have been used) or going to the end of the page (if space bar has been used).

```
$(document).bind('keydown keyup', function (event) {
    key = '' + event.which;
    if (keyMap[key] !== undefined) {
        kInfo[keyMap[key]] = event.type === 'keydown' ? 1 : 0;
        return false;
    }
});
```

The kInfo{} object is returned and will be referenced in the game-wide SYS_keys object.

```
    return kInfo;
}();
```

Moving Everything

Despite their differing natures, the moving objects within the game all have one thing in common—they need to perform certain actions every game cycle:

- Perform logic like checking whether they have been hit
- Update their visual and collision positions
- Change their current image if appropriate

We can take advantage of these shared requirements by giving the moving objects a move() method and adding them to a common "process" list. Moving all the game objects is simply a matter of traversing the process list and calling the move() method for each one.

Removing objects is even easier: an object can just set its own removed flag, and it will be eliminated when the process list is traversed again. We create a processor object that handles all this functionality. A game-wide processor is referenced in SYS_processor:

```
var processor = function () {
```

We maintain two lists—processList[] for objects that need to be moved, and added Items[] for any new objects that are created while processList[] is being traversed:

```
var processList = [],
    addedItems = [];
```

The add() method adds new objects to the process list. Their move() methods will be called from the process() method:

```
return {
    add: function (process) {
        addedItems.push(process);
    },
```

The process() method traverses the current processList[], makes a note of any objects that have *not* been flagged as removed, and places them in newProcessList[]. This means that items flagged as removed will be "lost" in the next traversal. Finally, we create a new processList[] from newProcessList[] plus addedItems[], and reset addedItems[] so it's ready for any new objects.

Notice that no new objects are removed or added to processList[] while it is being traversed. This makes handling the traversal loop much simpler:

```
process: function () {
    var newProcessList = [],
        len = processList.length;
    for (var i = 0; i < len; i++) {
        if (!processList[i].removed) {
            processList[i].move();
            newProcessList.push(processList[i]);
        }
    }
    processList = newProcessList.concat(addedItems);
    addedItems = [];
}
};
};
```

A Simple Animator

This general-purpose animation effect object is useful for generating spot effects like explosions. The imageList parameter is passed in as an array of image numbers to animate through, although in *Orbit Assault*, the animations are composed only of single images. The timeout parameter is the time, in milliseconds, before the animation expires:

```
var animEffect = function (x, y, imageList, timeout) {
    var imageIndex = 0,
        that = DHTMLSprite(SYS_spriteParams);
```

We define a timeout to remove the effect after the specified time:

```
setTimeout(function(){
    that.removed = true;
    that.destroy();
}, timeout);
```

The move() method updates the image number, cycling back to the beginning when it reaches the end of the image list:

```
that.move = function () {
    that.changeImage(imageList[imageIndex]);
    imageIndex++;
```

```
        if (imageIndex === imageList.length) {
            imageIndex = 0;
        }
        that.draw(x, y);
    };
```

The animation effect adds itself to the process list:

```
    SYS_process.add(that);
};
```

Collision Detection

A game like *Orbit Assault* needs only simple rectangle overlap tests to determine whether two objects are touching, but there are numerous combinations of game objects that can collide with each other:

- Laser against aliens
- Laser against saucer
- Laser against shields
- Alien bombs against tank
- Alien bombs against shields

Writing specific collision-detection functions for each combination would work, but this is a cumbersome solution. A better option is to develop a more generalized collision system that can work for all combinations, and could even be used in other types of games.

Another concern is the number of collision tests performed every cycle. One optimization is to ensure that collisions are one-way: if object A is tested against object B, there is no point in testing object B against object A. If we maintain two sets of binary flags, colliderFlag and collideeFlags, game objects can quickly determine whether they should be checking against each other at all. Table 5-2 illustrates how we might set up the collision flags for three objects. In this example, the laser will check against the saucer and shield, as it has their colliderFlag values in its collideeFlags. The saucer and shield will check against nothing, as they have 0 in their collideeFlags.

Table 5-2. Collision flags

	Laser	Saucer	Shield
colliderFlag	1	2	4
collideeFlags	2+4	0	0

A quick way of checking the flags is to perform a binary AND:

```
    doCheck = objectA.collideeFlag & objectB.colliderFlag;
```

A nonzero result means a check should be made.

However, even with this improvement, there are still a lot of tests to perform:

- The tank's laser bolt could be checking against the following game objects:
  — 4 shields of 48 elements each
  — Alien bomb
  — Saucer
  — 55 aliens
  Total = 249 objects
- The alien bombs could be checking against the following elements:
  — 4 barriers of 48 elements each
  — Tank
  Total = 193 objects

Performing a total of 442 collision tests per cycle is not good. This scenario could become exponentially worse if the collision system were used in another game with more lasers, bombs, and aliens, possibly resulting in thousands of tests being performed.

We can further reduce the number of tests by eliminating redundant checks between objects that cannot possibly be colliding. A neat way of doing this is to create a grid, where each grid square contains a list of objects occupying it. An object needs to check collisions only against other objects in the same grid square, or any immediately surrounding grid squares (a total of nine squares). As long as the largest objects fit within a single grid square, this technique will work. In *Orbit Assault*, the grid square size is 32 pixels. Figure 5-4 illustrates how we can eliminate obviously noncolliding objects from checking by using this method. Only the five aliens on the left have any chance of touching the tank, and they will be checked; the three aliens on the right will be ignored.

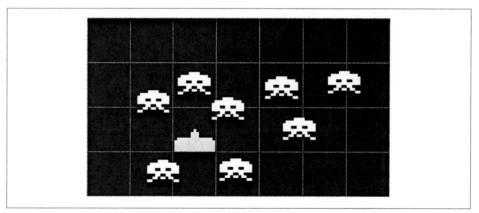

Figure 5-4. Game objects partitioned into a grid for collision detection purposes

This kind of object partitioning within a simple collision test is called *broad-phase* collision detection, and it is still a key element in maintaining speed in modern arcade games. You can employ more sophisticated methods, such as *data trees* (for optimized searching and sorting of objects), but the goal of eliminating redundant tests remains the same. Typically, a modern 3D game will perform broad-phase collision detection before applying more sophisticated geometric tests against objects.

Orbit Assault uses a collision manager object, which returns collider objects. Game objects use these collider objects to give them collision abilities. We reference a game-wide collision manager in SYS_collisionManager as follows:

```
var collisionManager = function () {
```

Next, we declare variables, including the grid itself and listIndex, which is used as a unique identifier for each collider object placed in the grid. checkList maintains a list of collider objects that need to check for collisions against others, while we use check ListIndex as a unique identifier for the collider objects within checkList. gridWidth and gridHeight define the size of the grid, with each unit representing a 32-pixel-square area:

```
var listIndex = 0,
    grid = [],
    checkListIndex = 0,
    checkList = {},
    gridWidth = 15,
    gridHeight = 12;
```

The grid is initialized with empty objects in each grid square. These grid objects will hold the list of collider objects in each grid square, with each collider object referenced as a property of the grid object. We name the properties via the unique listIndex variable. Why not use an array instead of an object? Unlike an array, it's easy to remove properties of an object (our collider objects) without affecting the indexing of the remaining properties within it. This is very handy when collider objects are continually being added or removed as they move around the grid:

```
for (var i = 0; i < gridWidth * gridHeight; i++) {
    grid.push({});
}
```

The getGridList() function accepts *x* and *y* pixel coordinates and returns the grid object that corresponds to those coordinates. It returns undefined if the coordinates are outside the bounds of the grid:

```
var getGridList = function (x, y) {
    var idx = (Math.floor(y / 32) * gridWidth) + Math.floor(x / 32);
    if (grid[idx] === undefined) {
        return;
    }
    return grid[idx];
};
```

The newCollider() function is called by game objects that need to collide with others. It accepts colliderFlag and collideeFlags to determine which other game objects (if any) to check against. The game object's width and height in pixels, as well as a callback that will be called when a collision is detected, are also passed.

Here we calculate the game object's half-width and half-height, which will be used in the collision-detection functions later on:

```
return {
    newCollider: function(colliderFlag, collideeFlags, width, height, callback){
        var list, indexStr = '' + listIndex++,
            checkIndex;
        var colliderObj = {
            halfWidth: width / 2,
            halfHeight: height / 2,
            centerX: 0,
            centerY: 0,
            colliderFlag: colliderFlag,
            collideeFlags: collideeFlags,
```

The update() method allows a game object to update its collider object's position. We calculate the center point of the game object and store it in the centerX and centerY properties. The collider object is removed from its old position grid list and placed in a new position grid list:

```
update: function (x, y) {
    colliderObj.centerX = x + 16;
    colliderObj.centerY = y + 32 - colliderObj.halfHeight;
    if (list) {
        delete list[indexStr];
    }
    list = getGridList(colliderObj.centerX, colliderObj.centerY);
    if (list) {
        list[indexStr] = colliderObj;
    }
},
```

The remove() method removes the collider object from the collisionManager grid:

```
remove: function () {
    if (collideeFlags) {
        delete checkList[checkIndex];
    }
    if (list) { // list could be undefined if item was off-screen
        delete list[indexStr];
    }
},
```

Next, the callBack() method fires the callback as specified in the original arguments passed to newCollider():

```
callback: function () {
    callback();
},
```

The checkCollisions() function runs through the collider objects in a grid square, performing various checks to see whether a collision has occurred. It first has to ensure that the collider object is not testing against itself, and then it checks the collision flags. Only then does it actually perform the rectangle tests to see whether the two collider objects are touching. It does this by checking the distance between the center points of the two objects in the x- and y-axes. If the distance is greater than the sum of their half-widths or half-heights, they are not touching:

```
checkCollisions: function (offsetX, offsetY) {
    var list = getGridList(colliderObj.centerX + offsetX,
                           colliderObj.centerY + offsetY);
    if (!list) {
        return;
    }
    var idx, collideeObj;
    for (idx in list) {
        if (list.hasOwnProperty(idx) &&
            idx !== indexStr &&
            (colliderObj.collideeFlags & list[idx].colliderFlag)) {
            collideeObj = list[idx];
            if(Math.abs(colliderObj.centerX - collideeObj.centerX) >
                (colliderObj.halfWidth + collideeObj.halfWidth)) {
                continue;
            }
            if(Math.abs(colliderObj.centerY - collideeObj.centerY) >
                (colliderObj.halfHeight + collideeObj.halfHeight)) {
                continue;
            }
            collideeObj.callback(colliderObj.colliderFlag);
            callback(collideeObj.colliderFlag);
            return true;
        }
    }
    return false;
}
};
```

If the collider object has a nonzero set of collideeFlags, it is added to the checkList for collision testing. Finally, the collider object is returned:

```
if (collideeFlags) {
    checkIndex = '' + checkListIndex++;
    checkList[checkIndex] = colliderObj;
}
return colliderObj;
},
```

checkCollisions() is the main collisionManager collision method. It tests all the relevant collider objects against one another (as defined by the collision flags) by calling their own checkCollisions() methods:

```
checkCollisions: function () {
    var idx, colliderObj;
    for (idx in checkList) {
```

```
                    if (checkList.hasOwnProperty(idx)) {
                        colliderObj = checkList[idx];
                        for (var y = -32; y <= 32; y += 32) {
                            for (var x = -32; x <= 32; x += 32) {
                                if (colliderObj.checkCollisions(x, y)) {
                                    break;
                                }
                            }
                        }
                    }
                }
            };
        };
```

Aliens

The aliens are probably the single most complex elements in the game. This section covers the various facets of their behavior, such as bomb-dropping logic, choreographed movement, and reactive speed.

Alien bombs

Alien bombs drop randomly from any one of the lowest aliens in each column. The starting position of the alien bomb (x, y) and a callback (called when the bomb is removed for any reason) are passed in as parameters. Finally, we set the bomb's image number:

```
var alienBomb = function (x, y, removedCallback) {
    var that = DHTMLSprite(SYS_spriteParams),
        collider;
    that.changeImage(19);
```

The remove() method is called when anything collides with the bomb. It creates an animated effect (a small explosion), as well as removing the bomb itself and also calling the removedCallback() that was passed in as a parameter:

```
that.remove = function () {
    animEffect(x, y + 8, [18], 250, null);
    that.destroy();
    collider.remove();
    that.removed = true;
    removedCallback();
};
```

The bomb is added to the collision system. Notice how a bomb checks only against shields, not the player; it is the player's tank itself that checks against alien bombs:

```
collider = SYS_collisionManager.newCollider(ALIEN_BOMB, SHIELD,
    6, 12, that.remove);
```

The move() method simply moves the bomb downward while updating the collision object and checking whether its position has passed the vertical level of the tank:

```
that.move = function () {
    y += 3.5 * SYS_timeInfo.coeff;
    that.draw(x, y);
    collider.update(x, y);
    if (y >= TANK_Y) {
        that.remove();
    }
};
```

The alien bomb adds itself to the process list:

```
    SYS_process.add(that);
};
```

Alien invaders

Each alien invader is pretty dumb. It does nothing more than maintain a sprite for drawing and accept marching orders from a high-level aliensManager object to move.

The alien object accepts *x* and *y* pixel coordinates and an image number. A point value and hit callback are also passed. The canFire property, which determines whether an alien can drop bombs, is initially set to false:

```
var alien = function (x, y, frame, points, hitCallback) {
    var animFlag = 0,
        that = DHTMLSprite(SYS_spriteParams),
        collider, collisionWidth = 16;
    that.canFire = false;
```

The remove() method is called when the alien is hit. If the alien has been hit by a shield, then remove() immediately returns. If the alien has been hit by the player tank's laser, it creates an explosion animation effect and sets its own remove property. Finally, the hitCallback() is called:

```
that.remove = function (colliderFlag) {
    if (colliderFlag & SHIELD) {
        return;
    }
    animEffect(x, y, [8], 250, null);
    that.destroy();
    collider.remove();
    that.removed = true;
    hitCallback(points);
};
```

The width of the alien for collision purposes adjusts to match the dimensions of the image frame used:

```
if (frame === 2) {
    collisionWidth = 22;
}
else if (frame === 4) {
```

```
        collisionWidth = 25;
    }
```

Here we create a collider object and perform an initial update to set the collider object's position:

```
collider = SYS_collisionManager.newCollider(ALIEN, 0, collisionWidth, 16,
    that.remove);
collider.update(x, y);
```

The move() method accepts two movement arguments (dx and dy) that determine the direction of movement. The sprite image is animated, and the alien's *x* and *y* positions are updated:

```
that.move = function (dx, dy) {
    that.changeImage(frame + animFlag);
    animFlag ^= 1;
    x += dx;
    y += dy;
```

Next, we perform a test on the alien's vertical position to see whether it lies on or near the shields. If it does, a new collider object replaces the old one, but this time it tests against the shields so the alien can destroy them on contact. By performing the vertical position test, we ensure that only aliens near the shields will bother checking for them, thus minimizing the workload:

```
if (!collider.collideeFlags && y >= SHIELD_Y - 16) {
    collider.remove();
    collider = SYS_collisionManager.newCollider(ALIEN, SHIELD,
    collisionWidth, 16, that.remove);
}
```

The collider object's position is updated, as is the sprite's position. Now we test whether either of the play area's horizontal extents has been exceeded. If one has, the alien returns true; otherwise, it returns false:

```
collider.update(x, y);
that.draw(x, y);
if ((dx > 0 && x >= SCREEN_WIDTH - 32 - 16) || (dx < 0 && x <= 16)) {
    return true;
}
return false;
};
```

The getXY() method returns the alien's *x* and *y* pixel positions:

```
that.getXY = function () {
    return {
        x: x,
        y: y
    };
};
```

The alien object instance is returned:

```
        return that;
    };
```

Aliens manager

The `aliensManager` object is a far more interesting beast than the aliens themselves. It choreographs the aliens to move in that classic way and decides which one will drop bombs.

`aliensManager` is passed two parameters: a callback to send messages back to the main game controlling object, and the starting *y* position of the first alien row. We set up various variables (including the main aliens list) and define a hit function (`hitFunc()`) to be called whenever an alien is hit by the player's laser bolt:

```
var aliensManager = function (gameCallback, startY) {
    var aliensList = [],
        aliensFireList = [],
        paused = false,
        moveIndex,
        dx = 4,
        dy = 0,
        images = [0, 2, 2, 4, 4],
        changeDir = false,
        waitFire = false,
        scores = [40, 20, 20, 10, 10],
        that,
        hitFunc = function (points) {
            if (!paused) {
                that.pauseAliens(150);
            }
            gameCallback({
                message: 'alienKilled',
                score: points
            });
        },
```

Here we initialize all the aliens and set up their image numbers, scores, and hit callbacks. We set the `canFire` property for the initial lowest row of aliens to `true`, ready to drop bombs. Finally, we set the index of the first alien to be moved to the bottom-right alien in the aliens list:

```
for (var y = 0; y < ALIEN_ROWS; y++) {
    for (var x = 0; x < ALIEN_COLUMNS; x++) {
        var anAlien = alien((x * 32) + 16, (y * 32) + startY,
            images[y], scores[y], hitFunc);
        aliensList.push(anAlien);
        if (y == ALIEN_ROWS - 1) {
            aliensList[aliensList.length - 1].canFire = true;
        }
    }
}
moveIndex = aliensList.length - 1;
```

Next, we create an instance of aliensManager (that):

```
that = {
```

The pause() method allows the entire group of aliens to remain static for a set amount of time; it will be called when an alien or the player is hit:

```
pauseAliens: function (pauseTime) {
    paused = true;
    setTimeout(function () {
        paused = false;
    }, pauseTime);
},
```

The move() method performs the main alien-controlling logic and is called each game cycle. It moves only a single alien (the one indexed by moveIndex) per cycle. If the aliens are paused, it immediately returns. If no aliens remain, aliensManger is flagged for removal, and a message is sent to the main game indicating that all the aliens have been cleared:

```
move: function () {
    if (paused) {
        return;
    }
    if (!aliensList.length) {
        that.removed = true;
        gameCallback({
            message: 'allAliensKilled'
        });
        return;
    }
```

If the current alien has been flagged for removal, we perform a search for the lowest alien in the same column. The canFire property for the lowest alien (if one is found) is set to true so it can now drop bombs. Finally, the alien flagged for removal is removed from the aliens list (the moveIndex is adjusted accordingly to point to the next valid alien):

```
var anAlien = aliensList[moveIndex];
if (anAlien.removed) {
    for (var i = aliensList.length - 1; i >= 0; i--) {
        if (aliensList[i].getXY().x === anAlien.getXY().x &&
            i !== moveIndex) {
            if (i < moveIndex) {
                aliensList[i].canFire = true;
            }
            break;
        }
    }
    aliensList.splice(moveIndex, 1);
    moveIndex--;
    if (moveIndex === -1) {
        moveIndex = aliensList.length - 1;
    }
}
```

```
            return;
        }
```

If the current alien's canFire property is true, it is added to a list of possible bomb-dropping aliens (aliensFireList). One of these aliens will be randomly selected later for dropping bombs:

```
        if (anAlien.canFire) {
            aliensFireList.push(anAlien);
        }
```

If the aliens are dropping down a line, there should be no horizontal movement. The current alien is moved. If the alien returns true, the horizontal extents have been reached, and we set a flag (changeDir) to indicate that all aliens must descend lower in the play area and change horizontal direction:

```
        var dx2 = dy ? 0 : dx;
        if (anAlien.move(dx2, dy)) {
            changeDir = true;
        }
```

If the current alien has reached the same vertical level as the player's tank, then it's game over:

```
        if (anAlien.getXY().y >= TANK_Y) {
            gameCallback({
                message: 'aliensAtBottom'
            });
            return;
        }
```

The current moveIndex is decremented to index the next alien. If all the aliens have been moved, the following events take place: moveIndex is reset back to the last alien; if the aliens have reached the horizontal extents (changeDir == true), the horizontal movement direction (dx) is flipped, and the next movement of aliens will be downward (dy); if no alien bomb is currently active (waitFire == false), an alien from the firing list will be randomly selected to drop a bomb.

```
        moveIndex--;
        if (moveIndex === -1) {
            moveIndex = aliensList.length - 1;
            dy = 0;
            var coeff = SYS_timeInfo.averageCoeff;
            dx = 4 * (dx < 0 ? -coeff : coeff);
            if (changeDir === true) {
                dx = -dx;
                changeDir = false;
                dy = 16;
            }
            if (!waitFire) {
                var fireAlien = aliensFireList[Math.floor(Math.random() *
                    (aliensFireList.length))];
                var xy = fireAlien.getXY();
                alienBomb(xy.x, xy.y, function () {
                    waitFire = false;
```

```
        });
        aliensFireList = [];
        waitFire = true;
      }
    }
  }
};
```

Here, the `alienManager` object instance is added to the process list, and the instance is returned in that:

```
    SYS_process.add(that);
    return that;
};
```

The Player

This section covers the relatively simple behavior of the player's tank and the laser bolt that it fires.

Tank

A callback is passed as a parameter to the tank object; this informs the main game object that the tank has been hit. We declare various variables and create a `DHTMLSprite` instance (that). We set the image number, and the tank is drawn at its starting position:

```
var tank = function (gameCallback) {
    var x = ((SCREEN_WIDTH / 2) - 160),
        canFire = true,
        collider,
        waitFireRelease = true,
        that = DHTMLSprite(SYS_spriteParams);
    that.changeImage(6);
    that.draw(x, TANK_Y);
```

The `move()` method first checks the left and right keys, setting the horizontal movement amount (dx) as appropriate. We adjust the amount of movement to the frame rate for a consistent speed on different hardware and browser combinations:

```
    that.move = function () {
        var dx = keys.left ? -2 : 0;
        dx = keys.right ? 2 : dx;
        x += dx * SYS_timeInfo.coeff;
```

Next, we constrain the updated position of the tank to the horizontal limits of the play area:

```
        if (dx > 0 && x >= (SCREEN_WIDTH / 2) + 168) {
            x = (SCREEN_WIDTH / 2) + 168;
        }
        if (dx < 0 && x <= (SCREEN_WIDTH / 2) - 200) {
            x = (SCREEN_WIDTH / 2) - 200;
        }
```

The tank is drawn at the new position, and the collider object is updated:

```
that.draw(x, TANK_Y);
collider.update(x, TANK_Y);
```

If the tank is able to fire (canFire), the fire key status is checked. We also check to ensure that the player released the fire key before pressing it again; this prevents the player from just holding down the fire key to launch lasers:

```
if (canFire) {
    if (keys.fire) {
        if (!waitFireRelease) {
```

If all the key-press conditions have been met, a tank laser bolt is created. A callback function is also passed, allowing the tank to fire again when the laser is removed for any reason:

```
            laser(x, TANK_Y+8, function(){canFire = true;} );
            canFire = false;
            waitFireRelease = true;
        }
```

If the player has not pressed the fire key, the waitFireRelease flag is cleared, ensuring that the next fire-key press will fire a laser:

```
    } else {
        waitFireRelease = false;
    }
    }
}; // End of move() method.
```

The hit() method is called when the tank is hit. It removes the collider object, removes the sprite, and sets the tank's removed flag. An explosion animation effect is initialized, and the main game object is informed that the tank has been hit:

```
that.hit = function () {
    collider.remove();
    that.destroy();
    that.removed = true;
    animEffect(x, TANK_Y, [8], 250, null);
    gameCallback({
        message: 'playerKilled'
    });
};
```

Now we set up the collider object, and the tank instance is added to the process list:

```
collider = SYS_collisionManager.newCollider(PLAYER, ALIEN_BOMB,
    30, 12, that.hit);
SYS_process.add(that);
};
```

Laser

The laser object is given an initial position (*x*, *y*) and callback for when the laser has been removed. We create a DHTMLSprite instance as follows:

```
var laser = function (x, y, callback) {
    var that = DHTMLSprite(SYS_spriteParams);
```

The remove() method will be called when the laser collides with other objects. If the laser has collided with the top of the screen, a shield, or an alien bomb, then a specific animation effect (a smaller explosion sprite) is created. The laser is then removed, and after a small delay (to further limit the speed at which the player can fire), the callback is called.

```
that.remove = function (collideeFlags) {
    if (collideeFlags & (TOP_OF_SCREEN + SHIELD + ALIEN_BOMB)) {
        animEffect(x, y, [18], 250, null);
    }
    that.destroy();
    collider.remove();
    that.removed = true;
    setTimeout(callback, 200);
};
```

Here we create a collider instance, referencing the remove() method as a callback, and the laser's image is set:

```
var collider = SYS_collisionManager.newCollider(LASER, ALIEN + ALIEN_BOMB +
    SHIELD + SAUCER, 2, 10, that.remove);
that.changeImage(7);
```

The move() method simply moves the laser bolt upward while updating the collision object. If the vertical position (*y*) moves off the top of the playing area, the remove() method is called:

```
that.move = function () {
    y -= 7 * SYS_timeInfo.coeff;
    that.draw(x, y);
    collider.update(x, y);
    if (y <= -8) {
        that.remove(TOP_OF_SCREEN);
    }
};
```

The laser instance (that) is added to the process list:

```
SYS_process.add(that);
};
```

Shields

The shields are gradually destroyed piece by piece as the player's laser or alien bombs hit them. Should the aliens get low enough, they will also destroy the shields. Each shield acts as a wrapper object for 40 "bricks."

The position of the shield (x, y) is passed in as a parameter:

```
var shield = function (x, y) {
```

Here we define the `shieldBrick` object, which accepts a position (x, y) and an image number as parameters. We initialize a DHTMLsprite using the image parameter:

```
var shieldBrick = function (x, y, image) {
    var that = DHTMLSprite(SYS_spriteParams),
        collider,
```

The `hit()` function will be called if anything hits the shield brick:

```
hit = function () {
    that.destroy();
    collider.remove();
};
```

We initialize a collider object, using the previously defined `hit()` function as a callback:

```
collider = SYS_collisionManager.newCollider(SHIELD, 0, 4, 8, hit);
that.removed = false;
that.changeImage(image);
that.draw(x, y);
collider.update(x, y);
},
```

The `brickLayout[]` array defines the arrangement and image numbers of the shield Bricks required to create a single shield:

```
brickLayout = [
    1, 2, 3, 3, 3, 3, 3, 3, 3, 3, 4, 5,
    3, 3, 3, 3, 3, 3, 3, 3, 3, 3, 3, 3,
    3, 3, 3, 6, 7, 0, 0, 8, 9, 3, 3, 3,
    3, 3, 3, 0, 0, 0, 0, 0, 0, 3, 3, 3];
```

The `brickLayout[]` array is traversed, initializing a `shieldBrick` on a 12 x 4 basis. A 0 entry in the `brickLayout[]` indicates that no brick should be initialized at that position. The positions calculated are relative to the x and y parameters passed into the `shield` object.

```
for (var i = 0; i < brickLayout.length; i++) {
    if (brickLayout[i]) {
        shieldBrick(x + ((i % 12) * 4), y + (Math.floor(i / 12) * 8),
            brickLayout[i] + 8);
    }
}
};
```

Mystery Saucer

When the mystery saucer is passed a callback to the main game object, a random direction of movement is calculated (dx), as is the appropriate starting position (x):

```
var saucer = function (gameCallback) {
    var dx = (Math.floor(Math.random() * 2) * 2) - 1,
        x = 0;
    dx *= 1.25;
    if (dx < 0) {
        x = SCREEN_WIDTH - 32;
    }
```

We create a DHTMLSprite instance and set the appropriate image number:

```
var that = DHTMLSprite(SYS_spriteParams);
that.changeImage(20);
```

The remove() function is called when the saucer has reached the opposite side of the play area:

```
var remove = function () {
    that.destroy();
    collider.remove();
    that.removed = true;
};
```

The collision system calls the saucer's hit function when the player's laser hits the saucer. The hit function also sends a message back to the main game (along with the position of the saucer), informing it that the saucer has been hit:

```
var hit = function () {
    remove();
    gameCallback({
        message: 'saucerHit',
        x: x,
        y: 32
    });
};
```

We create a collider object using the hit() function as a callback:

```
var collider = SYS_collisionManager.newCollider(SAUCER, 0, 32, 14, hit);
```

The move() method moves the saucer in the direction held in dx, updates the collision object, and checks for the opposite side of the play area:

```
that.move = function () {
    that.draw(x, 32);
    collider.update(x, 32);
    x += dx;
    if (x < 0 || x > SCREEN_WIDTH - 32) {
        remove();
    }
};
```

The saucer is added to the process list:

```
    SYS_process.add(that);
};
```

The Game

All of the game objects and game logic are tied together in a high-level game object. It performs various crucial tasks, such as calling the move() method for all the game objects (via the process object) and running the collisions tests (via collisionManager). By responding to messages from the game objects, it controls the flow of the game—detecting when all the aliens have been hit, when the player has been hit, and when the game is over:

```
var game = function () {
```

Here we declare various variables, including the text displayed on the title screen:

```
    var time,
        aliens,
        gameState = 'titleScreen',
        aliensStartY,
        lives,
        score = 0,
        highScore = 0,
        extraLifeScore = 0,
        saucerTimeout = 0,
        newTankTimeout,
        newWaveTimeout,
        gameOverFlag = false,
        startText =
            '<div class="message">' +
            '<p>ORBIT ASSAULT</p>' +
            '<p>Press FIRE to Start</p>' +
            '<p>Z = LEFT</p>' +
            '<p>X = RIGHT</p>' +
            '<p>M - FIRE</p>' +
            '<p>EXTRA TANK EVERY 5000 POINTS</p>' +
            '</div>',
```

The initShields() function creates four evenly spaced shields:

```
        initShields = function () {
            for (var x = 0; x < 4; x++) {
                shield((SCREEN_WIDTH / 2) - 192 + 12 + (x * 96), SHIELD_Y);
            }
        },
```

The updateScores() function first checks whether an extra tank should be awarded, which happens every 5,000 points. It updates the score and changes the high score if the old one has been surpassed. Finally, it writes out the updated score, high score, and number of lives text into the play area:

```
        updateScores = function () {
            if (score - extraLifeScore >= 5000) {
```

```
        extraLifeScore += 5000;
        lives++;
    }
    if (!$('#score').length) {
        $("#draw-target").append('<div id="score"></div>' +
            '<div id="lives"></div><div id="highScore"></div>');
    }
    if (score > highScore) {
        highScore = score;
    }
    $('#score').text('SCORE: ' + score);
    $('#highScore').text('HIGH: ' + highScore);
    $('#lives').text('LIVES: ' + lives);
},
```

The `newSaucer()` function initializes a new mystery saucer at random intervals between 5 and 20 seconds:

```
newSaucer = function () {
    clearTimeout(saucerTimeout);
    saucerTimeout = setTimeout(function () {
        saucer(gameCallback);
        newSaucer();
    }, (Math.random() * 5000) + 15000);
},
```

The `init()` function clears the play area of any objects and initializes a game object processor (`SYS_process`), a collision manager (`SYS_collisionManager`), and an aliens manager (`aliens`). It schedules the player's tank to be initialized after two seconds; sets off the random timer for the mystery saucer; and updates the score, high score, and lives text display:

```
init = function () {
    $("#draw-target").children().remove();
    SYS_process = processor();
    SYS_collisionManager = collisionManager();
    aliens = aliensManager(gameCallback, aliensStartY);
    setTimeout(function () {
        tank(gameCallback);
    }, 2000);
    initShields();
    newSaucer();
    updateScores();
},
```

The `gameOver()` function clears any pending timers to prevent further tanks, alien waves, or saucers from being initialized. Finally, a Game Over message is displayed, appended to the usual title-screen text:

```
gameOver = function() {
    gameOverFlag = true;
    clearTimeout(newTankTimeout);
    clearTimeout(newWaveTimeout);
    clearTimeout(saucerTimeout);
```

```
      setTimeout(function () {
          $("#draw-target").children().remove();
          $("#draw-target").append('<div class="message">' +
              '<p>*** GAME OVER ***</p></div>' + startText);
          gameState = 'titleScreen';
      }, 2000);
  },
```

The `gameCallBack()` function responds to messages dispatched from game objects. A `switch-case` block performs the appropriate action depending on the message received. However, if it's game over, the function just returns:

```
gameCallback = function (messageObj) {
    if (gameOverFlag) {
        return;
    }
    switch (messageObj.message) {
```

When an alien has been hit, the score updates:

```
case 'alienKilled':
    score += messageObj.score;
    updateScores();
    break;
```

When the player hits the mystery saucer, she is awarded a random score of 50, 100, or 150 points. The appropriate animation effect for the points given is displayed:

```
case 'saucerHit':
    var pts = Math.floor((Math.random() * 3) + 1);
    score += pts * 50;
    updateScores();
    animEffect(messageObj.x, messageObj.y, [pts + 20], 500, null);
    break;
```

If the player's tank has been hit, the aliens are paused and the number of lives is decremented. If no lives remain, the game is over; otherwise, a new tank is scheduled to reappear in two seconds:

```
case 'playerKilled':
    aliens.pauseAliens(2500);
    lives--;
    updateScores();
    if (!lives) {
        gameOver();
    } else {
        newTankTimeout = setTimeout(function () {
            tank(gameCallback);
        }, 2000);
    }
    break;
```

When all the aliens have been hit, the next wave starts 32 pixels below the previous one. The new wave is scheduled to start in two seconds:

```
case 'allAliensKilled':
    if (aliensStartY < 160) {
```

```
        aliensStartY += 32;
    }
    newWaveTimeout = setTimeout(function () {
        init();
    }, 2000);
    break;
```

If any aliens reach the bottom of the play area, it's game over:

```
    case 'aliensAtBottom':
        gameOver();
        break;
    }
},
```

The gameLoop() function is called every 15 milliseconds and operates in one of two states: 'playing' or 'titleScreen'. In 'playing' state, the game objects are processed and collisions are checked. 'titleScreen' state sits in a loop, ready to start the game if the fire key is pressed. It would be easy to add more animation or other effects to the 'titleScreen' state if desired:

```
gameLoop = function () {
    switch (gameState) {
    case 'playing':
        SYS_timeInfo = time.getInfo();
        SYS_process.process();
        SYS_collisionManager.checkCollisions();
        break;

    case 'titleScreen':
```

If the player presses the fire key, the scores, lives, and aliens' start position are reset; the game state is set to 'playing'; and a new game is initialized:

```
        if (keys.fire) {
            gameOverFlag = false;
            time = timeInfo(60);
            keys.fire = 0;
            lives = 3;
            score = 0;
            extraLifeScore = 0;
            aliensStartY = 64;
            gameState = 'playing';
            init();
        }
    }
    setTimeout(gameLoop, 15);
}();
```

The title screen start text is displayed, and the main loop starts:

```
    $("#draw-target").append(startText);
    gameLoop();
}();
```

Putting It All Together

The *Orbit Assault* HTML page (Example 5-1) is a simple container for the JavaScript source code, a small amount of CSS, and the play area element (draw-target).

Example 5-1. Orbit Assault page code

```
<!DOCTYPE html>
<html>
<head>
<title>Orbit Assualt</title>
<script type="text/javascript"
    src="http://ajax.googleapis.com/ajax/libs/jquery/1.4.2/jquery.min.js">
</script>
<style type="text/css">

#draw-target {
    width:480px;
    height:384px;
    background-color:#000;
    position:relative;
    color:#FFF;
    font-size:16px;
    font-family:"Courier New", Courier, monospace;
    font-weight:bold;
    letter-spacing:1px;
}
.message {
    margin-left: auto;
    margin-right: auto;
    padding-top:32px;
    text-align:center;
}
#score {
    position:absolute;
    top.8px;
    left:16px;
}
#highScore {
    position:absolute;
    top:8px;
    right:16px;
}
#lives {
    margin-left: auto;
    margin-right: auto;
    padding-top:8px;
    text-align:center;
}
</style>
<script type="text/javascript">
    $(document).ready(function() {

        // For IE6
        try {
```

```
            document.execCommand("BackgroundImageCache", false, true);
} catch(err) {};

var PLAYER = 1,
    LASER = 2,
    ALIEN = 4,
    ALIEN_BOMB = 8,
    /*** CODE REMOVED FOR CONCISENESS ***/
    };

var processor = function () {
    /*** CODE REMOVED FOR CONCISENESS ***/
};

var collisionManager = function () {
    /*** CODE REMOVED FOR CONCISENESS ***/
};

var DHTMLSprite = function (params) {
    /*** CODE REMOVED FOR CONCISENESS ***/
};

var timeInfo = function (goalFPS) {
    /*** CODE REMOVED FOR CONCISENESS ***/
};

var keys = function () {
    /*** CODE REMOVED FOR CONCISENESS ***/
}();

var animEffect = function (x, y, imageList, timeout) {
    /*** CODE REMOVED FOR CONCISENESS ***/
};

var alien = function (x, y, frame, points, hitCallback) {
    /*** CODE REMOVED FOR CONCISENESS ***/
};
  // aliens
var aliensManager = function (gameCallback, startY) {
    /*** CODE REMOVED FOR CONCISENESS ***/
};

var laser = function (x, y, callback) {
    /*** CODE REMOVED FOR CONCISENESS ***/
};

var alienBomb = function (x, y, removedCallback) {
    /*** CODE REMOVED FOR CONCISENESS ***/
};

var tank = function (gameCallback) {
    /*** CODE REMOVED FOR CONCISENESS ***/
};

var shield = function (x, y) {
```

```
                    /*** CODE REMOVED FOR CONCISENESS ***/
            };

            var saucer = function (gameCallback) {
                /*** CODE REMOVED FOR CONCISENESS ***/
            };

            var game = function () {
                /*** CODE REMOVED FOR CONCISENESS ***/
            }();

        });
</script>
</head>
<body>
    <div id="draw-target"> </div>
</body>
</html>
```

CHAPTER 6

HTML5 Canvas

One of HTML5's most tantalizing features is the Canvas element. Taking the form of a simple rectangular area within the page (similar to a `div`), Canvas allows you to draw sophisticated graphics inside it using JavaScript. It was initially developed by Apple for rendering user interface widgets and other imagery within the Mac operating system and by the Safari browser. Apple released its patents relating to Canvas under the World Wide Web Consortium's (W3C) royalty-free licensing terms. This means that Apple provides royalty-free licensing for Canvas when it appears within the context of W3C HTML recommendations.

This chapter covers the basics of Canvas and uses it to implement various practical applications. A fully exhaustive coverage of the tag is beyond the scope of this book, but if this chapter whets your appetite, you may wish to consider the following titles to increase your knowledge:

- *Canvas Pocket Reference* by David Flanagan (O'Reilly; *http://oreilly.com/catalog/ 0636920016045*)
- *HTML5 Canvas* by Steve Fulton and Jeff Fulton (O'Reilly; *http://oreilly.com/cata log/0636920013327*)

Canvas is a *low-level*, *immediate mode* application programming interface (API):

Low level
> Canvas provides a fast but fairly basic feature set. For instance, rectangles are the only native primitive shape. However, you can augment the feature set via Java-Script programming.

Immediate mode
> Canvas drawing instructions are executed the moment they are called; unlike SVG, Canvas has no intermediate data structure that stores a hierarchy of graphical objects before drawing. This means that drawing operations can be layered indefinitely with no degradation in performance—perfect for applications such as bitmap art packages or other elaborate "layered" effects.

The following Canvas example displays a blue rectangle:

```
<!DOCTYPE html>
<head>
    <meta http-equiv="Content-Type" content="text/html; charset=utf-8" />
    <script type="text/javascript"
        src="http://ajax.googleapis.com/ajax/libs/jquery/1.4.2/jquery.min.js">
    </script>
    <script>
        $(document).ready(function() {
            var a_canvas = $("#a_canvas")[0],
                ctx = a_canvas.getContext("2d");
            ctx.fillStyle = "rgb(0,0,255)";
            ctx.fillRect(50, 25, 150, 100);
        });
    </script>
</head>
<body>
    <canvas id="a_canvas">
    </canvas>
</body>
</html>
```

(The use of jQuery depends on personal preference.)

Canvas's low-level nature makes it a neat and simple system to use, and its speed is well suited to dynamic graphics applications. Anyone who has programmed bitmap graphics on other systems will feel at home straightaway with Canvas.

Canvas Support

The Canvas element is supported in most popular browsers, including Firefox, Chrome, Opera, and Safari. After much conjecture, on July 1, 2010, via the Internet Explorer 9 (IE9) development blog, Microsoft announced that its latest browser would support the Canvas element. Indeed, the company went one better and augmented its Canvas support with hardware acceleration. This relatively low-key announcement belies its importance: Internet Explorer still holds the lion's share of the browser market, and its support of Canvas provided the lynchpin needed to ensure developer use of the element. However, IE9 works only on Windows Vista and Windows 7; it is not supported by Windows XP (still the most popular operating system). It will be some time before the Canvas benefits of IE9 reach all Windows users.

Bitmaps, Vectors, or Both?

Canvas has a small but well-chosen set of both vector *and* bitmap commands that are suitable for a wide variety of applications. What's the difference between the two?

Vector
Vector graphics are defined by mathematical representations of lines and curves. You can fill vector shapes with color and/or pick out their outlines with a color stroke. The key advantage of vector graphics is that they can be scaled to any size

with no loss of quality: edges and detail remain razor-sharp. Vectors are best suited for imagery that contains larger areas of solid or gradient color and low detail density—typically, charts, graphs, flags, road maps, and cartoon-style images. Because of their mathematical nature, vectors are perfect for manipulating with JavaScript.

Bitmap

Bitmap images (like the ubiquitous JPEG format) are defined by a grid of square pixels in varying colors. They do not scale very well, as the image becomes blocky (pixelated) when enlarged and fragmentary when reduced from its original size. This is because individual pixels are either enlarged or lost. Some implementations of Canvas may minimize these undesirable effects by applying a blur filter. Bitmaps are best used for photographic-style imagery with significant areas of detail.

 The final viewable output from Canvas is always bitmap, regardless of how the image was generated. If you want to take advantage of sharp vector scaling, you need to redraw the image at any new scale using vector commands. Simply increasing the zoom using browser controls or enlarging the canvas with CSS will give exactly the same result as zooming a bitmap image: a blocky/blurry effect.

Canvas Limitations

There are a few limitations to using Canvas, some of which come with the low-level territory it occupies:

- The lack of data structure for visual elements means that you must create your own objects in JavaScript to update the positions and other attributes of nonstatic graphical items.
- Related to the preceding point, you cannot apply events (like mouse clicks) to items drawn within Canvas, as they do not exist as tangible entities; they are just transient drawing operations. You must program such functionality.
- You must have a good knowledge of JavaScript to fully exploit Canvas.

Canvas Versus SVG

Some members of the web standards community had initial reservations about Apple creating yet another standard for browser graphics. Surely, Scalable Vector Graphics (SVG) had this base covered already? Superficially, SVG and Canvas appear to offer similar graphics capabilities, but there is a fundamental difference: SVG is a high-level XML-based markup language, where you draw by creating XML elements with attributes to define the image, whereas Canvas offers a drawing API that you access directly from JavaScript.

You can create SVG XML manually with any text editor, or output it from a drawing package like Adobe Illustrator or Inkscape. The following SVG example displays a blue rectangle:

```
<?xml version="1.0" standalone="no" ?>
<!DOCTYPE svg PUBLIC
    "-//W3C//DTD SVG 1.1//EN" "http://www.w3.org/Graphics/SVG/1.1/DTD/svg11.dtd">
<svg width="100%" height="100%" version="1.1" xmlns="http://www.w3.org/2000/svg">
    <rect id='a_rectangle' width="300" height="100" style="fill:rgb(0,0,255)" />
</svg>
```

To manipulate the rectangle via JavaScript, you need to access the a_rectangle element and adjust its attributes as appropriate. Sound familiar? Just like with HTML, we have to go through a DOM-like structure to define visuals. What happens if we want, for example, 1,000 rectangles? That's right—we have to insert 1,000 rectangle elements into the XML. This approach is not particularly efficient or intuitive for programming-intensive dynamic graphics.

However, SVG does offer you the ability to both draw and animate without resorting to JavaScript at all, and you can edit it very simply using the plethora of SVG-compatible design tools available. Now benefiting from basic support in IE9, SVG is a good solution where vector imagery is required. Sites like Wikipedia use SVG extensively for vector illustrations.

Canvas Versus Adobe Flash

Most web users are familiar with Adobe Flash. It powers a huge amount of online advertising content, videos, and games. Indeed, there are many examples of entire websites created with Flash. It is a mature plug-in dating back to 1996 and enjoys near-ubiquitous installation on many systems. However, there are issues with Flash and developments in HTML5 (which includes Canvas) that may herald a sea change in the creation of rich Internet content:

- Flash is a proprietary format owned by Adobe. There is no charge for *playing* Flash content, but to develop it you must purchase the appropriate authoring software. Using a closed system like Flash to power web-based content is incongruous with the evolution of a free and open Web.

- Flash has its roots in the desktop PC era. It is deliberately not supported in-browser on popular mobile hardware from Apple, such as the iPod, iPhone, and iPad. Apple relented slightly in September 2010, allowing software to be developed with Flash and then packaged as native applications.

- Despite the availability of Flash Lite on some mobile devices and Flash 10.1 support on Android 2.2–powered devices, mobile users are less dependent on Flash for rich content. They can often compensate for its absence with easily downloaded native applications (e.g., the excellent Android YouTube player application) or thousands of native games.

- Popular websites like YouTube, Facebook, and CBS are now supplying their video content in HTML5-compatible formats (H.264 video).

If there is one subject that provokes a lot of hot-headed reactions, it's the HTML5 versus Flash debate. Veteran Flash developers with a vested interest in keeping Flash alive will naturally contest HTML5's ability to supplant Flash. Proponents of an open Web will argue that HTML5 renders Flash redundant.

In reality, it is unlikely that Flash will disappear anytime soon, if at all; it is too ingrained in the Web to make a fast exit, and various aspects of HTML5 are slow to be ratified. However, with the benefit of cross-browser support and familiar and free development tools, only the most optimistic Flash developers would ignore HTML5. One thing that *is* likely to happen sooner rather than later is the cessation of 100%-Flash websites. With increased JavaScript performance and libraries like jQuery, along with facilities like Canvas, there are few reasons to develop sites in this way.

Canvas Exporters

Understanding JavaScript is a prerequisite for fully utilizing Canvas, as it is wholly controlled by the language. There is no markup-based way to access its capabilities. However, Canvas exporters and converters are emerging that can create the JavaScript required to render Canvas graphics created in applications. This is great news for designers with limited JavaScript abilities, and great news for programmers too, as creating elaborate vector art with manually entered Canvas commands is tedious and error-prone.

Adobe Flash CS5+ (http://www.adobe.com/products/flash.html)
Adobe's Flash CS5+ has a Canvas exporter that allows a subset of Flash to be exported as JavaScript Canvas source code. This will benefit developers who want to cover both the Flash and Canvas bases. However, because this solution requires the purchase of the Flash authoring tool, it may not be cost effective for those who want to develop solely using Canvas.

Canvg (http://code.google.com/p/canvg/)
Canvg (Figure 6-1) is a JavaScript library that takes SVG data and draws it using Canvas. Unfortunately, the Canvas JavaScript statements are not saved in any way, and hence you must always include the Canvg library to draw the SVGs.

SVG-to-Canvas (http://www.professorcloud.com/svg-to-canvas/)
This online utility converts static SVG into a JavaScript Canvas function. It uses a modified version of the Canvg library.

AI-Canvas (http://visitmix.com/labs/ai2canvas/)
This sophisticated Adobe Illustrator plug-in (Figure 6-2) converts both static drawings and animations. If the plug-in encounters elements of the imagery that cannot be converted, rather than failing, it converts those elements into simple bitmaps.

All the image elements are converted into Canvas JavaScript functions that can be tweaked by hand if necessary.

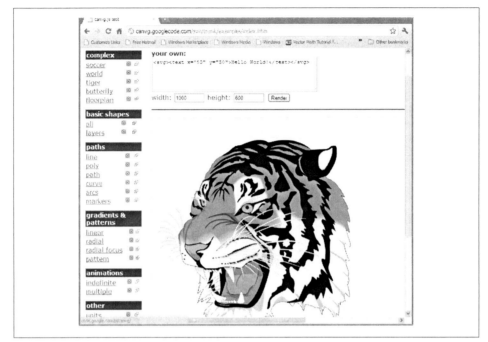

Figure 6-1. Canvg in action

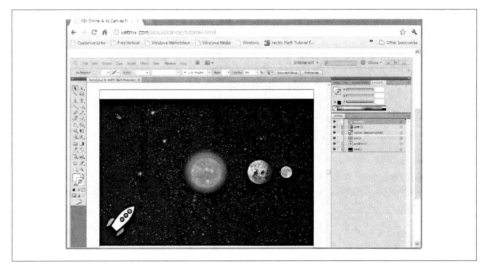

Figure 6-2. AI-Canvas also handles animations

Canvas Drawing Basics

The basic Canvas drawing commands are straightforward to implement and are discussed in the following sections.

The Canvas Element

Inserting a Canvas element into a web page is no different than inserting any other HTML element:

```
<canvas id = 'mycanvas' width = 512 height = 384>
    Fallback content
</canvas>
```

If you don't specify any `width` or `height` attributes, the default size will be 300 × 150 pixels. It *is* possible to change the canvas size via CSS (e.g., `width:50%`), but it's not recommended; depending on the browser implementation, the output may become distorted or scaled. However, you can style the element with the usual borders, margins, and background colors, although this in no way affects drawing to the canvas itself. The coordinate system has its default origin in the top left—coordinate (0,0)—so, for example, something drawn at coordinate (10, 15) would be positioned 10 pixels from the left and 15 pixels from the top.

If Canvas is not available to the browser, the fallback content between the start and end tags is displayed. Ideally, this should be the regular text or HTML representation of the data that was to be displayed by Canvas. For example, where Canvas might have displayed a pie chart, the fallback content would display a regular table. There are situations where fallback content simply cannot replace Canvas; games and drawing applications don't have non-Canvas equivalents. In these cases, the fallback content should display a useful message explaining to the user that Canvas is not available and the browser should be upgraded.

Solely placing Canvas into a page gives us no functionality; it must be controlled by JavaScript to do anything useful. You will rarely see Canvas being used without an `id` attribute, as this attribute is how scripts identify it. Typically, JavaScript will get a "handle" variable to Canvas like this:

```
var canvas = document.getElementById('mycanvas');
// Or, using jQuery:
var canvas = $('#mycanvas')[0];
```

The Drawing Context

We must obtain a "drawing context" from Canvas before we can use drawing commands:

```
var canvas = document.getElementById('mycanvas');
var ctx = canvas.getContext('2d');
```

Although it is not an official recommendation, you'll often see `ctx` used to refer to the drawing context in example Canvas code.

 There is also a 3D drawing context available that gives you access to the currently experimental WebGL interface. WebGL is based on the OpenGL ES 2.0 standard (a pared-down version of OpenGL) and provides 3D graphics capabilities via JavaScript. It is available in the development versions of most browsers. OpenGL is really a set of low-level functions that still require you to do a fair amount of work to create a 3D application.

There was some initial doubt in the web community about whether JavaScript was capable of managing the hierarchy of objects in a more than trivial 3D scene; regardless of whether or not the objects are being drawn by WebGL, numerous other calculations are required to manage a 3D application or game. However, with the ongoing improvements in JavaScript performance, the language has inspired more confidence, and various higher-level 3D libraries have emerged that can simplify 3D application development. All of these libraries are built on top of WebGL:

- O3d (originally a plug-in, but now a JavaScript library)
- GLGE
- C3DL
- SpiderGL
- SceneJS
- Processing.js

Drawing Rectangles

Canvas is not overtly generous in its built-in shape-drawing offerings—in fact, we are limited to rectangles:

```
// Draw a 100 by 150 pixel filled rectangle at coordinate (10,10).
ctx.fillRect(10,10,100,150);

// Draw a 100 by 150 pixel outlined rectangle at coordinate (10,10).
ctx.strokeRect(10,10,100,150);

// Clear a 100 by 150 pixel rectangle at coordinate (10,10).
ctx.clearRect(10,10,100,150);
```

The apparent bias toward rectangles isn't a problem, though, because we can create all other shapes by using paths defined by combinations of lines and curves.

Drawing Paths with Lines and Curves

A path defines a shape that can then be filled and/or stroked with an outline. Canvas includes the following functions to perform path drawing:

Function	Description
beginPath()	Starts a new path
moveTo()	Sets the current position of the path
lineTo()	Defines a line from the current position
arc()	Defines an arc (portions of a circle)
arcTo()	Defines an arc from the current position
quadraticCurveTo()	Defines a quadratic curve from the current position
bezierCurveTo()	Defines a Bézier curve from the current position
closePath()	Ends a path
stroke()	Strokes a path with an outline

An important thing to note is that the drawing position where one "to" command (lineTo(), bezierCurveTo(), etc.) *ends* also defines where the next "to" command's drawing position *begins*. It can be useful to think of the "to" commands as drawing with a pencil without being able to lift it off the paper. The moveTo() command allows you to lift the pencil off the paper and position it somewhere else before drawing again.

The following example uses lines to draw a filled triangle in the top left and a stroked triangle in the bottom right (Figure 6-3), assuming a canvas size of 500 × 500 pixels:

```
// Draw a filled triangle, top-left.
ctx.beginPath();
ctx.moveTo(20,20);
ctx.lineTo(470,20);
ctx.lineTo(20,470);
ctx.fill();
    // Draw a stroked triangle, bottom-right.
ctx.beginPath();
ctx.moveTo(180,30);
ctx.lineTo(480,480);
ctx.lineTo(30,480);
ctx.closePath();
ctx.stroke();
```

Notice how you don't need a closePath() command for the filled triangle, as fill() automatically closes the path.

Canvas allows you to specify fractional pixel positions. You may find this odd at first glance, as pixels are unit elements and obviously cannot be subdivided. However, Canvas uses anti-aliasing techniques to give the illusion that fractional pixel positions exist. This allows for cleaner-looking edges and smoother movement, especially where shapes move slowly.

Figure 6-3. Filled and stroked triangles

You can use the arc() command to draw circles, or portions of circles:

```
arc(x, y, radius, startAngle, endAngle, anticlockwise);
```

The parameters are as follows:

x,y
> The position of the center of the circle.

radius
> The radius in pixels.

startAngle, endAngle
> The drawing will "sweep" between these two angles. The angles are defined in radians, with 2π (approximately 6.282) radians equivalent to 360 degrees.

anticlockwise
> The direction in which to draw the arc.

Here are the calculations required to convert to and from radians:

```
var radians = degrees * Math.PI / 180;
```

And from radians to degrees:

```
var degrees = radians * 180 / Math.PI;
```

The following code draws two rows of circles, each starting at 0 radians and increasing the endAngle for each circle. The top row is drawn clockwise, and the bottom is drawn anticlockwise (Figure 6-4).

```
var endAngle = 0.0;
for (var x = 50; x < 500; x += 100) {
    ctx.beginPath();
    ctx.moveTo(x, 190);
    endAngle += (2 * Math.PI) / 5;
    ctx.arc(x, 190, 50, 0, endAngle, false);
    ctx.fill();
}
endAngle = 0.0;
for (x = 50; x < 500; x += 100) {
    ctx.beginPath();
    ctx.moveTo(x, 310);
    endAngle += (2 * Math.PI) / 5;
    ctx.arc(x, 310, 50, 0, endAngle, true);
    ctx.fill();
}
```

Figure 6-4. Arcs drawn with increasing end angle, clockwise (top row) and anticlockwise (bottom row)

 If moveTo() is not used to position the start of an arc, a line will be drawn between the last drawing position and the start of the new arc.

The arcTo() command is similar to the arc() command, but we specify the curve in a different way:

```
arcTo(x1,y1, x2,y2, radius);
```

The curve is defined by two lines, the first from the current position to point (x1,y1), and the second from point (x1,y1) to point (x2,y2). Defining a curve this way makes it easy to create rounded corners between lines. The curve will occupy the corner where the two lines join.

The following function draws rectangles of any size (w,h) with rounded corners. The corner radius (in radians) is defined by the parameter cr.

```
var drawRoundedRect = function (ctx, x, y, w, h, cr) {
    ctx.beginPath();
    ctx.moveTo(x + w / 2, y);              // Start in the middle of the top edge.
    ctx.arcTo(x + w, y, x + w, y + h, cr); // Top edge and upper-right corner.
    ctx.arcTo(x + w, y + h, x, y + h, cr); // Right edge and lower-right corner.
    ctx.arcTo(x, y + h, x, y, cr);         // Bottom edge and lower-left corner
    ctx.arcTo(x, y, x + w, y, cr);         // Left edge and upper-left corner.
    ctx.closePath();
    ctx.stroke();
};
```

Figure 6-5 shows the results of calling the function with various corner radii, starting at a corner radius of 0 radians and increasing by 2π radians for each square.

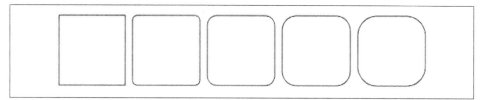

Figure 6-5. Squares drawn with rounded corners utilizing the arcTo() command

The following page code shows how drawRoundedRect() is actually called within a loop to give the output shown in Figure 6-5:

```
<!DOCTYPE html>
<html>

    <head>
        <title>
            Canvas Rounded Rectangles
        </title>
        <script type="text/javascript">
            window.onload = function() {
                var canvas = document.getElementById('mycanvas');
                var ctx = canvas.getContext('2d');

                var drawRoundedRect = function(ctx, x, y, w, h, cr) {
                    ctx.beginPath();
                    ctx.moveTo(x + w / 2, y);
                    ctx.arcTo(x + w, y, x + w, y + h, cr);
                    ctx.arcTo(x + w, y + h, x, y + h, cr);
                    ctx.arcTo(x, y + h, x, y, cr);
                    ctx.arcTo(x, y, x + w, y, cr);
                    ctx.closePath();
                    ctx.stroke();
```

```
                };

                var cr = 0;
                for (x = 0; x < 500; x += 100) {
                    drawRoundedRect(ctx, x + 5,
                        ctx.canvas.height / 2 - 45, 90, 90, cr);
                    cr += Math.PI * 2;
                }

            };
        </script>
        <style type="text/css">
            #mycanvas {border:1px solid;}
        </style>
    </head>

    <body>
        <canvas id="mycanvas" width=5 00, height=5 00>
        </canvas>
    </body>

</html>
```

The enticingly named `quadtraticCurveTo()` and `bezierCurveTo()` commands enable us to draw the curves with one or two control points. The control points allow the curve to be bent and shaped beyond the symmetrical curves of the `arc()` and `arcTo()` commands. We usually find these types of curves in the vector drawing facilities of packages such as Photoshop, Freehand, and Inkscape. Using the curves in JavaScript can be tricky, as we get no visual feedback on the positions of the control points and the effect they have on the curves.

The following page code displays a quadratic curve at the top, and a Bézier curve at the bottom of a canvas (Figure 6-6). It also displays the control points, which can be dragged around with the mouse. It uses the jQuery UI "draggable" functionality to move the control points. Note how the control points are actually regular div elements rather than Canvas paths. It is perfectly legitimate, and often useful, to combine regular DOM elements with Canvas in this way:

```
<!DOCTYPE html>
<html>

    <head>
        <script type="text/javascript"
            src="http://ajax.googleapis.com/ajax/libs/jquery/1.4.2/jquery.min.js">
        </script>
        <script type="text/javascript"
            src="http://ajax.googleapis.com/ajax/libs/jqueryui/1.8.0/jquery-ui.min.js">
        </script>
        <script type="text/javascript">
            $(function() {
                var canvas = document.getElementById('mycanvas');
                var ctx = canvas.getContext('2d');
```

```
            $('.dragger').draggable({
                cursor: 'crosshair'
            });
            // Trapping the 'mousedown' event and returning false
            // prevents the text select caret from appearing.
            $('.dragger').bind("mousedown", function() {
                return false;
            });
            $('.dragger').bind("drag", function() {

                ctx.clearRect(0, 0, canvas.width, canvas.height);
                var canvasX = $(canvas).position().left,
                    canvasY = $(canvas).position().top,
                    cpx1, cpy1, cpx2, cpy2, $dragr = $('#dragger1');
                // The control point positions are made relative to the canvas,
                // although this calculation is not strictly necessary for
                // this demonstration, as the canvas is in the top-left of the
                // page.
                cpx1 = $dragr.position().left - canvasX;
                cpy1 = $dragr.position().top - canvasY;

                // Draw the quadratic curve (one control point).
                ctx.beginPath();
                ctx.moveTo(50, 150);
                ctx.quadraticCurveTo(cpx1, cpy1, 450, 150);
                ctx.closePath();
                ctx.stroke();

                // Get the position of the other two control points.
                $dragr = $('#dragger2');
                cpx1 = $dragr.position().left - canvasX;
                cpy1 = $dragr.position().top - canvasY;
                $dragr = $('#dragger3');
                cpx2 = $dragr.position().left - canvasX;
                cpy2 = $dragr.position().top - canvasY;

                // Draw the Bezier curve (two control points).
                ctx.beginPath();
                ctx.moveTo(50, 350);
                ctx.bezierCurveTo(cpx1, cpy1, cpx2, cpy2, 450, 350);
                ctx.closePath();
                ctx.stroke();
            });

            // Trigger an initial drag event so the curves are drawn.
            $('.dragger').trigger("drag");

        });
    </script>
    <style type="text/css">
        .dragger {width:10px; height:10px;z-index:1}
        #mycanvas {border:1px solid;position:absolute;top:0px;}
    </style>
</head>
```

```
<body style="position:relative;">
    <div class="dragger" id="dragger1" style="background-color:#f00;">
    </div>
    <div class="dragger" id="dragger2" style="background-color:#0f0;">
    </div>
    <div class="dragger" id="dragger3" style="background-color:#00f;">
    </div>
    <canvas id="mycanvas" width=500, height=500>
    </canvas>
</body>
</html>
```

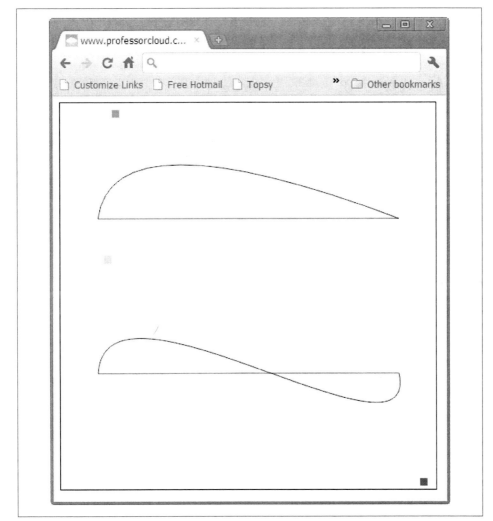

Figure 6-6. Quadratic curve (top) with one control point; Bézier curve (bottom) with two control points

Drawing Bitmap Images

We draw bitmap images via the `drawImage()` command. It comes in three-, five-, and nine-parameter flavors. In all cases, the first parameter specifies an image source that provides the pixel data for drawing. The image source can be an image loaded with `Image()`, a regular `<img>` tag, or even another Canvas or `<video>` tag. This flexibility in specifying an image source gives you great creative potential: for example, Figure 6-7 shows a `<video>` tag being used as the image source for an "explode" effect on a video stream, whereas Figure 6-8 shows a random portion of a large source bitmap being used to create natural-looking animated nebula clouds.

 If performance becomes an issue when you're using `drawImage()`, it may be beneficial to ensure that the image source is another Canvas tag. This prevents any image conversion overhead on certain browsers. For example, the video "explode" effect shown in Figure 6-7 copies the video image to a Canvas element before splitting into small tiles with `draw Image()`.

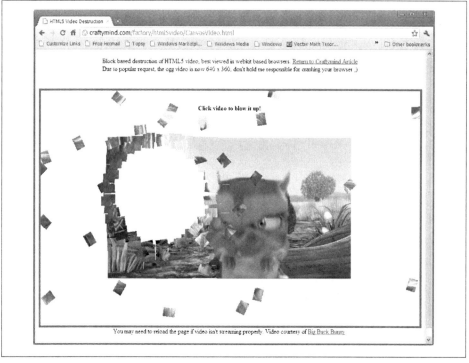

Figure 6-7. Using a `<video>` tag as a bitmap image source for drawImage(); each small "exploded" tile has a portion of video playing inside it

Figure 6-8. A random portion of a large bitmap is layered and scaled up to create a convincing animated nebula effect (http://www.professorcloud.com/mainsite/canvas-nebula.htm)

The three-parameter version of `drawImage()` is the easiest to use, and simply copies the image source to the point (*x*, *y*) on the canvas. The width and height of the bitmap are determined by the source bitmap:

```
drawImage(source, x, y);
```

The five-parameter version allows you to specify the destination width and height, enabling you to scale an image to the desired size:

```
drawImage(source, x, y, width, height);
```

The nine-parameter version allows you to copy a portion of the image source, where parameters 2–5 specify a rectangle within the source image, and parameters 6–9 specify the destination rectangle within the canvas being drawn on:

```
drawImage(source, sx, sy, swidth, sheight, x, y, width, height);
```

 Some browsers (specifically, Firefox and Opera) may suffer a severe performance penalty and other strange glitches if you're using draw Image() with fractional pixel positions. To avoid these issues, ensure that positions are rounded to whole integers:

```
Math.floor(x)
```

or:

```
(x>>0)
```

Colors, Strokes, and Fills

In the earlier code samples, we used the stroke() command to create a default one-pixel black outline around shape paths. You can change the style of outline using the lineWidth and strokeStyle properties, and specify an internal color fill using the fill Style property. Here is a modified version of the rounded rectangle code that uses these properties (Figure 6-9):

```
var drawRoundedRect = function (ctx, x, y, w, h, cr) {
    ctx.beginPath();
    ctx.moveTo(x + w / 2, y);                // Start in the middle of the top edge.
    ctx.arcTo(x + w, y, x + w, y + h, cr);   // Top edge and upper-right corner.
    ctx.arcTo(x + w, y + h, x, y + h, cr);   // Right edge and lower-right corner.
    ctx.arcTo(x, y + h, x, y, cr);           // Bottom edge and lower-left corner
    ctx.arcTo(x, y, x + w, y, cr);           // Left edge and upper-left corner.
    ctx.closePath();
    ctx.strokeStyle = '#f00';                // Set stroke color to bright red.
    ctx.lineWidth = 4;                       // Set line width to 4 pixels.
    ctx.stroke();
    ctx.fillStyle = '#0f0';                  // Here we specify a green fill.
    ctx.fill();
};
```

Figure 6-9. Stroking shapes with lineWidth = 4 and strokeStyle = '#f00' and fillStyle = '#0f0'

Notice how the stroke lines appear thinner than the four pixels specified. This is because the stroke is centered on the path and the inner two pixels are hidden by the green fill. Simply increase the line width to get the desired result.

You can also specify colors with different levels of transparency via an alpha value. Alpha values range from 0 (completely transparent) to 1 (completely opaque). As well as specifying a local alpha value for the current stroke or fill command, you can use the globalAlpha property to set an alpha value for all strokes and fills; the local alpha value will be multiplied by the globalAlpha property.

In addition, you can draw bitmaps with varying levels of transparency via the globalAlpha property. All the pixel alphas in the bitmap will be multiplied by the globalAlpha property. PNG images contain an alpha channel for transparency effects, so pixels in the image specified with an alpha of 0.5 and drawn with a globalAlpha of 0.5 will actually be drawn with an alpha of 0.25.

Drawing items with an alpha value of less than 1 involves extra work for the browser, as it must perform additional calculations to display the final color result for each pixel. This is true regardless of whether or not the Canvas implementation uses hardware acceleration. When designing your application, consider whether using alpha values is absolutely necessary, especially when drawing speed is important.

If you specify (or calculate via globalAlpha) an alpha value of 0 (fully transparent), the browser may still try to draw the item. This involves unnecessary work and can be a hidden source of performance issues. Avoid drawing many items with 0 alpha if possible.

We define colors in Canvas using CSS3 color specifiers. Any of the following statements is valid for specifying a fill of bright red:

```
ctx.fillStyle = 'red';                   // HTML4 color name.
ctx.fillStyle = '#f00';                  // Hexadecimal RGB.
ctx.fillStyle = '#ff0000';               // Hexadecimal RRGGBB.
ctx.fillStyle = 'rgb(255, 0, 0);         // Decimal integers (0-255)
ctx.fillStyle = 'rgba(255, 0, 0, 0.5);   // Decimal integers with 0.5 alpha.
ctx.fillStyle = 'rgb(100%, 0%, 0%)';     // Percentages.
ctx.fillStyle = 'rgb(100%, 0%, 0%, 0.5)'; // Percentages with alpha.
ctx.fillStyle = 'hsl(0, 100%, 100%)';    // Hue, saturation, luminance (HSL).
ctx.fillStyle = 'hsl(0, 100%, 100%, 0.5)'; // HSL with alpha.
```

As well as flat-color fills and strokes, you can specify color gradients using the create LinearGradient() or createRadialGradient() commands.

Creating a gradient using createLinearGradient() requires some setup:

1. Create a CanvasGradient object using createLinearGradient(). The four parameters passed define a line along which the gradient will be drawn.
2. Add color stops along this line, where 0 specifies the beginning of the line and 1 specifies the end. You must have at least two color stops to define a gradient.
3. Use the CanvasGradient object as the fill or stroke style.

We add color stops with the CanvasGradient addColorStop() command. This command accepts a value between 0 and 1, where 0 represents the beginning of the gradient and 1 represents the end. The following code defines a gradient that fades from black to white to red:

```
cg.addColorStop(0, 'black');
cg.addColorStop(0.5, 'white');
cg.addColorStop(1, 'red');
```

The following function produces a gradient sky and grass effect (Figure 6-10):

```
var drawSkyAndGrass = function (ctx){
    // The gradient line is defined from the top to the bottom of the canvas.
    var cg = ctx.createLinearGradient(0, 0, 0, ctx.canvas.height);
    // Start off with sky blue at the top.
    cg.addColorStop(0, '#00BFFF');
    // Fade to white in the middle.
    cg.addColorStop(0.5, 'white');
    // Green for the top of the grass.
    cg.addColorStop(0.5, '#55dd00');
    // Fade to white at the bottom.
    cg.addColorStop(1, 'white');
    // Use the CanvasGradient object as the fill style.
    ctx.fillStyle = cg;
    // Finally, fill a rectangle the same size as the canvas.
    ctx.fillRect(0, 0, ctx.canvas.width, ctx.canvas.height);
};
```

Figure 6-10. A gradient sky and grass effect created with createLinearGradient()

We call this function by passing it a Canvas context in the usual way.

What happens when the rectangle drawn is not the same size as the canvas? Figure 6-11 shows the results of drawing a rectangle that is one-quarter of the canvas size. We do this by replacing the last line of the previous function with the following:

```
ctx.fillRect(0, 0, ctx.canvas.width/2, ctx.canvas.height/2);
```

Figure 6-11. The same gradient as Figure 6-10, but drawn with a smaller rectangle

Notice how the drawn rectangle acts like a "window" over the gradient defined in the CanvasGradient object.

The createRadialGradient() command allows you to create a radial gradient that spans two circles. The command accepts two circles specified with a position and radius:

```
ctx.createRadialGradient(circle1x, circle1y, circle1Radius,
                         circle2x, circle2y, circle2Radius);
```

Typically, the circles' centers are at the same position and the first circle lies inside the second, although this is not a prerequisite for the function to work. Any area inside the first, smaller circle is filled with the first color defined by addColorStop(); this color fades to the extents of the larger circle into the final color defined by addColorStop(). Any area outside the larger circle is also filled with the final addColorStop() color.

The following function creates a sun using a radial gradient that fades from solid white to transparent yellow. We can overlay this on the sky and grass gradient for a nice sunny day effect (Figure 6-12):

```
var drawSun = function(ctx) {
    // Create a radial gradient with a 32-pixel-radius inner circle
    // and a 64-pixel-radius outer circle. Both are positioned at (64,64).
    var radGrad = ctx.createRadialGradient(64, 64, 32, 64, 64, 64);
    // The inner circle is white and opaque.
    radGrad.addColorStop(0,'white');
    // The outer circle is yellow and fully transparent,
    // thus making the sun fade from solid white to transparent yellow.
    radGrad.addColorStop(1,'rgba(255,255,0,0)');
    ctx.fillStyle = radGrad;
    // Fill a 128-pixel-wide rectangle with the sun gradient.
    ctx.fillRect(0, 0, 128, 128);
};
```

Figure 6-12. A radial gradient used to create a sun effect over the sky and grass

Animating with Canvas

When using JavaScript (or a JavaScript library like jQuery), you are probably accustomed to manipulating a page element's position, size, image, or color and watching it magically assume its new properties while forgetting its old properties, without any additional work involved. Logically, it makes complete sense that increasing an element's *x* and *y* positions will move it down and right across the page. However, if we naively try to animate a moving rectangle in Canvas assuming the same sort of behavior, the results may not be what we expect (Figure 6-13):

```
<!DOCTYPE html>
<head>
```

```
<title>
    Naive implementation of animation in Canvas.
</title>
<meta http-equiv="Content-Type" content="text/html; charset=utf-8" />
<script type="text/javascript"
    src="http://ajax.googleapis.com/ajax/libs/jquery/1.4.2/jquery.min.js">
</script>
<script>
    $(document).ready(function() {
        var a_canvas = $("#a_canvas")[0];
        var ctx = a_canvas.getContext("2d");
        for (var p = 0; p < 450; p++) {
            ctx.fillStyle = "rgb(0,0,255)";
            // Draw a rectangle
            ctx.fillRect(p, p, 50, 50);
        }
    });
</script>
</head>
<body>
    <canvas id="a_canvas" width=500 height=5 00>
    </canvas>
</body>

</html>
```

Figure 6-13. Naively animating moving squares in Canvas may not give the result you expect

Remember, Canvas is a low-level and immediate mode system: each loop iteration simply draws another rectangle on the screen, on top of the previous iteration's rectangle. This results in a big smeared shape, not a moving rectangle. We need to do a bit more work to create an animated square that moves across the page:

1. Store an initial position for the square (x, y).
2. Clear the canvas.
3. Update the square's position by changing x, y, or both.
4. Draw the square at the new position.
5. Wait a bit.
6. Loop back to step 2.

Fundamentally, all animated bitmap systems do something like this under the hood. Step 2 may be optional in certain circumstances. For instance, if the background were being completely filled with a solid color, gradient, or bitmap image, then clearing it is moot. Step 5 is needed so the user has a chance to actually see the animation and give the browser time to do other things; otherwise, the browser would freeze with no delay. Typically, a delay of around 20–50 milliseconds works well for animation. The following page will give us an animated moving square in Canvas as expected:

```
<!DOCTYPE html>
<head>
    <meta http-equiv="Content-Type" content="text/html; charset=utf-8" />
    <script type="text/javascript"
        src="http://ajax.googleapis.com/ajax/libs/jquery/1.4.2/jquery.min.js">
    </script>
    <script>
        $(function() {
            var a_canvas = $("#a_canvas")[0],
                ctx = a_canvas.getContext("2d"),
                p = 0;
            // We use setInterval() to create a delay between iterations.
            setInterval(function() {
                // Clear canvas.
                ctx.clearRect(0, 0, a_canvas.width, a_canvas.height);
                // Change position, and restart at top left if position reaches 451.
                if (p++ > 450) {
                    p = 0
                };
                // Draw a rectangle.
                ctx.fillStyle = "rgb(0,0,255)";
                ctx.fillRect(p, p, 50, 50);
            }, 30);

        });
    </script>
</head>
<body>
    <canvas id="a_canvas" width=500 height=500>
```

```
      </canvas>
    </body></html>
```

Canvas and Recursive Drawing

One benefit of immediate mode drawing is the lack of an intervening data structure that we'd have to create and manipulate to keep track of drawing elements; with immediate mode drawing, you can just fire and forget drawing commands, layering them as thick as you like. This makes Canvas particularly useful for high-density, recursive drawing functions like fractals. *Recursive functions* are defined as those that call themselves. By feeding the last set of results generated by a function back into the function itself, we create a kind of software feedback loop. The following example calls itself recursively 10 times:

```
var rescurse(value1, value2) {
    value1--;
    value2++;
    if (value1 <= 0) return;
    recurse(value1, value2);
};
recurse(10,0);
```

The previous example is not particularly exciting, but it demonstrates two important aspects of recursive functions:

- Values are adjusted within the recursive function and fed back into it.
- We need a test to break out of otherwise infinite recursive loops.

Instead of applying simple increments and decrements, what if we did something more interesting involving a little bit of trigonometry and some random elements? Figure 6-14 shows a recursively drawn tree that uses simple Canvas-line drawing commands. The natural-looking effect is a recognizable feature of recursive graphical functions. Notice how the final tips of the branches look very refined and thin. This is due to the previously discussed fractional pixel anti-aliasing.

The highly detailed and complex appearance belies the simple nature of the code:

```
var drawTree = function (ctx, startX, startY, length, angle, depth, branchWidth) {
    var rand = Math.random,
        newLength, newAngle, newDepth, maxBranch = 3,
        endX, endY, maxAngle = 2 * Math.PI / 4,
        subBranches, lenShrink;
    // Draw a branch, leaning either to the left or right (depending on angle).
    // First branch (the trunk) is drawn straight up (angle = 1.571 radians)
    ctx.beginPath();
    ctx.moveTo(startX, startY);
    endX = startX + length * Math.cos(angle);
    endY = startY + length * Math.sin(angle);
    ctx.lineCap = 'round';
    ctx.lineWidth = branchWidth;
    ctx.lineTo(endX, endY);
```

Figure 6-14. A recursive tree drawn with Canvas

```
// If we are near the end branches, make them green to look like leaves.
if (depth <= 2) {
    ctx.strokeStyle = 'rgb(0,' + (((rand() * 64) + 128) >> 0) + ',0)';
}
// Otherwise, choose a random brownish color.
else {
    ctx.strokeStyle = 'rgb(' + (((rand() * 64) + 64) >> 0) + ',50,25)';
}
ctx.stroke();

// Reduce the branch recursion level.
newDepth = depth - 1;
// If the recursion level has reached zero, then the branch grows no more.
if (!newDepth) {
    return;
}
// Make current branch split into a random number of new branches (max 3).
// Add in some random lengths, widths, and angles for a more natural look.
subBranches = (rand() * (maxBranch - 1)) + 1;
// Reduce the width of the new branches.
branchWidth *= 0.7;
// Recursively call drawTree for the new branches with new values.
for (var i = 0; i < subBranches; i++) {
```

```
                newAngle = angle + rand() * maxAngle - maxAngle * 0.5;
                newLength = length * (0.7 + rand() * 0.3);
                drawTree(ctx, endX, endY, newLength, newAngle, newDepth, branchWidth);
        }
    };
```

Canvas Tree Page Layout

Play around with the initial values passed to drawTree(). You will notice how making small changes to the initial values can give very different results. Increasing the initial value of depth (penultimate parameter) much beyond a value of 12 is not recommended unless you are very patient!

```
<!DOCTYPE html>
<html>
    <head>
        <title>
            Recursive Canvas Tree
        </title>
        <script type="text/javascript"
            src="http://ajax.googleapis.com/ajax/libs/jquery/1.4.2/jquery.min.js">
        </script>
        <script type="text/javascript">

            /*** drawTree() function goes here ***/

            $(document).ready(function() {
                var canvas = document.getElementById('mycanvas');
                var ctx = canvas.getContext('2d');
                drawTree(ctx, 320, 470, 60, -Math.PI / 2, 12, 12);
            });
        </script>
    </head>
    <body>
        <canvas id="mycanvas" width=640, height=4 80></canvas>
        </div>
    </body>
</html>
```

Replacing DHTML Sprites with Canvas Sprites

In the section "A More Dynamic Sprite Application" on page 32, we developed a DHTML animated sprite system and used it to create various graphical demonstrations. In Chapter 5, we used the same sprite system to develop a DHTML video game. We made some effort to "hide" the mechanics of drawing the sprites within the DHTMLSprite object in order to make the applications using it more amenable to implementing a different sprite system. Here we will convert one of the demonstrations to use a new CanvasSprite object that takes advantage of the increased performance of the Canvas element.

The New CanvasSprite Object

CanvasSprite is a direct replacement for the DHTMLSprite object. All parameters in the params object passed to it are the same as before, apart from the inclusion of a Canvas context parameter (ctx):

```
var CanvasSprite = function (params) {
    // The canvas drawing context is passed in the params object.
    var ctx = params.ctx,
        width = params.width,
        height = params.height,
        imagesWidth = params.imagesWidth,
        vOffset = 0,
        hOffset = 0,
        hide = false,
        // An Image object is created, and this will be used as the source
        // for the canvas drawImage function below.
        img = new Image();
    img.src = params.images;

    return {
        draw: function (x, y) {
            if (hide) {
                return;
            }
            // The canvas drawImage function allows us to extract individual
            // sprite images from a larger composite image.
            ctx.drawImage(img, hOffset, vOffset, width, height,
                x >> 0, y >> 0, width, height);
        },
        changeImage: function (index) {
            index *= width;
            vOffset = Math.floor(index / imagesWidth) * height;
            hOffset = index % imagesWidth;
        },
        show: function () {
            hide = false;
        },
        hide: function () {
            hide = true;
        },
        destroy: function () {
            return;
        }
    };
};
```

Notice how we use a binary shift operator (x >> 0, y >> 0) to make the rendering positions whole integers. Firefox and Opera browsers suffer a big performance hit when trying to render at fractional pixel positions. This is not important for regular drawing, but for high-speed graphics, the degradation is significant.

Other Code Changes

The other code changes required to get the CanvasSprite object working are highlighted in the following code example in bold. You may wish to refer back to the original source code in "A More Dynamic Sprite Application" in Chapter 2 for more details.

```
var bouncySprite = function(params) {
    // Other code as before goes here...
    // We are now referencing CanvasSprite instead of DHTMLSprite.
    // that = DHTMLSprite(params);
    that = CanvasSprite(params);
    // Other code as before goes here...
};

var bouncyBoss = function (numBouncy, $drawTarget, ctx) {
    var bouncys = [];

    for (var i = 0; i < numBouncy; i++) {
        bouncys.push(bouncySprite({
            // Other code as before goes here...
            maxY: $drawTarget.height() - 64,
            ctx: ctx     // Pass a Canvas context as one of the parameters to bouncy
                         // sprite.
        }));
    }
    var moveAll = function () {
        // The moveAll() function now clears the Canvas before drawing
        // all the sprites.
        ctx.clearRect(0, 0, ctx.canvas.width, ctx.canvas.height);
        // Other code as before goes here...
    };
    moveAll();
};

$(document).ready(function () {
    // Pass a Canvas context to bouncyBoss.
    var canvas = $('#draw-target')[0];
    bouncyBoss(80, $('#draw-target'), canvas.getContext("2d"));
});
```

A Graphical Chat Application with Canvas and WebSockets

Drawing pretty graphics is all very well, but in the following example, we will look at a more practical application for Canvas: a pseudo-3D chat application (Figure 6-15). This example will also demonstrate how to combine Canvas with other HTML5 features like WebSockets.

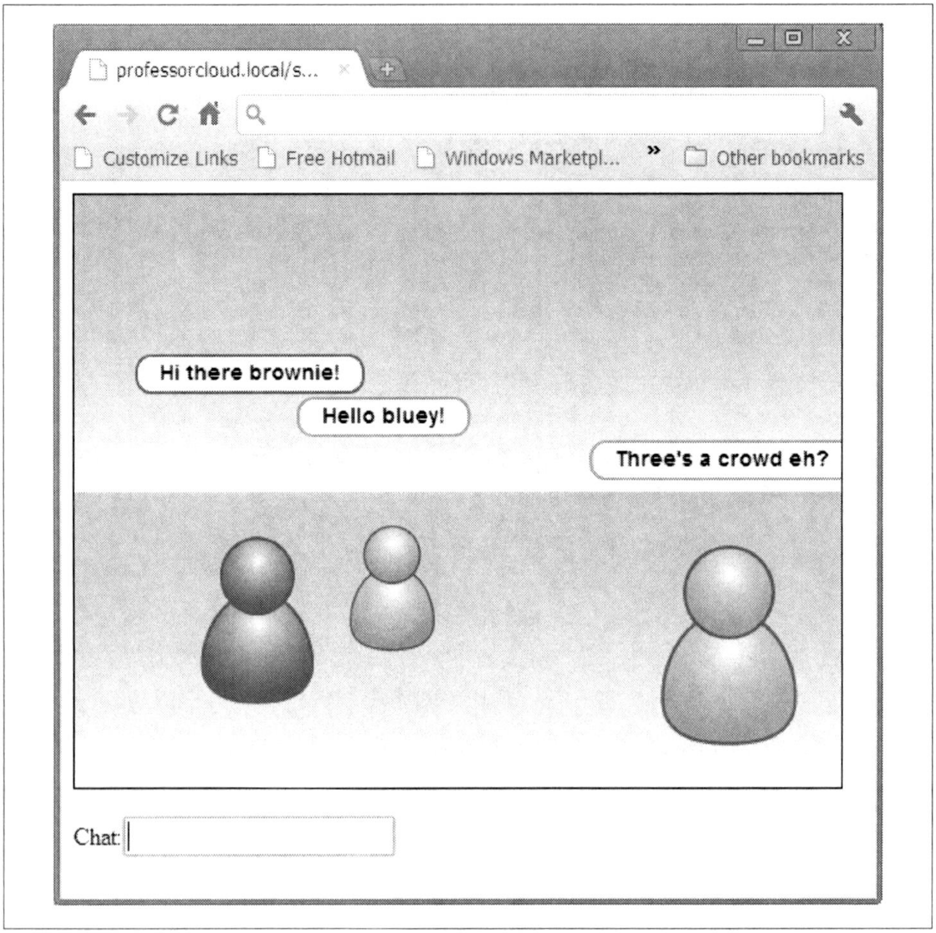

Figure 6-15. A pseudo-3D graphical chat application using HTML5 Canvas and WebSockets

The WebSockets Advantage

Canvas has enjoyed its fair share of the HTML5 limelight, and another equally exciting (but possibly less well known) HTML5 element is WebSockets. Although this book is about graphics, it's worth discussing why WebSockets are significant for modern web applications and how they can be integrated with Canvas.

The Web typically transmits its data between servers and client browsers using the HTTP protocol, but HTTP has certain limitations (unlike shiny new WebSockets) that make it unsuitable for high-speed, bidirectional network communication:

It's a one-way street

The client web browser requests data from the server and the server then obliges. The server cannot "push" information to the client without being asked for it specifically.

It carries significant overhead

HTTP data carries a lot of baggage in the form of header information. Requesting just one byte of data can result in potentially hundreds of bytes of additional "invisible" header information also being sent. Among other things, the headers typically contain information about the nature of the data being transmitted, such as content type, caching, encoding, etc.

Its connections are nonpersistent

For each HTTP request, a connection has to be negotiated, the data sent, and the connection closed again. This is analogous to holding a telephone conversation and having to call back after each sentence.

You can improve HTTP performance somewhat by using programming techniques such as Comet/Long polling, which tries to simulate the persistent, bidirectional connections of more efficient network sockets. Although these techniques can offer some improvement, there is a danger that the server will not be able to service the high volume of HTTP connections required; web server software like Apache is not particularly efficient at handling such connections. Ultimately, you can't make a silk purse out of a sow's ear: HTTP is simply too inefficient for the sort of network transmission required for multiplayer games and other fast-communicating applications.

WebSockets address these problems by allowing genuine, persistent, and bidirectional connections between client and server. The client can send data to the server at any time and vice versa. Also, there is very little data overhead, because there are no headers once the connection is established. The data is simply preceded by a 0 byte (0x00) and terminated by 0xff.

WebSockets Support and Security

WebSockets are currently supported by Firefox 4, Google Chrome 4+, Opera 10.70+, and Safari 5. Unfortunately, security issues surrounding the WebSockets communication protocol have prompted the developers of Firefox and Opera to disable default WebSockets functionality, and other browser vendors may consider the same course of action. You can find technical details of the security issues at *http://www.ietf.org/ mail-archive/web/hybi/current/msg04744.html*.

So, it looks like default WebSockets functionality is in a state of flux until a newer revision of the underlying protocol abates the security concerns. However, there is no reason not to start experimenting with WebSockets now in preparation for the protocol revisions.

Turning on WebSockets in Firefox 4 and Opera 11

Luckily, Firefox and Opera users can turn on WebSockets functionality for development purposes.

For Firefox 4:

1. Enter **about:config** in the browser's address bar.
2. Find and toggle the network.websocket.override-security-block flag.

For Opera:

1. Enter **opera:config** in the browser's address bar.
2. In the Preferences Editor, open the User Prefs section and turn on Enable WebSockets.

The Chat Application

Our chat application is broadly composed of four main elements:

- The socket server that runs on the web server
- Client avatars that move around and "chat"
- The chat text itself
- The text input area

When a user connects to the chat page, an avatar is automatically created for him in a random color. The user can then move the avatar around by clicking on the page and also enter text in the chat box. The avatar's movement and chat text will be mirrored to all other connected users. Effectively, everyone sees the same page, but each user can control only his own avatar.

The socket server

The socket server is required to handle connections and transmit information between the connected clients. It must run on a server that all clients can connect to.

The choice of programming language for the socket server could be any one of the popular server-side languages such as PHP, Java, or Python. As a JavaScript programmer, you will also be pleased by the existence of *node.js*, a server-based implementation of JavaScript and associated libraries that make it suitable for efficient network socket programming.

For the chat application, I've chosen PHP for the socket server, as it enjoys near-ubiquitous preinstallation on Linux-based web hosting services.

The socket server (*server.php*) is actually composed of two parts: a general-purpose socket handler class (`WebSocketServer`), which can be used for a variety of applications, and a chat-application-specific call-back function (`process()`), which is tailored to our chat application. Check out the book's code repository for the PHP source code.

Thorough coverage of PHP is beyond the scope of this book, but even if you have never used it before, the language is relatively easy to learn and there are a vast number of online resources. If you are interested in taking a closer look at the socket server code, there are a couple of PHP syntax idiosyncrasies worth mentioning:

- Variables are preceded by a $ symbol (not to be confused with jQuery's use of $).
- Strings are oddly concatenated with a period symbol (.) instead of the usual addition sign (+).

The socket server performs, among other things, the following operations:

- Accepts new connections and maintains a list of connected clients
- Receives data updates from clients (chat text and position)
- Transmits data updates to all connected clients
- Removes clients from the list when connection is broken (e.g., browser closed)

Installing a web hosting environment locally

Unless you have root access to a dedicated or virtual web server, it is unlikely that you will be able to get the socket server working. Properly configured shared web-hosting environments will invariably have a firewall that prevents use of any communications ports. Luckily, you can still experiment with server-side code by installing a hosting environment on your own local machine.

Installing a web-hosting environment used to be a painful and lengthy process at the best of times. However, the "Apache Friends" XAMPP software consolidates the required modules (Apache and PHP) into a single download that you can install in a few minutes on Windows, Mac, and Linux systems. To download the XAMPP software, go to *http://www.apachefriends.org/en/xampp.html*.

Figure 6-16 shows the XAMPP control panel. Note that PHP is not featured in the control panel and "just works" transparently.

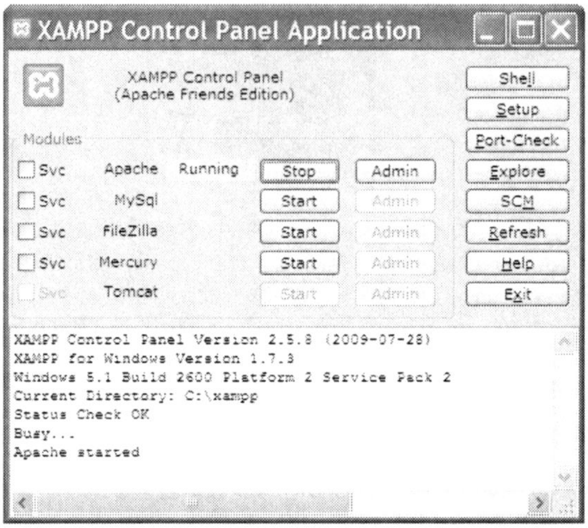

Figure 6-16. With XAMPP, you can easily install a full hosting environment on your local machine

To start the socket server via XAMPP, click the Shell button on the XAMPP control panel. This presents you with a command-line shell that you can use to run the socket server (Figure 6-17). Enter **php *path-to-socket-server*\server.php** to run the socket server, and then press Enter.

You'll need to change the path to *server.php* to point to the location of this file on your local machine.

The socket server is now waiting for connections from the JavaScript side of the chat application.

Figure 6-17. Running the socket server from the XAMPP command-line shell

Finally, we need to run the actual chat web page (the JavaScript) in the browser. The simplest way to do this is by specifying the filesystem location of the page in the browser, for example, *file:///C:/professorcloud.com/book/canvas/canvas-websockets-chat.htm*.

Apache is not actually serving the chat page when we use the *file:///* protocol, as the browser is directly accessing the HTML file.

You can also test several instances of the chat web page by opening multiple browser windows and "chatting" with yourself.

A more elaborate way to test the chat application is to serve the chat page and run the chat server on a computer (the web server) across a network. Here are the steps involved:

1. On the web server, modify the Apache *httpd.conf* file to include a virtual host entry to map the web server's IP address to the location of the chat application on the web server. The first virtual host defined will be the default one used for the web server's IP address.

2. Start Apache via the XAMPP control panel.

   Users of other computers on the network can connect to the chat application by entering the web server's IP address into a suitable browser.

You can find documentation on how to set up XAMPP for hosting here:

- Windows: *http://www.apachefriends.org/en/xampp-windows.html*
- Mac: *http://www.apachefriends.org/en/xampp-macosx.html*
- Linux: *http://www.apachefriends.org/en/xampp-linux.html*

The camera

The camera object determines the perspective view of the chat area. It contains three utility functions:

setFOVandYPos()
> The field of view (FOV) angle and vertical position of the camera are passed in. Calculating the camera distance from the FOV allows you to change the canvas size without affecting the view presented (assuming the same aspect ratio is maintained). We use a value of 125 degrees FOV and camera y position of –128.

worldToScreen()
> This calculates the canvas screen coordinates from the world coordinates passed in. It also calculates a scale that can be applied to the avatars so they appear smaller the farther away they are, effectively simulating perspective.

screenToWorld()
> The opposite of worldToScreen(). From a position on the canvas, the equivalent world coordinates are returned. screenToWorld() converts the mouse-click position into a new world position for the user's avatar. We use the toFixed() method to

prevent meaninglessly fine values from being returned; for example, a value of
188.42620390960207 takes longer to transmit over the network than 188.426.

```
var camera = function () {
    var camDist, camY;
    return {
        setFOVandYPos: function (angle, y) {
            camY = y;
            angle *= (Math.PI / 180);
            camDist = (ctx.canvas.width * 0.5) / Math.tan(angle * 0.5);
        },
        worldToScreen: function (x, y, z) {
            return {
                sx: (camDist * x) / z,
                sy: (camDist * (y - camY)) / z,
                scale: (camDist / z)
            };
        },
        screenToWorld: function (sx, sy) {
            sx -= ctx.canvas.width / 2;
            sy -= ctx.canvas.height / 2;
            var wz = (-camY / sy) * camDist;
            return {
                wx: (sx / camDist * wz).toFixed(3),
                wy: (sy / camDist * wz).toFixed(3),
                wz: wz.toFixed(3)
            };
        }
    };
}();
```

The avatars

Avatars are the graphical representation of the clients. They appear in randomly generated colors to distinguish themselves from other avatars, and we move them by clicking the mouse on the desired new position. They are composed of two vector shapes,
a round head and domed body. We use radial gradient fills to add depth and apply a
darker outline stroke to separate the avatar from the background.

```
var avatar = function (color) {
    var that = {},
        destX = 0,
        destZ = 0,
        x = 0,
        z = 0,
        textX, avatarHW = 40.5,
        avatarH = 106,
        outlineColor = color.substr(1),
        gradient1, gradient2;
    outlineColor = (parseInt(outlineColor, 16) & 0xfefefe) >> 1;
    outlineColor = '#' + outlineColor.toString(16);

    gradient1 = ctx.createRadialGradient(37.7, 55.6, 0.0, 37.7, 55.6, 46.1);
    gradient1.addColorStop(0.00, "#fff");
```

```
gradient1.addColorStop(1.00, color);
gradient2 = ctx.createRadialGradient(37.6, 15.3, 0.0, 37.6, 15.3, 31.1);
gradient2.addColorStop(0.00, "#fff");
gradient2.addColorStop(1.00, color);

that.remove = false;

that.setDest = function (dstX, dstZ) {
    destX = dstX;
    destZ = dstZ;
};
that.getZ = function () {
    return z;
};
that.getTextX = function () {
    return textX;
};
that.move = function (coeff) {

    var vx = destX - x,
        vz = destZ - z,
        dist = Math.sqrt(vx * vx + vz * vz),
        p, x1, y1;

    // Normalize (make unit length) the vector from old pos to new pos.
    if (dist) {
        vx /= dist;
        vz /= dist;
    }
    // Apply the vector capped to a maximum of 4 units.
    if (dist > 4) {
        dist = 4;
    }
    x += vx * (dist * coeff);
    z += vz * (dist * coeff);
    p = camera.worldToScreen(x - avatarHW, -avatarH, z);
    textX = p.sx + (avatarHW * p.scale) + (ctx.canvas.width / 2);

    // Draw the body.
    ctx.save();
    ctx.translate(p.sx + (ctx.canvas.width / 2), p.sy + (ctx.canvas.height / 2));
    ctx.scale(p.scale, p.scale);
    ctx.beginPath();
    ctx.moveTo(73.1, 83.6);
    ctx.bezierCurveTo(71.7, 102.1, 52.2, 105.2, 37.4, 105.2);
    ctx.bezierCurveTo(22.5, 105.2, 3.0, 102.1, 1.6, 83.6);
    ctx.bezierCurveTo(0.1, 62.7, 14.0, 35.3, 37.4, 35.3);
    ctx.bezierCurveTo(60.8, 35.3, 74.7, 62.7, 73.1, 83.6);
    ctx.closePath();
    ctx.fillStyle = gradient1;
    ctx.fill();
    ctx.lineWidth = 2.0;
    ctx.lineJoin = "miter";
    ctx.miterLimit = 4.0;
    ctx.strokeStyle = outlineColor;
```

```
        ctx.stroke();
        // Draw the head.
        ctx.beginPath();
        ctx.moveTo(61.2, 25.3);
        ctx.bezierCurveTo(61.2, 38.4, 50.5, 49.1, 37.4, 49.1);
        ctx.bezierCurveTo(24.2, 49.1, 13.6, 38.4, 13.6, 25.3);
        ctx.bezierCurveTo(13.6, 12.1, 24.2, 1.5, 37.4, 1.5);
        ctx.bezierCurveTo(50.5, 1.5, 61.2, 12.1, 61.2, 25.3);
        ctx.closePath();
        ctx.fillStyle = gradient2;
        ctx.fill();
        ctx.strokeStyle = outlineColor;
        ctx.stroke();
        ctx.restore();
    };
    return that;
};
```

The chat text

The chat text appears above the avatar that has "spoken" and gradually moves up the screen as the user enters more text. To make the text clearer and to add a speech-bubble effect, we surround the text with a rounded rectangle filled with white. The rectangle is stroked with a thick outline in the same color as the avatar that created it.

The textScroller object manages and draws the text generated as the avatars chat. The addText() method adds new lines of text to the beginning of a list while deleting lines of text that are more than five entries old. This creates a vertical scrolling effect, with the topmost lines of text being lost as they move off the top of the canvas. The method accepts the horizontal position of the avatar as the center position of the text, as well as the avatar's color.

The drawText() method iterates through the text list and draws each line of text. To make the text stand out, we display a rounded white rectangle around the words and apply a bold stroke in the same color as the user's avatar. We use the Canvas measure Text() method to calculate the width of the text, and hence the width of the rounded rectangle.

```
var textScroller = function () {
    var textList = [];
    return {
        addText: function (text, x, color) {
            if (textList.length > 5) {
                textList.splice(0, 1);
            }
            textList.push({
                text: text,
                x: x,
                color: color
            });
        },
        drawText: function () {
            var y = (ctx.canvas.height / 2) - 16,
```

```
            tx, w, x1, y1, w1, i;
        ctx.font = "bold 14px sans-serif";
        ctx.fillStyle = '#000';
        for (i = textList.length - 1; i > -1; i--) {
            tx = textList[i];
            w = ctx.measureText(tx.text).width / 2;
            ctx.beginPath();
            y1 = y - 17;
            x1 = tx.x - 2; // Same as stroke width.
            w1 = w + 16;
            // Begin in middle of top.
            ctx.moveTo(x1, y1);
            // Top and upper-right corner.
            ctx.arcTo(x1 + w1, y1, x1 + w1, y1 + 24, 10);
             // Right and lower-right corner.
            ctx.arcTo(x1 + w1, y1 + 24, x1 - w1 - 10, y1 + 24, 10);
             // Bottom and lower-left corner.
            ctx.arcTo(x1 - w1, y1 + 24, x1 - w1, y1, 10);
            // Left and upper-left corner.
            ctx.arcTo(x1 - w1, y1, x1 + w1, y1, 10);
            ctx.closePath();
            ctx.fillStyle = 'white';
            ctx.fill();
            ctx.lineWidth = 2;
            ctx.strokeStyle = tx.color;
            ctx.stroke();
            ctx.fillStyle = 'black';
            ctx.fillText(tx.text, x1 - w, y);
            y -= 28;
        }
    }

    };
}();
```

The background

The drawBackground object draws a gradient blue sky and green floor. Both the sky and
the floor fade to white to give a three-dimensional sense of depth.

```
var drawBackground = function () {
    var linGrad = ctx.createLinearGradient(0, 0, 0, ctx.canvas.height);
    linGrad.addColorStop(0, '#00BFFF');
    linGrad.addColorStop(0.5, 'white');
    linGrad.addColorStop(0.5, '#55dd00');
    linGrad.addColorStop(1, 'white');
    return function () {
        ctx.fillStyle = linGrad;
        ctx.fillRect(0, 0, ctx.canvas.width, ctx.canvas.height);
    };
}();
```

Initialization

The initAndGo() function performs various setup tasks, such as establishing event handlers and connecting to the server. It finally executes the loop that moves and draws the avatars and text:

```
var initAndGo = function () {
    // Set the field of view and camera vertical position.
    camera.setFOVandYPos(125, -128);
    // Socket server is running on the local machine
on port 8999.
    var host = "ws://127.0.0.1:8999",
        socket, avatarList = [];
    // The send function transmits an arbitrary number of arguments to the
    // server.
    var send = function () {
        var data = '';
        for (var i = 0; i < arguments.length; i++) {
            data += arguments[i] + ',';
        }
        socket.send(data);
    };
    try {
        socket = new WebSocket(host);
        // When the socket connects, it creates a new avatar in a random color.
        // It also sets the border color around the text input area.
        socket.onopen = function (msg) {
            // Random color for avatar.
            var rColor = Math.round(0xffffff * Math.random());
            rColor = ('#0' + rColor.toString(16)).
                replace(/^#0([0-9a-f]{6})$/i, '#$1');
            send('CONNECT', rColor, 250);
            $('#text-input').css({
                border: "2px solid " + rColor,
                color: rColor
            });
        };
        socket.onmessage = function (msg) {
            if (msg.data) {
                var textData = msg.data,
                    data;
                // Parse the returned socket data into a JavaScript object
                // via JSON.
                textData = textData.replace(/[\x00-\x1f]/, '');
                data = $.parseJSON(textData);
                for (var userId in data) {
                    if (avatarList[userId] === undefined) {
                        // Initialize a new avatar if the the userId doesn't
                        // yet exist in the avatarList[].
                        avatarList[userId] = avatar(data[userId].colr);
                    }
                    if (data[userId].pos !== undefined) {
                        // Update avatar's destination x and z positions.
                        var pos = data[userId].pos.split(',');
                        avatarList[userId].setDest(pos[0], pos[1]);
```

```
            }
            if (data[userId].chattext !== undefined) {
                // Add chat text if present in data.
                textScroller.addText(unescape(data[userId].chattext),
                    avatarList[userId].getTextX(), data[userId].colr);
            }
            if (data[userId].disconnect) {
                // Flag avatar for removal if the server says so.
                avatarList[userId].remove = true;
            }
        }
    }
};
} catch (ex) {
    alert('Socket error: ' + ex);
}
// Stop text input losing focus when clicking on canvas.
$('#the-canvas').bind('mousedown', this, function (event) {
    return false;
});
// Get clicks on canvas and convert to world coordinates.
// Send these coordinates back to the server.
$(ctx.canvas).bind('click', function (evt) {
    var canvas, bb, mx, my, p;
    canvas = ctx.canvas;
    // Get canvas size and position
    bb = canvas.getBoundingClientRect();
    // Convert mouse event coordinates to canvas coordinates
    mx = (evt.clientX - bb.left) * (canvas.width / bb.width);
    my = (evt.clientY - bb.top) * (canvas.height / bb.height);
    // Stop avatars going too far back.
    if (my < canvas.height / 2 + 32) {
        return;
    }
    p = camera.screenToWorld(mx, my);
    send('UPDATE', p.wx, p.wz);
});
// Get key presses and send chat text to server if return key is pressed.
// The text is escaped to ensure correct transmission.
$(window).bind('keypress', function (evt) {
    if (evt.which == 13) {
        send('CHATTEXT', escape($('#text-input').val()));
        $('#text-input').val('');
    }
});
var oldTime = new Date().getTime();

// The main loop is executed via setInterval at 20-millisecond intervals.
setInterval(function () {
    var newTime = new Date().getTime(),
        elapsed = newTime - oldTime,
        i = 0,
        avatarListNew = [],
        sortList = [],
        // Work out a coefficient of movement based on elapsed time
```

```
            // to ensure consistent speed across different browsers and hardware.
            coeff = elapsed / 20;
        oldTime = newTime;

        // Draw the background. There is no need to erase
        // the canvas first, as the background completely fills it.
        drawBackground();

        // Place non-removed avatars into sortlist ready for drawing.
        // Also place them in avatarListNew.
        for (var av in avatarList) {
            if (!avatarList[av].remove) {
                sortList[i++] = avatarListNew[av] = avatarList[av];
            }
        }

        // Sort the list into z-order.
        sortList.sort(function (a, b) {
            return b.getZ() - a.getZ();
        });

        // Move the avatars.
        for (i = 0; i < sortList.length; i++) {
            sortList[i].move(coeff);
        }

        // avatarListNew now becomes our current avatar list.
        // It does not contain removed avatars.
        avatarList = avatarListNew;

        // Finally, draw all the chat text.
        textScroller.drawText();
    }, 20);
}();
```

The page code

Here is the HTML page layout for the chat application, which is saved in a file called
canvas-websockets-chat.htm:

```
<html>
    <head>
        <meta http-equiv="Content-Type" content="text/html; charset=utf-8" />
        <script type="text/javascript"
            src="http://ajax.googleapis.com/ajax/libs/jquery/1.4.2/jquery.min.js">
        </script>
        <script type="text/javascript">                    jQuery( function($) {
            var ctx = $('#the-canvas')[0].getContext('2d');

            var camera = function () {
                /*** CODE REMOVED FOR CONCISENESS ***/
            }();
            var textScroller = function () {
                /*** CODE REMOVED FOR CONCISENESS ***/
            }();
```

```
            var avatar = function (color) {
                /*** CODE REMOVED FOR CONCISENESS ***/
            };
            var drawBackground = function () {
                /*** CODE REMOVED FOR CONCISENESS ***/
            }();
            var initAndGo = function () {
                /*** CODE REMOVED FOR CONCISENESS ***/
            }();
        });
    </script>
    <style type="text/css">
        body {font-family: sans-serif}
        #text-input {font-size:16px;}
        #the-canvas {border:1px solid;}
    </style>
</head>

<body>
    <canvas id="the-canvas" width='512' height='384'>
    </canvas>
    <p>
        <label for='text-input'>
            Chat:
        </label>
        <input id='text-input' />
    </p>
</body>
</html>
```

CHAPTER 7

Vectors for Games and Simulations

Most programmers will agree that programming is a lot more fun than mathematics, but there are certain circumstances where a little bit of math knowledge can go a long way. As a "value added" math subject, vectors punch way above their weight in terms of useful functionality. Mix together a few other math ingredients, and you have a versatile vector toolkit that can be used for all sorts of applications. Don't worry if math isn't your strong point; the JavaScript equivalents of equations will always be provided. Although it can be a benefit if you understand the underlying mathematics, it is not crucial.

Vectors are typically described as a quantity that has both a magnitude (length) *and* direction. Exactly what does this mean? Some simple examples illustrate the concept best.

- Nonvectors:
  — 2 miles
  — 12 inches
  — 1 kilometer
- Vectors:
  — 2 miles north
  — 12 inches to the right
  — 1 kilometer northeast

Why are vectors useful? Because they make all sorts of movement and spacial behavior a lot easier to understand and implement in code. Vectors can be added, scaled, rotated, and pointed at things. They also form the foundation of more sophisticated programming subjects like physics simulations. Most importantly, when you get the hang of them, they are huge amounts of fun.

The real-world distances and directions described in the preceding lists are familiar and make sense; however, as JavaScript programmers, we are more interested in measurements and directions that are relevant to our applications—not miles and inches.

What units of measurement should we use? In fact, the actual units of measurement are irrelevant: as long as we stick to the same units for all calculations, we can convert them to screen pixel positions at the end, ready for drawing.

In our real-world examples, the direction part of the vectors are specified as compass directions and "to the right." These values aren't practical for JavaScript use, so we must represent direction in some other way. A direction and length (a vector) in 2D space (e.g., your computer screen) can be represented by horizontal (x) and vertical (y) components. Figure 7-1 shows four different vectors on a grid with their x and y components.

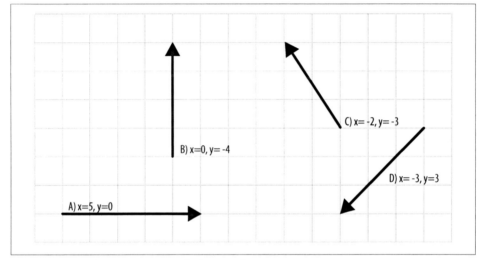

Figure 7-1. Four direction vectors with their x and y components

For this chapter's examples, we will stick to the familiar CSS/bitmap screen coordinate system with the origin in the top left, an x-axis increasing to the right, and a y-axis increasing toward the bottom (aka a *Cartesian coordinate system*). In this example, the vectors represent a direction and length, not a position. The positions on the grid are arbitrary and purely for illustration purposes. However, the x and y components *can* be used to represent a position, depending on how the vector is used in the application.

In Figure 7-1, the directions have been specified with x and y components, but what about the length of the vectors? If a vector points in exactly the same direction as any one axis, then the length is simply the length along that axis; for example, it's fairly obvious that vector A has a length of 5 and vector B has a length of 4. But what if the vectors aren't parallel to any one axis, like vectors C and B? Things aren't quite so obvious in this case, since neither the x or y component represents the length of the vector.

Luckily, we can use the Pythagorean theorem to calculate the length of our vector based on the *x* and *y* components. The definition of the Pythagorean theorem is as follows:

> For a right-angled triangle, the square (area) of the hypotenuse is equal to the sum of the squares of the other two sides (Figure 7-2).

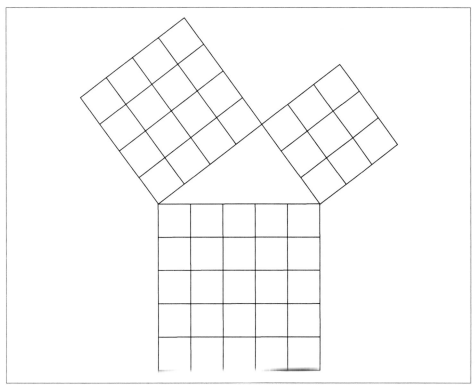

Figure 7-2. Pythagorean theorem

In Figure 7-2, the hypotenuse is the longest edge of the central triangle (in this instance, at the bottom of the triangle), opposite the right angle at the top. The theorem works regardless of which side the hypotenuse is on. How does all of this relate to our vectors? Imagine that the two shorter edges of the triangle in Figure 7-2 are our *x* and *y* components. The length of the vector squared is simply the length of the hypotenuse squared:

$$\text{length}^2 = x^2 + y^2$$

or in JavaScript:

```
lengthSquared = (x*x + y*y);
```

The squared length of the vector can be useful, but we might want the actual length. We can calculate this using the square root of the squared length:

$$\text{length} = \sqrt{(x^2 + y^2)}$$

or in JavaScript:

```
length = Math.sqrt(x*x + y*y);
```

Figure 7-3 shows a vector with components $x = -3$ and $y = 3$. Plug those figures into the Pythagorean theorem, and the length equals approximately 4.24.

```
length = Math.sqrt(-3*-3 + 3*3);    // length = 4.24.
```

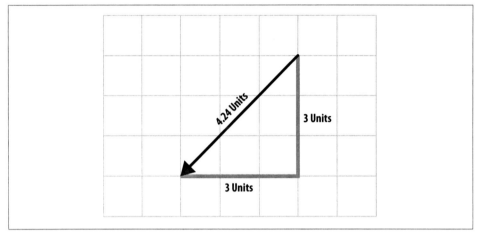

Figure 7-3. The Pythagorean theorem can calculate the length of a vector based on the x and y components

Operations on Vectors

We can apply several useful operations to vectors, some of which are listed in the following sections along with some potential applications.

Addition and Subtraction

You can add vectors to or subtract them from each other by adding or subtracting their *x* and *y* components. This works just like regular arithmetic, so adding a vector to itself will double its length, and subtracting a vector from itself will result in a zero vector. Some examples include:

- Adding a gravity vector to the vector of a ball in flight so it drops realistically
- Adding the vectors of two colliding bodies together for a realistic collision response
- Adding the thrust vector of a rocket engine to a spacecraft so it moves

Scaling

By multiplying the *x* and *y* components by a scale value, you can scale the length of the vector up or down as required. Some examples include:

- Repeatedly scaling a movement vector by a value slightly less than 1 so the object using the vector comes to rest very smoothly
- Taking the direction vector of a cannon and scaling it up to give the initial vector of a cannonball fired from it

Normalization

Sometimes it's useful to make a vector *unit length*, or in other words, make its length one unit long. This process is called *normalization*, and vectors of unit length are called *unit vectors*. You calculate the unit length by dividing the *x* and *y* components by the length of the vector. Typically, we'd do this when we are interested in the direction of a vector, but not its length. Unit vectors might represent:

- The orientation of a directional jet
- The incline of a slope
- The elevation of a cannon

Once we have the unit vector, we can scale it up to represent the thrust of the jet or the cannonball's initial movement.

Rotation

The ability to rotate a vector by an arbitrary angle is extremely useful, as it enables you to point a vector in any direction you desire. Examples include:

- Making one object always point to another
- Changing the "thrust" direction of a virtual jet engine
- Changing the initial "launch" direction of a projectile based on the angle of the object that launched it

In JavaScript math functions (and more advanced mathematics in general), angles are specified in radians as opposed to the more familiar 360 degrees in a circle. A *radian* is an arc with the same length as the circle's radius (Figure 7-4). A circle's circumference can be calculated as $2\pi r$, where r = radius. Hence, there are 2π radians in a circle (approximately 6.282).

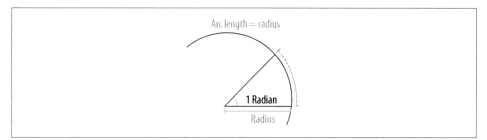

Figure 7-4. A radian in all its glory

Radians aren't particularly intuitive to work with and visualize, but it's easy to convert to and from radians and degrees using these JavaScript functions:

```
// Degrees to radians.
degToRad = function(deg) {
    return deg * (Math.PI/180);
};

// Radians to degrees.
radToDeg = function(rad) {
    return rad * (180/Math.PI);
};
```

One other difference between radians and degrees is that 0 radians actually points along the horizontal axis to the right. This is different from 0 degrees, which is usually assumed to be pointing straight up along the vertical axis.

Dot Product

A *dot product* gives the cosine of the angle between two vectors, or to put it another way, it tells us how similar in direction two vectors are. The possible values range from –1 to 1 (assuming the vectors are unit length). Here are some examples of what the values mean:

- Vectors pointing in the same direction: dot product = 1
- Vectors positioned at 45 degrees to each other: dot product = 0.5
- Vectors at right angles (90 degrees) to each other: dot product = 0
- Vectors pointing in the opposite direction: dot product = –1

The dot product is useful in situations where we need to know to what extent objects are facing each other. For example, in a game, we could determine from the dot product whether two characters could "see" each other, or whether a particular side of a shape is pointing in a certain direction.

Creating a JavaScript Vector Object

To make the most of vectors in JavaScript, we can encapsulate some of the functionality described earlier in a reusable object, thus making the vectors easier to use in applications. We can then easily attach any additional vector-related functionality to this object as needed.

The *x* and *y* components of the vector are actually called **vx** and **vy** in the vector object; this makes it more obvious in the later code examples that we are dealing with vector properties and not some other *x* and *y* values:

```
var vector2d = function (x, y) {

    var vec = {
        // x and y components of vector stored in vx,vy.
        vx: x,
        vy: y,

        // scale() method allows us to scale the vector
        // either up or down.
        scale: function (scale) {
            vec.vx *= scale;
            vec.vy *= scale;
        },

        // add() method adds a vector.
        add: function (vec2) {
            vec.vx += vec2.vx;
            vec.vy += vec2.vy;
        },

        // sub() method subtracts a vector.
        sub: function (vec2) {
            vec.vx = vec2.vx;
            vec.vy -= vec2.vy;
        },

        // negate() method points the vector in the opposite direction.
        negate: function () {
            vec.vx = -vec.vx;
            vec.vy = -vec.vy;
        },

        // length() method returns the length of the vector using Pythagoras.
        length: function () {
            return Math.sqrt(vec.vx * vec.vx + vec.vy * vec.vy);
        },

        // A faster length calculation that returns the length squared.
        // Useful if all you want to know is that one vector is longer than another.
        lengthSquared: function () {
            return vec.vx * vec.vx + vec.vy * vec.vy;
        },
```

```
// normalize() method turns the vector into a unit length vector
// pointing in the same direction.
normalize: function () {
    var len = Math.sqrt(vec.vx * vec.vx + vec.vy * vec.vy);
    if (len) {
        vec.vx /= len;
        vec.vy /= len;
    }
    // As we have already calculated the length, it might as well be
    // returned, as it may be useful.
    return len;
},

// Rotates the vector by an angle specified in radians.
rotate: function (angle) {
    var vx = vec.vx,
        vy = vec.vy,
        cosVal = Math.cos(angle),
        sinVal = Math.sin(angle);
    vec.vx = vx * cosVal - vy * sinVal;
    vec.vy = vx * sinVal + vy * cosVal;
},

// toString() is a utility function for displaying the vector as text,
// a useful debugging aid.
toString: function () {
    return '(' + vec.vx.toFixed(3) + ',' + vec.vy.toFixed(3) + ')';
}
};
return vec;
};
```

A Cannon Simulation Using Vectors

Now that we've defined the vector object, we can use it to develop a simple cannon simulation (Figure 7-5). First, I should qualify the term "simulation": our goal is not to try to replicate with absolute realism the physics of a cannon, but rather to create a simulation that is realistic enough for applications like games. Even the most advanced physics in games have to suspend reality somewhat. For example, human characters in games do not simulate physics to remain upright and walk, and aircraft in games do not simulate all the physics of flight to remain airborne.

 Strictly speaking, for accurate simulations, you should factor the time elapsed per frame into your calculations. However, for the purposes of this demonstration, we'll assume a frame rate of 30 milliseconds. In actuality, timers on certain browsers are not particularly accurate anyway, so the lack of time calculations is no great loss.

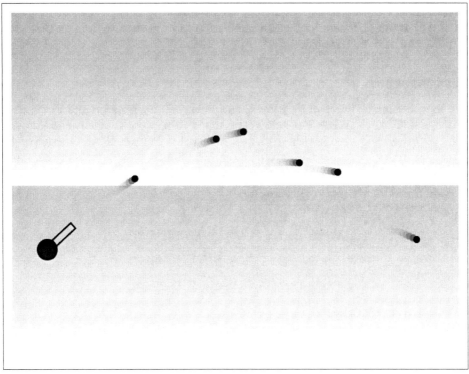

Figure 7-5. Simple cannon simulation using vectors and HTML5 Canvas

The simulation uses HTML5 Canvas to draw the graphics, although you could adapt it to work with any number of rendering methods in the browser (SVG, CSS3, etc.). The graphics are deliberately basic to keep the code's focus on the use of vectors and the calculations required.

The cannon simulation will use vectors for the following:

- To represent the aiming direction of the cannon
- To represent the movement of the cannonball (initially derived from the aiming direction of the cannon)

Simulation-Wide Variables

Here we define a handful of simulation-wide variables at the top of the main simulation function. Although these variables are available to all functions in the simulation, they are wrapped in the main simulation function and do not appear in the global scope:

```
var gameObjects = [],                    // An array of game objects.
    canvas = document.getElementById('canvas'), // A reference to the Canvas.
    ctx = canvas.getContext('2d');       // A reference to the drawing context.
```

We add every object in the simulation (apart from the background) to the game Objects[] array. The main loop of the simulation can then iterate through this array to move and draw all the objects.

The Cannonball

We initialize the cannonball by passing an initial *x* and *y* position and a vector of movement. On each cycle, we add the vector to the current position, and add a gravity value to the vector's *y* component to make the ball fall as it moves along. On each cycle, we increase the gravity value by a fixed amount to simulate gravitational acceleration. The ball is represented by a simple filled circle.

```
var cannonBall = function (x, y, vector) {
    var gravity = 0,
        that = {
            x: x,                   // Initial x position.
            y: y,                   // Initial y position.
            removeMe: false,        // A flag to indicate removal.

            // move() method updates position with velocity,
            // and checks for cannonball hitting the ground.
            move: function () {
                vector.vy += gravity;   // Add gravity to vertical velocity.
                gravity += 0.1;         // Increase gravity.
                that.x += vector.vx;    // Add velocity vector to position.
                that.y += vector.vy;

                // When cannonball gets too low, flag it for removal.
                if (that.y > canvas.height - 150) {
                    that.removeMe = true;
                }
            },
            // draw() method draws a filled circle, centered on the position
            // of the ball.
            draw: function () {
                ctx.beginPath();
                ctx.arc(that.x, that.y, 5, 0, Math.PI * 2, true);
                ctx.fill();
                ctx.closePath();
            }
        };
    return that;
};
```

The Cannon

The cannon is represented by a simple rectangular barrel mounted on a wheel, and it pivots to always aim at the mouse pointer. To calculate the angle to the mouse pointer, we use the Math.atan2(y,x) function. Math.atan2(y,x) returns the angle in radians between a horizontal axis and a point relative to that axis. Assuming the horizontal axis passes through the pivot point of the cannon, the relative point specified is simply the position of the mouse pointer relative to the pivot point of the cannon:

```
angle = Math.atan2(mouseY - cannonY, mouseX - cannonX);
```

When the mouse is clicked, the cannon fires a cannonball. The cannonball is initialized with a start position (the pivot point of the cannon) and a movement vector. We calculate the movement vector from the position of the mouse pointer relative to the position of the cannon:

```
vector = vector2d(mouseX - cannonX, mouseY - cannonY);
```

However, although this vector is aimed in the correct direction, its length is the distance from the cannon to the mouse pointer. This is not much use, as this distance will vary: it can't simply be scaled up or down by a fixed amount. The solution is to normalize the vector to a consistent unit length, and then scale it up to the desired length:

```
vec.normalize();    // Make it unit length.
vec.scale(25);      // Scale it up to 25 units.
```

Here is the full cannon object:

```
var cannon = function (x, y) {
    var mx = 0,
        my = 0,
        angle = 0,
        that = {
            x: x,
            y: y,
            angle: 0,
            removeMe: false,

            // move() method does nothing more than angle the cannon
            // toward the mouse pointer.
            move: function () {
                // Calculate angle to mouse pointer.
                angle = Math.atan2(my - that.y, mx - that.x);
            },

            draw: function () {
                ctx.save();
                ctx.lineWidth = 2;
                // Origin will be bottom-center of barrel.
                ctx.translate(that.x, that.y);

                // Apply the rotation previously calculated in the
                // move() method.
                ctx.rotate(angle);
                // Draw a rectangular 'barrel'.
                ctx.strokeRect(0, -5, 50, 10);

                // Draw 'wheel' at bottom of cannon.
                ctx.moveTo(0, 0);
                ctx.beginPath();
                ctx.arc(0, 0, 15, 0, Math.PI * 2, true);
```

```
                ctx.fill();
                ctx.closePath();
                ctx.restore();
            }
        };

    // When mouse is clicked, fire a cannonball.
    canvas.onmousedown = function (event) {
        // Create a vector from cannon postion in direction of mouse.
        var vec = vector2d(mx - that.x, my - that.y);
        vec.normalize(); // Make it unit length.
        vec.scale(25);   // Scale it up to 25 units per frame.
        // Create a new cannonball, and add it to the gameObjects list.
        gameObjects.push(cannonBall(that.x, that.y, vec));
    };

    // Keep a note of the mouse position over the canvas.
    canvas.onmousemove = function (event) {
        var bb = canvas.getBoundingClientRect();
        mx = (event.clientX - bb.left);
        my = (event.clientY - bb.top);
    };

    return that;
};
```

The Background

The more eagle-eyed readers among you probably noticed that in Figure 7-5, the cannonballs appear to have a trail as they fly through the air. We achieve this effect by making interesting use of the Canvas `globalAlpha` property on the background of sky and grass. Normally, when animating with Canvas, we need to redraw the entire canvas every frame to "erase" the previous frame's imagery. If we don't do this, all moving imagery smears across the canvas and leaves a repeating trail. By specifying an alpha value for the background, we only partially erase the previous frame. As these semi-transparent backgrounds are layered, they eventually completely erase the imagery from the previous frames. Think of the background as tracing paper: one or two sheets will look transparent, but if we keep adding sheets, the pile will become opaque. The net effect is that any moving imagery leaves a diminishing partial trail that looks like motion blur. The smaller the alpha value used, the longer it will take for the trails to fade.

```
    // Draws a blue sky and grass, with the horizon in the middle of the canvas.
    // Drawn as semitransparent to give the illusion of blurring on moving objects.
    var drawSkyAndGrass = function (){
        ctx.save();
        // Set transparency.
        ctx.globalAlpha = 0.4;
        // Create a CanvasGradient object in linGrad.
        // The gradient line is defined from the top to the bottom of the canvas.
        var linGrad = ctx.createLinearGradient(0, 0, 0, canvas.height);
        // Start off with sky blue at the top.
```

```
linGrad.addColorStop(0, '#00BFFF');
// Fade to white in the middle.
linGrad.addColorStop(0.5, 'white');
// Green for the top of the grass.
linGrad.addColorStop(0.5, '#55dd00');
// Fade to white at the bottom.
linGrad.addColorStop(1, 'white');
// Use the CanvasGradient object as the fill style.
ctx.fillStyle = linGrad;
// Finally, fill a rectangle the same size as the canvas.
ctx.fillRect(0, 0, canvas.width, canvas.height);
ctx.restore();
};
```

The Main Loop

We wrap the main loop in an anonymous function within a `setInterval()` call. The main loop is processed every 30 milliseconds and calls the `move()` and `draw()` methods of the simulation objects. It also creates a new list of objects that do not have their `removeMe` flags set. Any objects that *do* have their `removeMe` flags set are not included in the new list, and hence disappear from the simulation. This is what happens to the cannonballs when they move below ground level.

Page Layout

Here is the final page layout for the cannon simulation. Note that I've removed some of the function code to avoid repetition. Simply substitute in the appropriate function in its entirety from earlier in the chapter.

```
<!DOCTYPE html>
<html>
<head>
<script type="text/javascript" >
    window.onload = function() {
        var gameObjects = [],
            canvas = document.getElementById('canvas'),
            ctx = canvas.getContext('2d');

        var vector2d = function (x, y) {
            /*** Code Removed For Conciseness ****/
        };

        var cannonBall = function (x, y, vector) {
            /*** Code Removed For Conciseness ****/
        };

        var cannon = function (x, y) {
            /*** Code Removed For Conciseness ****/
        };

        var drawSkyAndGrass = function (){
            /*** Code Removed For Conciseness ****/
```

```
            };

            // Add an initial cannon to the game objects list.
            gameObjects.push(cannon(50,canvas.height-150));

            // This is the main loop that moves and draws everything.

            setInterval( function() {
                drawSkyAndGrass();

                // Here, we loop through all the object in the gameObjects[]
                // Array. As each object is found, it is drawn, moved, and then
                // added to the gameObjectsFresh[] array,UNLESS it has its removeMe flag
                // set. gameObjectsFresh[] is then copied into gameObjects[] ready for
                // the next frame. gameObjects[] will now not contain any removed
                // objects, and they will disappear, as nothing references them anymore.
                gameObjectsFresh = [];
                for(var i=0;i<gameObjects.length;i++) {
                    gameObjects[i].move();
                    gameObjects[i].draw();
                    if ( gameObjects[i].removeMe === false) {
                        gameObjectsFresh.push(gameObjects[i]);
                    }
                }
                gameObjects = gameObjectsFresh;

            },30);
        };
    </script>

</head>
    <body>
        <canvas id = "canvas" width = "640" height = "480" style="border:1px solid">
            No HTML5 Canvas detected!
        </canvas>
    </body>
</html>
```

Rocket Simulation

The following rocket simulation (Figure 7-6) is a more elaborate demonstration of the use of vectors. The simulation features a steerable rocket and colorful obstacles to avoid. The rocket rotates to face the mouse pointer, and you can apply engine thrust in the facing direction of the rocket by holding down the left mouse button. The simulation is gravity and friction-free, so it requires dexterous use of the mouse to keep the rocket traveling in the desired direction. The same vector object we defined earlier in the cannon example is used throughout.

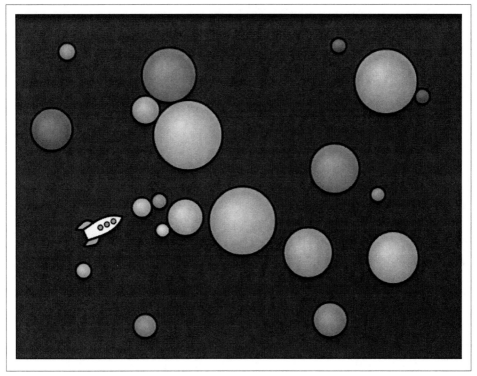

Figure 7-6. Rocket simulation in action

The Game Object

We use functional inheritance in the rocket simulation to create both the rocket and obstacles from a base object called gameObject, which provides common methods and properties:

```
var gameObject = function (x, y, radius, mass) {
    var that = {
        x: x,
        y: y,
        vel: vector2d(0, 0),
        radius: radius,
        mass: mass,
        removeMe: false,

        move: function () {
            that.x += that.vel.vx;
            that.y += that.vel.vy;
            if (that.vel.vx < 0 && that.x < -50) {
                that.x += canvas.width + 100;
            } else if (that.vel.vx > 0 && that.x > canvas.width + 50) {
                that.x -= canvas.width + 100;
            }
            if (that.vel.vy < 0 && that.y < -50) {
```

```
            that.y += canvas.height + 100;
        } else if (that.vel.vy > 0 && that.y > canvas.height + 50) {
            that.y -= canvas.height + 100;
        }
    },

    draw: function () {
        return;
    }
};
return that;
};
```

Essentially, the object represents a ball with a radius and mass. We initialize game Object by passing an initial x and y position, a radius, and mass. We use a velocity vector, vel, to store the gameObject's current direction and speed of movement, with an initial value of 0 (no movement).

The move() method adds the velocity vector, vel, to the current x and y position of the gameObject, thus moving it. The additional tests and calculations in the move() method make the gameObject "wrap around" the canvas. For example, an object that drifts off the righthand side of the canvas will magically reappear on the lefthand side. This makes the whole simulation more fluid and prevents objects from constantly bouncing off the edges of the canvas.

The draw() method within the context of gameObject is a dummy function, and is implemented only for the sake of reference. The rocket and obstacles will override this function with their own specific implementations that actually draw something.

The Obstacle Object

The obstacle object inherits all the methods and properties of gameObject but augments itself with a proper draw() method and performs some additional setup. We create an initial gameObject and give the fourth parameter (mass) the same value as the radius. This is a quick way of assigning a mass that is proportional to the obstacle size. After we've created the gameObject, we create a random color in randColor1. Next, we initialize randColor2 with the same color, but with half the brightness: the >> 1 expression is a binary shift-right, equivalent to integer division by two. The string slice() function is called to ensure that the colors are always represented as a full six-digit hexadecimal number (#123456).

Notice that we do not define a move() method, as the one inherited from gameObject already has the functionality we need.

The draw() method draws a circle using the passed-in radius and fills it with a radial gradient using randColor1 and randColor2, defined earlier. randColor1 is the lighter of the two colors, and acts as a highlight to give the illusion of spherical solidity. The highlight is offset slightly to the top left of the circle, with a radius 1/8 of the full radius of the obstacle. Finally, we apply a three-pixel black stroke.

```
var obstacle = function (x, y, radius) {
    var that = gameObject(x, y, radius, radius),
        randColor1 = Math.floor(Math.random()*0xffffff),
        randColor2 = ((randColor1 & 0xfefefe)>>1).toString(16);
    randColor1 = randColor1.toString(16);
    randColor1 = '#000000'.slice(0,7-randColor1.length) + randColor1;
    randColor2 = '#000000'.slice(0,7-randColor2.length) + randColor2;

    that.draw = function () {
        ctx.beginPath();
        var radgrad = ctx.createRadialGradient(that.x, that.y, radius,
            (that.x - (radius / 4)), (that.y - (radius / 4)), (radius / 8)   );
        radgrad.addColorStop(0, randColor2);
        radgrad.addColorStop(1, randColor1);
        ctx.fillStyle = radgrad;
        ctx.arc(that.x, that.y, that.radius, 0, Math.PI * 2, true);
        ctx.fill();
        ctx.strokeStyle = '#000';
        ctx.lineWidth = 3;
        ctx.stroke();
        ctx.closePath();
    };
    return that;
};
```

The Rocket Object

The bulk of the rocket object code is taken up by the draw() method. In fact, the draw() method uses the output from the AI→Canvas plug-in for Adobe Illustrator and is probably longer than if we'd worked out the drawing commands manually. However, it's a great time-saver, so in this instance we've used the unoptimized output.

The move() method adds a thrust vector to the rocket's velocity, capping it at five units to prevent the rocket from whizzing off too quickly.

We use three mouse events to control the rocket:

onmousedown

> This creates a thrust vector in the direction of the mouse pointer. We calculate the thrust vector by creating a vector between the rocket and mouse pointer, making the vector unit length, and then scaling it to an appropriate length.

onmouseup

> This zeros out the thrust vector, preventing further thrust from being added to the rocket's velocity.

onmousemove

> This records the mouse pointer position over the canvas and stores the results in mx and my. The angle to the mouse pointer is also stored for the draw() method's use, allowing the rocket to be drawn at the correct angle to face the mouse pointer.

```
var rocket = function (x, y) {
    // mx and my store the mouse position over the canvas.
```

```
    var mx = 0,
        my = 0,
        // Initial angle and thrust vector are zero.
        angle = 0,
        thrust = vector2d(0, 0),
        // gameObject is initialized with radius of 15 and mass of 15.
        that = gameObject(x, y, 15, 15),
        // Keep a reference to the parent (gameObject) move() method,
        // so it can be called in the overridden move() method later on.
        move = that.move;

    // Method to draw a rocket.
    // Output generated by AI->Canvas plug-in for Adobe Illustrator.
    that.draw = function () {
        ctx.save();
        ctx.translate(that.x, that.y);
        ctx.rotate(angle);
        ctx.scale(0.5, 0.5);
        ctx.beginPath();
        ctx.moveTo(-49.5, -16.0);
        ctx.lineTo(-48.9, 16.5);
        ctx.bezierCurveTo(-10.0, 19.9, 32.4, 31.4, 68.3, -1.6);
        ctx.bezierCurveTo(31.3, -33.5, -10.9, -21.8, -49.5, -16.0);
        ctx.closePath();
        ctx.fillStyle = "rgb(255, 255, 0)";
        ctx.fill();
        ctx.lineWidth = 6.0;
        ctx.lineJoin = "round";
        ctx.stroke();

        ctx.beginPath();
        ctx.moveTo(40.1, 5.6);
        ctx.bezierCurveTo(36.1, 5.7, 32.8, 2.5, 32.7, -1.4);
        ctx.bezierCurveTo(32.7, -5.3, 35.8, -8.6, 39.8, -8.7);
        ctx.bezierCurveTo(39.8, -8.7, 39.8, -8.7, 39.8, -8.7);
        ctx.bezierCurveTo(43.8, -8.7, 47.1, -5.6, 47.2, -1.6);
        ctx.bezierCurveTo(47.2, 2.3, 44.1, 5.6, 40.1, 5.6);
        ctx.bezierCurveTo(40.1, 5.6, 40.1, 5.6, 40.1, 5.6);
        ctx.closePath();
        ctx.fillStyle = "rgb(0, 127, 127)";
        ctx.fill();
        ctx.lineWidth = 3.6;
        ctx.stroke();

        ctx.beginPath();
        ctx.moveTo(19.7, 5.9);
        ctx.bezierCurveTo(15.7, 6.0, 12.4, 2.9, 12.4, -1.1);
        ctx.bezierCurveTo(12.3, -5.0, 15.5, -8.3, 19.5, -8.3);
        ctx.bezierCurveTo(19.5, -8.3, 19.5, -8.3, 19.5, -8.3);
        ctx.bezierCurveTo(23.5, -8.4, 26.7, -5.3, 26.8, -1.3);
        ctx.bezierCurveTo(26.9, 2.6, 23.7, 5.9, 19.7, 5.9);
        ctx.bezierCurveTo(19.7, 5.9, 19.7, 5.9, 19.7, 5.9);
        ctx.closePath();
        ctx.fill();
        ctx.stroke();
```

```
    ctx.beginPath();
    ctx.moveTo(-1.0, 6.3);
    ctx.bezierCurveTo(-4.9, 6.3, -8.2, 3.2, -8.3, -0.7);
    ctx.bezierCurveTo(-8.4, -4.7, -5.2, -7.9, -1.2, -8.0);
    ctx.bezierCurveTo(-1.2, -8.0, -1.2, -8.0, -1.2, -8.0);
    ctx.bezierCurveTo(2.8, -8.1, 6.1, -4.9, 6.2, -1.0);
    ctx.bezierCurveTo(6.2, 3.0, 3.0, 6.2, -0.9, 6.3);
    ctx.bezierCurveTo(-1.0, 6.3, -1.0, 6.3, -1.0, 6.3);
    ctx.closePath();
    ctx.fill();
    ctx.stroke();

    ctx.beginPath();
    ctx.moveTo(-49.5, -16.0);
    ctx.lineTo(-68.3, -25.1);
    ctx.bezierCurveTo(-56.3, -31.0, -39.9, -37.8, -29.5, -35.3);
    ctx.bezierCurveTo(-22.7, -33.7, -14.5, -21.6, -14.5, -21.6);
    ctx.lineTo(-49.5, -16.0);
    ctx.closePath();
    ctx.fillStyle = "rgb(255, 0, 0)";
    ctx.fill();
    ctx.lineWidth = 6.0;
    ctx.stroke();

    ctx.beginPath();
    ctx.moveTo(-47.9, 16.4);
    ctx.lineTo(-66.4, 26.2);
    ctx.bezierCurveTo(-54.3, 31.7, -37.7, 38.0, -27.4, 35.2);
    ctx.bezierCurveTo(-20.6, 33.3, -12.8, 21.0, -12.8, 21.0);
    ctx.lineTo(-47.9, 16.4);
    ctx.closePath();
    ctx.fill();
    ctx.stroke();
    ctx.restore();
};
that.move = function () {
    var speed;
    // Calculate angle to mouse pointer.
    angle = Math.atan2(my - that.y, mx - that.x);
    // Add thrust to current velocity.
    that.vel.add(thrust);
    speed = that.vel.length();
    // If speed is > 5, then scale velocity back down.
    if (length > 5) {
        that.vel.normalize();
        that.vel.scale(5);
    }
    move();
};
// When mouse is held down, thrust.
canvas.onmousedown = function (event) {
    // Create a vector from rocket postion in direction of mouse.
    thrust = vector2d(mx - that.x, my - that.y);
    thrust.normalize(); // Make it unit length.
```

```
                    thrust.scale(0.1); // Scale it down.
        };
        // When mouse is released, cancel thrust.
        canvas.onmouseup = function (event) {
            thrust = vector2d(0, 0);
        };

        // Keep a note of the mouse position over the canvas.
        canvas.onmousemove = function (event) {
            var bb = canvas.getBoundingClientRect();
            mx = (event.clientX - bb.left);
            my = (event.clientY - bb.top);
        };

        return that;
    };
```

Background

The drawBackground() function fills the canvas with a subtle blue-to-dark purple gra‐
dient to create the illusion of a space background. Because the background is the same
size as the canvas, we don't need to clear the canvas on each frame; the background fill
will do this for us.

```
    // Draws a spacey-looking background - a dark blue gradient fading to dark purple
    // in the middle.
    var drawBackground = function (){
        ctx.save();
        // Create a CanvasGradient object in linGrad.
        // The gradient line is defined from the top to the bottom of the canvas.
        var linGrad = ctx.createLinearGradient(0, 0, 0, canvas.height);
        // Start off with dark blue at the top.
        linGrad.addColorStop(0, '#000044');
        // Fade to purple in the middle.
        linGrad.addColorStop(0.5, '#220022');
        // Fade to dark blue at the bottom.
        linGrad.addColorStop(1, '#000044');
        // Use the CanvasGradient object as the fill style.
        ctx.fillStyle = linGrad;
        // Finally, fill a rectangle the same size as the canvas.
        ctx.fillRect(0, 0, canvas.width, canvas.height);
        ctx.restore();
    };
```

Collision Detection and Response

The collision function first checks whether any two game objects are overlapping, and
if so, bounces them off each other. The initial overlap test determines whether the circles
defined by the position and radius of the game objects are touching: two circles are
intersecting if the distance between their center points is less than the sum of their radii.
In Figure 7-7, the two circles are colliding because distance D1 is less than R1+R2. D2
represents the amount of intersection. By moving the circles apart by length D2 after

collision, we ensure that they will no longer intersect and will be flush to each other for visually perfect edge-to-edge collision detection.

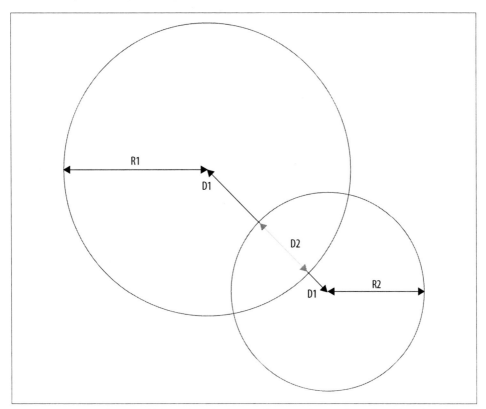

Figure 7-7 Two circles are colliding when the distance between their center points is less than the sum of their radii

The collideAll() function uses a nested loop to check each object against the others. One small but important optimization here is to make the inner loop start at +1 from the current position of the outer loop. This ensures that collision tests are one-way only —object 1 tests against object 2, but not object 2 against object 1—and in doing so can more than halve the number of tests required.

If the game objects overlap, do the following:

1. Move the objects apart by the amount of overlap as described.

2. Make the game objects bounce off each other by calculating new velocity vectors:

```
var bounce = function(ball1,ball2) {
    var colnAngle = Math.atan2(ball1.y - ball2.y, ball1.x - ball2.x),
        length1 = ball1.vel.length(),
        length2 = ball2.vel.length(),
        dirAngle1 = Math.atan2(ball1.vel.vy, ball1.vel.vx),
```

```
                    dirAngle2 = Math.atan2(ball2.vel.vy, ball2.vel.vx),
                    newVX1 = length1 * Math.cos(dirAngle1-colnAngle),
                    newVX2 = length2 * Math.cos(dirAngle2-colnAngle);
                ball1.vel.vy = length1 * Math.sin(dirAngle1-colnAngle);
                ball2.vel.vy = length2 * Math.sin(dirAngle2-colnAngle);
                ball1.vel.vx =((ball1.mass-ball2.mass)*newVX1 +
                    (2*ball2.mass)*newVX2) /
                    (ball1.mass+ball2.mass);
                ball2.vel.vx =((ball2.mass-ball1.mass)*newVX2 +
                    (2*ball1.mass)*newVX1) /
                    (ball1.mass+ball2.mass);
                ball1.vel.rotate(colnAngle);
                ball2.vel.rotate(colnAngle);
        };

        var collideAll = function () {
            var vec = vector2d(0, 0),
                dist, gameObj1, gameObj2, c, i;
            // Check each object against every other object.
            for (var c = 0; c < gameObjects.length; c++) {
                gameObj1 = gameObjects[c];
                // The inner loop starts at one past the outer loop.
                // This ensures efficient one-way testing:
                // A against B, but not B against A.
                for (i = c + 1; i < gameObjects.length; i++) {
                    gameObj2 = gameObjects[i];
                    // Get the distance between the two objects.
                    vec.vx = gameObj2.x - gameObj1.x;
                    vec.vy = gameObj2.y - gameObj1.y;
                    dist = vec.length();
                    // If distance < sum of the two radii, then we
                    // have a collision.
                    if (dist < gameObj1.radius + gameObj2.radius) {
                        // Move objects apart so they are no longer intersecting,
                        // but flush against each other.
                        vec.normalize();
                        vec.scale(gameObj1.radius + gameObj2.radius - dist);
                        vec.negate();
                        gameObj1.x += vec.vx;
                        gameObj1.y += vec.vy;
                        // Finally, bounce the two colliding objects.
                        bounce(gameObj1, gameObj2);
                    }
                }
            }
        };
```

The bounce() function uses trigonometry and elastic collision calculations to work out
the magnitude and direction of bounce for the two colliding objects. This function
works by rotating the movement vectors so that a one-dimensional elastic collision
calculation can be performed. The resultant vectors are then rotated back into two
dimensions to make the objects bounce off each other. This is just one way of calculating bounce vectors; there are other methods available. Look up billiard or pool
physics in Google if you are interested in the math involved.

Page Code

Here is the layout of the page. I've removed the body of certain functions to avoid repetition.

```
<!DOCTYPE html>
<html>
<head>

<script type="text/javascript" >
    window.onload = function() {
        var gameObjects = [],
            canvas = document.getElementById('canvas'),
            ctx = canvas.getContext('2d');

        // Vector object.
        var vector2d = function (x, y) {
            /*** CODE REMOVED FOR CONCISENESS ***/
        };


        var gameObject = function (x, y, radius, mass) {
                /*** CODE REMOVED FOR CONCISENESS ***/
        };

        var obstacle = function (x, y, radius) {
            /*** CODE REMOVED FOR CONCISENESS ***/
        };

        var bounce = function(ball1,ball2) {
            /*** CODE REMOVED FOR CONCISENESS ***/
        };

        var rocket = function (x, y) {
            /*** CODE REMOVED FOR CONCISENESS ***/
        };

        var collideAll = function () {
            /*** CODE REMOVED FOR CONCISENESS ***/
        };

        // Draws a spacey-looking background,
        // a dark blue gradient fading to dark purple
        // in the middle.
        var drawBackground = function (){
            /*** CODE REMOVED FOR CONCISENESS ***/
        };

        // Add rocket to the game objects list.
        gameObjects.push(rocket(50,canvas.height-150));
        // Create a bunch of obstacles.
        for(var i=0;i<20;i++) {
            var radius = ((Math.random()*4)+1)*10;
            var x = Math.random() * (canvas.width-(radius*2)) +radius;
            var y = Math.random() * (canvas.height-(radius*2))+radius;
```

```
            gameObjects.push(obstacle(x,y,radius));
        }


        // This is the main loop that moves and draws everything.
        setInterval( function() {
            var gameObjectsFresh = [];
            drawBackground();
            // Here, we loop through all the object in the gameObjects[]
            // array. As each object is found, it is drawn, moved, and then
            // added to the gameObjectsFresh[] array, UNLESS it has its removeMe flag
            // set. gameObjectsFresh[] is then copied into gameObjects[], ready for
            // the next frame. gameObjects[] will now not contain any removed
            // objects, and they will disappear as nothing references them anymore.
            for(var i=0;i<gameObjects.length;i++) {
                gameObjects[i].move();
                gameObjects[i].draw();
                if ( gameObjects[i].removeMe === false) {
                    gameObjectsFresh.push(gameObjects[i]);
                }
            }
            collideAll();
            gameObjects = gameObjectsFresh;
        },30);
    };

</script>

</head>
    <body>
        <canvas id = "canvas" width ="640" height = "480" style="border:1px solid">
            No HTML5 Canvas detected!
        </canvas>
    </body>
</html>
```

Possible Improvements and Modifications

- Add some friction into the movement of the objects so they slow down and stop. Hint: In the move() method of gameObject, scale the velocity by a number just less than one.

- The draw() method of the rocket object is a fairly substantial chunk of code that draws lots of shapes and outlines. To speed up performance, draw the rocket object only once onto a hidden Canvas element, and then use this hidden element as a bitmap source for the Canvas drawImage() function. This will be substantially faster. Hint: Create a drawOnce() method in the rocket object to initially draw the rocket onto the hidden Canvas. Change the draw() method to use drawImage().

- Consider doing something more adventurous with the drawBackground() function. Try adding some stars or other detail.

- The collide() function uses the slower length() method to calculate the distance between two objects. Modify this code to use the faster lengthSquared() method. Hint: You'll need to compare the value returned against the sum of the two radii squared.
- Develop a new control system for the rocket, using the keyboard or different mouse actions, such as dragging.

CHAPTER 8

Google Visualizations

The Google Chart Tools API (application programming interface) is an extensive and growing set of data visualization tools that can add impressive visual impact to your data. If you're picturing boring old pie and bar charts, then read on: interactivity, animation, and just plain fun are all part of the Google Chart Tools mix (Figure 8-1). In fact, there's a lot more than just charts in Google Chart Tools:

- Maps
- Dynamic icons
- Dials and "o-meter"-style displays
- Formulas
- QR codes (2D bar codes for physical-world hyperlinks)
- Lots of third-party visualizations
- The ability to create your own custom visualizations

The API's expansive nature easily warrants a book of its own, so this chapter covers just the essentials required to get started, enabling you to make better use of the official online documentation (*http://code.google.com/apis/charttools/index.html*) to explore further. We will also develop some useful functions and examples to help you get the most out of Google Chart Tools.

Google Chart Tools is split into two distinct sections:

Image charts (aka Chart API)
> Image charts are created with a specially formatted URL that is passed to Google's chart servers. The servers return a static image of the chart for inclusion in web pages. Typically, the URL is used as the value for an <img> tag src attribute. Image charts are easy to use, requiring no external library and little or no programming to get them working. However, setting up the URL can be tricky and unintuitive. A little bit of JavaScript programming can augment an image chart's utility and ease of use. Figure 8-2 shows an image chart example.

Figure 8-1. Your accountant won't appreciate a chart like this

Interactive charts (aka Google Visualizations API)
Interactive charts use a JavaScript API (loaded as an external library) to render all sorts of dynamic charts and graphics in the browser. While making use of interactive charts requires some programming skill, the biggest challenge is choosing from the vast array of options available. Figure 8-3 shows an interactive chart example.

The first part of this chapter explores image charts, and the second explores interactive charts.

Limitations

There are a few limitations to Google Chart Tools, mostly involving image charts, and you should consider them if you intend to be adventurous with the API:

- Image charts are limited to a maximum pixel area of 300,000 pixels, with the longest edge being no longer than 1,000 pixels. In real terms, this is plenty for a reasonably large chart.

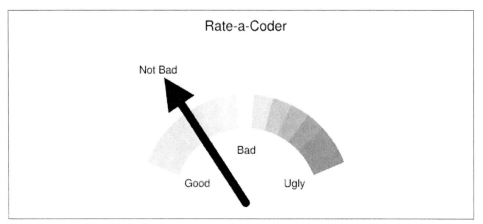

Figure 8-2. All sorts of information can be given a visual kick with Google Chart Tools. This is a Google-O-Meter image chart.

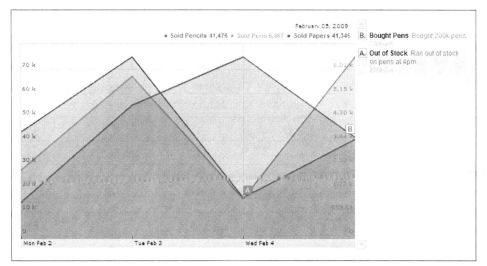

Figure 8-3. A sophisticated interactive chart with mouse-wheel zooming and drag scrolling

- The maximum URL size for image charts is 2 KB using GET, and 16 KB using POST. There are no such limitations for interactive charts, which connect to the Google chart servers with AJAX.

- The maximum number of chart requests is 250,000 per day. If you require more than this amount, you will need to contact Google. If you're using mostly unchanging image charts, one workaround is to simply take a copy of the generated image chart and save it on your own web servers as an image instead of constantly requesting the chart from Google.

POST and GET are methods for sending data to the web server. What's the difference between them? GET data is usually used for simple requests to the server, such as the URL in the browser address bar or the src URL in <img> tags (or an image chart URL). It is typically visible, either in the browser address bar or in a web page's source code. POST is often used where more significant data is being sent to the server to be processed and saved. Examples of typical POST data include the contents of a form, such as credit card details or an email. The contents of POST data are not visible under normal circumstances.

Chart Glossary

Regardless of the type of chart (meaning any image chart or visualization) you use, you should understand some common elements beforehand:

Data table

The data for a chart is stored internally as a table, and the goal of any chart is to make this table visually more meaningful than a basic grid of numbers and strings. A table has rows, columns, and cells. Each cell contains a single value in the table (a value might be a number, string, date, etc.). Rows and columns are numbered from 0, and a cell can be referenced by its row and column location. In Table 8-1, the cell at (0,2) has a value of 75, the cell at (0,0) has a value of Monday, and the cell at (2,2) has a value of 35. Figure 8-4 shows the same table represented as a column chart. I've deliberately used unique values so they are easier to pick out in code examples.

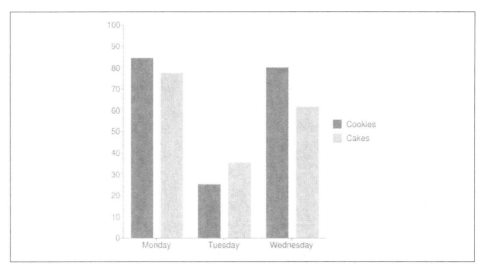

Figure 8-4. Two data series represented as a bar chart

Data series

A data series represents a set of related data values from a table, and any chart will feature one or more data series. In Table 8-1, each column represents one of three data series: Days, Cookie sales, and Cake sales.

Table 8-1. Tabular representation of bakery sales over a three-day period; each column represents a data series

Day	Cookie sales	Cake sales
Monday	90	75
Tuesday	40	65
Wednesday	60	35

Axis labels

Axis labels are either text or numeric labels that run along the length of each axis. The chart in Figure 8-4 features text labels along the horizontal axis and numeric labels on the vertical axis. You can automatically generate numeric labels by specifying a range and step value. Depending on the kind of chart, a data series might be used to create axis labels; notice how the Day series is used to create labels for the horizontal axis.

Legend

A legend describes a data series in a chart. In Figure 8-4, there are two color-coded legends (Cookies and Cakes) that describe the corresponding series in Table 8-1.

Image Charts

Image charts are designed to allow nonprogrammers with no JavaScript knowledge to create impressive-looking chart images. If you know a little HTML, you can use image charts. In contrast to the interactive charts API, there is no need to include any special JavaScript libraries, as the chart is requested from the Google chart servers with a regular URL request. Figure 8-5 shows the results of the following HTML page:

```
<html>
    <body>
        <img src = 'https://chart.googleapis.com/chart?
            cht=p3&chd=t:60,40&chs=500x250&chl=Hello|World'/>
    </body>
</html>
```

Not bad for such a short piece of code. However, constructing the URL can be a complicated and unintuitive process. Thankfully, if you are using charts where the data set is static (unchanging values that are known beforehand), Google has provided a useful Chart Wizard that makes the process of creating image chart URLs a whole lot easier (Figure 8-6). You can find the Chart Wizard at *http://code.google.com/apis/chart/docs/chart_wizard.html*.

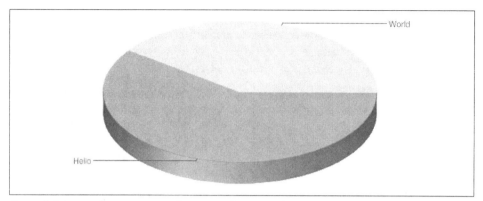

Figure 8-5. Image charts require nothing more than a simple URL request to yield impressive results

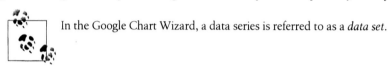

In the Google Chart Wizard, a data series is referred to as a *data set*.

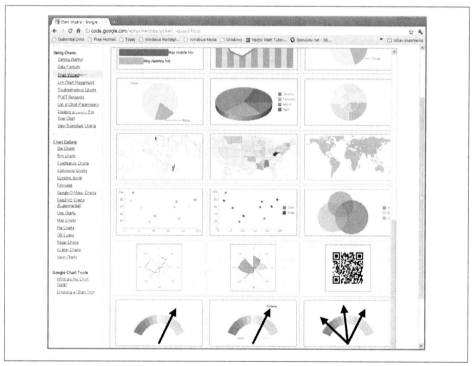

Figure 8-6. You want charts? You've got charts galore—and more—with Google's Chart Wizard (for image charts).

Although the Chart Wizard is very useful when the data series are static, it is not so helpful when the data is dynamic, such as unknown values being read from a server via JavaScript. You need a bit of JavaScript and an understanding of how the URL is constructed if you'll be using image charts with dynamic data.

One drawback of the image charts is the cryptic nature of the URL that must be passed to the Google servers. Let's take a closer look at the format of the URL used to generate the pie chart shown previously in Figure 8-5:

https://chart.googleapis.com/chart?
cht=p3&
chs=500x250&
chd=t:60,40&
chl=Hello|World

Here is a breakdown of the URL:

https://chart.googleapis.com/chart?
> All chart requests are sent to this address.

cht=p3&
> The type of chart—in this case, a 3D pie chart.

chs=500x250&
> The size of the chart in pixels, width × height.

chd=t:60,40&
> The data for each pie slice (one data series), specified in a basic text format that allows floating-point values between 0 and 100. There are other ways to specify data in the URL, which I'll cover later in this chapter.

chl=Hello|World
> These are the labels for each slice, separated by a pipe character.

 Using ampersands (&) in URLs can cause problems with XHTML-encoded pages. Replace the ampersand symbol with & if you encounter problems with WC3 validation or other issues with XHTML pages.

Study the online documentation for details about the different chart styles and the multitude of URL parameters required to set them up.

Data Formats and Chart Resolution

You can specify data for image charts in any one of four ways:

Basic text
> As used in the pie chart example, for floating-point numbers 0–100 inclusive.

Text format with custom scaling
> For positive or negative floating-point numbers with no range limits.

Simple encoding format
> A compact format where integer values 0–61 inclusive are represented by single characters.

Extended encoding format
> A compact format where integer values 0–4,095 inclusive are represented by combinations of two characters.

Why are all these different formats offered? URLs are limited to 2 KB in size (assuming the URL is sent via the GET method). The two encoded formats allow for more compact representation of chart data, thus increasing the chance that more complex charts will fit within the 2 KB limit. The two nonencoded text formats are easier to create and read, but are larger in size. A POST method is also supported that allows for 16 KB of data to be transferred via an HTML form. This method requires additional programming to post the chart data to the server and display the response.

The range of values allowed for each data format dictates the resolution of the chart using that format. The extended encoding format provides ample resolution for most applications (4,096 distinct values), and even the simple encoding format, with its modest resolution of 62 values, is adequate for smaller charts. Larger charts will still work at this resolution, but you may notice inaccuracies imposed by the limited granularity.

The JavaScript calculation required to scale arbitrary data values into the available resolution is as follows:

```
scaledValue = resolution * dataValue / maxDataValue;
```

`maxDataValue` is the chart limit above which none of the unscaled data values will pass. This value can simply be equal to the largest data value in the set, but for certain types of chart, a larger `maxDataValue` may be more aesthetically pleasing. For example, if you're using a data set that includes a maximum value of 185, then using a `maxData Value` of 200 will ensure that the vertical axis is always slightly larger than the tallest bar in the case of vertical bar charts.

Basic text format

Basic text format allows you to specify floating-point numbers 0–100 inclusive. Values below 0 are lost, and values above 100 are truncated.

The syntax for basic text format is as follows:

```
chd=t:val_1_1,val_1_2,val_1_3|val_2_1,val_2_2,val_2_3|...
```

Notice the use of the pipe character to separate the data series. Although this simple format is the easiest to use and create, it also takes up a lot of space, so watch that 2 KB limit.

Text format with custom scaling

Text format with custom scaling is similar to basic text format, but it uses an additional chds parameter to represent the scale within which each data series will fit. There are no limitations on the range of numbers that can be specified. The scales are represented by min-max pairs.

The syntax for text format with custom scaling is as follows:

```
chd=t:val_1_1,val_1_2,val_1_3|val_2_1,val_2_2,val_2_3|...
chds=<series_1_min>,<series_1_max>,<series_2_min>,<series_2_max>,...
```

If there are fewer min-max scale pairs than there are data series, the final min-max pair will be used for all remaining data series. In many cases, the same scale will be applied to all data series in the chart, in which case only one min-max pair needs to be specified.

Simple encoding format

Simple encoding format allows for integer values 0–61. Although we could adjust the data values to fit within this range, the limited granularity of values means that larger charts may show inaccuracies. So, this compact format is probably more useful for small charts.

The syntax for the simple encoding format is as follows:

```
chd:s<series_1>,<series_2>,<series_n>,...
```

The data series values are represented by single characters as follows:

- A–Z, where A = 0, B = 1, C = 2, ... Z = 25
- a–z, where a = 26, b = 27, c = 28, ... z = 51
- 0–9, where 0 = 52, 1 = 53, ... 9 = 61
- The underscore character (_) indicates a null value

This text format data:

```
chd=t:1,19,27,53,61,-1|12,39,57,45,51,27
```

is represented as chd=s:BTb19_,Mn5tzb in simple encoding format.

Notice that there is no delimiter between the values, and a comma separates each data series. The following function converts a JavaScript numeric array into a simple encoded string:

```
var simpleEncode = function (valueArray, maxValue) {

    var simpleEncoding =
        'ABCDEFGHIJKLMNOPQRSTUVWXYZabcdefghijklmnopqrstuvwxyz0123456789',
        chartData = '';
    for (var i = 0; i < valueArray.length; i++) {
        var currentValue = valueArray[i];
        if (!isNaN(currentValue) && currentValue >= 0) {
            // Calculate the character for the value, ensuring value is scaled to
```

```
            // fit within maxval.
            chartData += simpleEncoding.charAt(
            Math.round((simpleEncoding.length - 1) * currentValue / maxValue));
        } else {
            // Invalid values will be ignored.
            chartData += '_';
        }
    }
}
return chartData;
};
```

We'll see an example of how to use this function in the upcoming section "Using Dynamic Data" on page 203.

Extended encoding format

Extended encoding format is similar to simple encoding format, but uses two alphanumeric characters to represent each value, giving a range of 0–4,095 inclusive. The following table gives a concise list of the possible values:

AA = 0, AB = 1, ...AZ = 25	90 = 3956, 91 = 3957, ... 99 = 3965
Aa = 26, Ab = 27, ... Az = 51	9- = 3966, 9. = 3967
A0 = 52, A1 = 53, ... A9 = 61	-A = 3968, -B = 3969, ... -Z = 3993
A- = 62, A. = 63	-a = 3994, -b = 3995, ... -z = 4019
BA = 64, BB = 65, ... BZ = 89	–0 = 4020, –1 = 4021, ... –9 = 4029
Ba = 90, Bb = 91, ... Bz = 115	-- = 4030, -. = 4031
B0 = 116, B1 = 117, ... B9 = 125	.A = 4032, .B = 4033, ...Z = 4057
B- = 126, B. = 127	.a = 4058, .b = 4059, ...z = 4083
9A = 3904, 9B = 3905, ... 9Z = 3929	.0 = 4084, .1 = 4085, ...9 = 4093
9a = 3930, 9b = 3931, ... 9z = 3955	.- = 4094, .. = 4095

The syntax for extended encoding format is as follows:

```
chd:e<series_1>,<series_2>,<series_n>,...
```

This basic text format data:

```
chd=t:90,1000,2700,3500|3968,-1,1100,250
```

is represented as chd=e:BaPoqM2s,-A__RMD6 in extended encoding format.

Notice that there is no delimiter between the values, and a comma separates each data series.

The following function converts a JavaScript numeric array into an extended encoded string:

```
var extendedEncode = function (valueArray, maxVal) {
    var extendedEncoding =
        'ABCDEFGHIJKLMNOPQRSTUVWXYZabcdefghijklmnopqrstuvwxyz0123456789-.',
```

```
                extendedEncodingLen = extendedEncoding.length,
                exLenSquared = extendedEncodingLen * extendedEncodingLen,
                chartData = '';
        for (var i = 0, len = valueArray.length; i < len; i++) {
            var numericVal = valueArray[i];
            // Scale the value to fit within maxVal.
            var scaledVal = Math.floor(exLenSquared * numericVal / maxVal);
            if (scaledVal > exLenSquared - 1) {
                chartData += "..";
            } else if (scaledVal < 0) {
                // Negative values will be ignored.
                chartData += '_';
            } else {
                // Calculate first and second characters and add them to the output.
                var quotient = Math.floor(scaledVal / extendedEncodingLen);
                var remainder = scaledVal - extendedEncodingLen * quotient;
                chartData += extendedEncoding.charAt(quotient) +
                    extendedEncoding.charAt(remainder);
            }
        }
    }
    return chartData;
};
```

We'll explore an example of how to use this function in the next section, "Using Dynamic Data".

Using Dynamic Data

To use dynamic data with image charts, you must automatically generate the chart request URL from the data. You can do this in one of two ways:

- In the browser using JavaScript
- On the server using a language such as PHP (not discussed)

The following example shows how to create and use an image chart URL with Java-Script. It creates some random data for another bakery sales chart. Instead of using random data, however, it could just as easily read data from a server. The extended Encode() helper function defined earlier converts the data sets into the correct format. We also could have used simpleEncode(), but bear in mind the reduced resolution accuracy. Every time the page is refreshed, a new random chart is generated:

```
<html>

    <head>
        <script type="text/javascript">
            var extendedEncode = function(valueArray, maxVal) {
                // CODE REMOVED FOR CONCISENESS
            };

            // Fill two arrays representing the two data sets with random values.
            var dataSet1 = [];
            var dataSet2 = [];
            var maxVal = 100;
```

```
        for (var i = 0; i < 3; i++) {
            dataSet1.push(Math.random() * maxVal);
            dataSet2.push(Math.random() * maxVal);
        }
        // Create the URL using the random data sets.
        window.onload = function() {
            var URL = 'https://chart.googleapis.com/chart?' +
                      'cht=bvg& +
                      'chd=e:' +
                      extendedEncode(dataSet1, maxVal) + ',' +
                      extendedEncode(dataSet2, maxVal) +
                      '&chs=500x300' +
                      '&chxt=x,y' +
                      '&chco=4D89F9,C6D9FD' +
                      '&chdl=Cookies|Cakes' +
                      '&chbh=30,10,20' +
                      '&chl=Monday|Tuesday|Wednesday';

            // Locate the image element in the DOM and set its src attribute.
            var image = document.getElementById('chart');
            image.setAttribute('src', URL);
        }
    </script>
</head>

<body>
    <!-- The image source will be changed on each page refresh. -->
    <img id="chart">
    </div>
</body>

</html>
```

In the next example, we'll create a random Google-O-Meter chart at one-second intervals. The random values range from 0 to 100, and 100 minus this random value is the value used as the label for the arrow. Try modifying the code to display two or more arrows (hint: the Google-O-Meter draws one arrow for each value in the data set).

```
<html>

<head>
    <script type="text/javascript">
        setInterval(function() {
            // Create a random value between 0-100
            var value = Math.floor(Math.random() * 100);
            // Create the URL with random value for the data
            // and 100 - value specified as the label for the arrow.
            var URL = 'https://chart.googleapis.com/chart?' +
                      'cht=gom&' +           // Specify Google-O-Meter chart.
                      'chtt=Rate-a-Coder&' + // The chart title.
                      'chts=000000,18&' +    // Title size and color.
                      'chs=500x250&' +       // Chart size.
                      // Show both x-axis (arrow) and y-axis (values) labels.
                      'chxt=x,y&' +
                      // Label for arrow (data set 0),
```

```
                    // and labels for values (data set 1).
                    'chxl=0:|' + (100 - value) + '|1:|Good|Bad|Ugly&' +
                    // Color and size of label text.
                    'chxs=0,000000,14,0,t|1,000000,14,0,t&' +
                    // Color range of chart, red-yellow-green.
                    'chco=00FF00,FFFF00,FF0000&' +
                    // Finally, set the actual value for the arrow.
                    'chd=t:' + value;

                // Locate the image element in the DOM, and set its src attribute.
                var image = document.getElementById('chart');
                image.setAttribute('src', URL);
            }, 1000);
        </script>
    </head>

    <body>
        <!-- The image source will be changed once a second. -->
        <img id="chart">
        </div>
    </body>

</html>
```

The following code does not really create a chart at all. Instead it creates quick response (QR) codes based on the text entered (Figure 8-7).

 QR codes are a type of two-dimensional barcode that have become popular on the Web with the advent of mobile devices equipped with cameras and barcode-reading software. QR codes' ability to store all sorts of information (up to 4,296 characters), such as website URLs, contact details, and geographic locations, provides a quick way of entering information into mobile phones that would otherwise require time-consuming typing and other interactions with the device. For example, phone application websites often display a QR code that you can scan with your phone to completely automate the process of installing the software. QR codes can also be printed on business cards, allowing recipients to quickly scan the card to enter the contact details into their phones.

```
<html>
    <head>

        <script type="text/javascript">

            window.onload = function() {

                // Generate a new barcode when the submit button is clicked.
                document.getElementById('submit').onclick = function() {

                    // Get the text from the input.
                    var text = document.getElementById('text-input').value;
```

```
            // Create the URL for QR bar codes.
            var URL = "https://chart.googleapis.com/chart?" +
                "chs=256x256&" +                   // Size.
                "cht=qr&" +                         // Chart type.
                "chl=" + escape(text) + '&' +       // The text.
                "choe=UTF-8&";                      // Encoding.

            // Locate the image element in the DOM, set its src attribute.
            document.getElementById('chart').setAttribute('src', URL);
        }
      }
    </script>

  </head>

  <body>
    <!-- The image source will be changed when submit is pressed -->
    <img id="chart" width = "256" height="256"/>
    <hr/>
    <input id="text-input" type="text" size="48"
        style="font-size:18px" value = "Enter text:"/>
    <input id = "submit" type="button" value = "Create Barcode!"/>
    <hr/>
    </div>
  </body>

</html>
```

Figure 8-7. QR codes can store approximately 4 KB of information

Summary

The preceding overview of image charts showed how to create basic charts with a correctly formatted URL, and how to use JavaScript to create image charts with dynamic data. The Chart API gives you virtually unlimited options and chart combinations, and with Google offering "no questions asked" use of the API for anyone requesting fewer than 250,000 charts per day, there is plenty of scope for experimentation.

Next, we move on to interactive charts (aka Google Visualizations API), which is a more programmer-focused interface to Google's charting services.

Interactive Charts

In contrast to image charts, which (as their name implies) are displayed as regular images, interactive charts are composed of dynamic graphics that are drawn using various browser facilities such as DHTML, Flash, Canvas, SVG, and VML. Typical interactivity includes scrolling, zooming, sorting, tool tips, and hover effects.

The drawing method employed is mostly transparent to the developer, as a well-written visualization will use the appropriate rendering method for the target browser. This is a great time-saver, allowing the developer to concentrate on the functionality and aesthetics of the charts rather than the minutiae of drawing them.

Interactive charts require the use of an external API, which you would typically include in the <head> section of your page, as with any other external library:

```
<script type="text/javascript" src="https://www.google.com/jsapi"></script>
```

The stages required to draw a chart using the visualizations API are as follows:

1. Load the general Google AJAX API.
2. Request the appropriate visualizations API.
3. When the visualizations API has loaded, prepare the data, and finally draw the chart into an element on the page.

The following code draws a chart using the same bakery sales data used earlier in the chapter:

```
<html>

    <head>
        <!-- Load the general Google AJAX API -->
        <script type="text/javascript" src="https://www.google.com/jsapi">
        </script>
        <script type="text/javascript">
            // Load the visualization API, using the 'corechart' package within it.
            google.load("visualization", "1", {
                packages: ["corechart"]
            });
```

```
        // Define a function to draw the chart.
        var drawChart = function() {
            // Create a data table (initially empty).
            var data = new google.visualization.DataTable();
            // Define the columns in the table.
            data.addColumn('string', 'Day');
            data.addColumn('number', 'Cookies');
            data.addColumn('number', 'Cakes');
            // Specify the number of rows in the table.
            data.addRows(3);
            // Now add the data into each cell of the table.

            // Row 0
            data.setValue(0, 0, 'Monday');
            data.setValue(0, 1, 90);
            data.setValue(0, 2, 75);
            // Row 1
            data.setValue(1, 0, 'Tuesday');
            data.setValue(1, 1, 40);
            data.setValue(1, 2, 65);
            // Row 2
            data.setValue(2, 0, 'Wednesday');
            data.setValue(2, 1, 60);
            data.setValue(2, 2, 35);

            // Find an element in the page to draw the chart into.
            chartElement = document.getElementById('chart');
            // Create a chart object.
            var chart = new google.visualization.ColumnChart(chartElement);
            // Draw it!
            chart.draw(data, {
                width: 500,
                height: 300,
                title: 'Bakery Sales',
                vAxis: {
                    minValue: 0,
                    maxValue: 100
                }
            });
        }

        // Wait for the API loaded event to happen, then draw the chart.
        google.setOnLoadCallback(drawChart);
    </script>
</head>

<body>
    <!-- This is the element into which the chart will be drawn. -->
    <div id="chart">
    </div>
</body>

</html>
```

At first glance, the output doesn't look particularly different from the image charts we created earlier. However, if you hover your mouse over the chart elements, you'll see some default interactivity, such as color-changing bars and tool tips that display the exact data cell value (Figure 8-8).

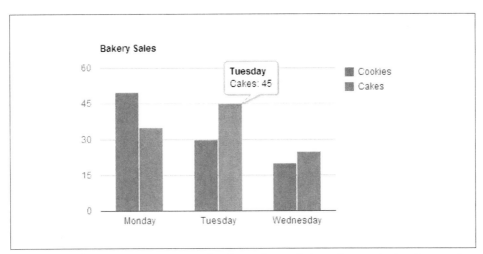

Figure 8-8. Default interactivity on a simple column chart includes tool tips and color-changing bars revealed on hover

If you have access to both Internet Explorer and Firefox browsers, study the source code generated by the charts; it is embedded within the specified chart element in the page as an `<iframe>`. If viewed in Internet Explorer, the chart will have been created with VML; in Firefox, the chart will have been created with SVG, which is not available in Internet Explorer.

> To examine dynamically generated parts of an HTML page, you cannot use the browser's default "view-source" functionality; doing so will just display the original page downloaded from the server without the chart. You will need to use the browser's developer facilities, such as Firebug in Firefox, or by pressing F12 in Internet Explorer (from version 8). Note, however, that there is a bug in IE that sometimes does not show the developer tools window correctly.

The code example illustrates some key elements of using the visualizations API:

Creating a visualizations API data table (`var data = new google.visualization.Data Table()`*)*
This creates the table data structure, ready to be filled with useful values.

Adding columns to the table (`data.addColumn(type, label)`)

This adds a column (a data series) to the data table. All values that are later placed in the column must be of type *type*. The way *label* is displayed for each column in the visualization depends on the visualization type being used. For example, in column charts, the label in column 0 is used for the *x*-axis labels; in pie charts, it is used to name the slices of the pie. Different visualizations expect different numbers of columns to be defined. For example, pie charts and gauges expect two columns to be defined (Figure 8-9):

- A text column for the pie slice name or gauge name
- A number column for the size of the pie slice or gauge pointer value

When using different visualizations, consult the online documentation for exact details on the number and types of columns accepted.

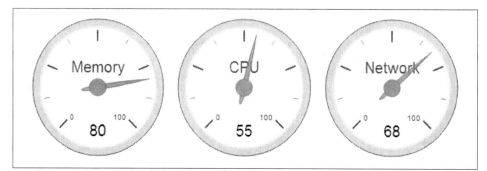

Figure 8-9. Three data values shown as gauges

Adding rows to the table (`data.addRows (numRows)`)

This adds a *numRows* number of empty data rows to the table. Alternatively, instead of *numRows*, it accepts an array of data to fill in the rows directly. In the previous code example, the data could have been filled in like this:

```
data.addRows( [['Monday', 90, 75],
               ['Tuesday', 40, 65],
               ['Wednesday', 60, 35]]);
```

Setting the cell values (`data.setValue(row, column, value)`)

This sets the value for a specific cell in the table. If *value* is not the correct type as defined by the column, an error will be generated.

There are other ways to add data to the data table, including using an efficient object literal method, which can be faster for very large tables.

The visualizations API can also make use of a *visualizations data source* to obtain data. A data source provides a URL to which the visualization can use GET requests to obtain data in the correct format. Typically, this data comes from a database or file. You obtain the data source with the Google Visualization API *wire protocol*, and the server software needs to use this protocol as well. Google provides libraries in various server languages to facilitate use of the protocol, including parsers for the Google Visualization API *Query Language*.

Consult the online documentation for information about adding data and using data sources.

Creating a chart (`var chart = new google.visualization.ColumnChart(chartElement)`)
This creates a chart object of the desired type (in this case, a column chart), ready to be drawn. `chartElement` specifies the page element (usually a `<div>`) into which the chart will be drawn.

Drawing a chart (`chart.draw(data, options)`)
This actually draws the chart into the chart element specified when the chart object was created. The `options` parameter is an object literal that contains both common (e.g., `width` and `height`) and visualization-specific options. Study the online documentation of the desired visualization to see the options available.

Interactive Charts Events

You can add interactivity beyond what is built in to the visualizations by using events. Each visualization may trigger its own events that JavaScript can listen for and act on. Consult the online documentation for specific information about the events triggered by the different visualizations. Table 8-2 lists the available events for the column chart used previously.

Table 8-2. Available events for the column chart visualization

Event name	Description	Values passed back
error	Triggered when an error occurs drawing the chart.	id, message
onmouse over	Triggered when the mouse moves over a bar.	row, column
onmouse out	Triggered when the mouse leaves a bar.	row, column
ready	Triggered when the chart is ready for interaction. You might be able to interact with charts without waiting for this event, but behavior is not guaranteed.	none

Event name	Description	Values passed back
select	Triggered when a bar or legend is clicked. In the case of bars, both the row and column values will be set. They can then be used to identify the correct value in the data table. In the case of legends, only the column will be set.	none

Retrieving event information

One slight complication of using visualization events is that some events will pass the event information directly to the event listener code, and others will require a method call on the visualization object itself. For example, the select event passes nothing back to event listeners, but the visualization's getSelection() method can then be called to establish which chart item was selected.

In the case of bar/column charts, we can listen for the two types of event like this:

```
// onmouseover events pass values back to listeners.
var eventListener = function(e) {
    // Display row and column of item clicked.
    alert(e.row + ',' + e.column);
};
google.visualization.events.addListener(chart, 'onmouseover', eventListener);

// select events do not pass values directly back to listeners.
// The visualizations getSelection() method must be called to get useful data.
var eventListener = function() {
    var sel = chart.getSelection();
    // getSelection() passes back an array of selected items. Here we just display
    // details of the first one.
    // Display row and column data of selected item.
    alert(sel[0].row + ',' + sel[0].column;
};
google.visualization.events.addListener(chart, 'select', eventListener);
```

The following code displays the same column chart as before, but now features three event listeners for onmouseover, onmouseout, and select. Notice how the getSelec tion() method returns an array. Some visualizations may have more than one item selected in the chart (for example, the table visualization). For the column chart, however, only one item will be selectable.

```
<html>
    <head>
        <!-- Load the general Google AJAX API -->
        <script type="text/javascript" src="https://www.google.com/jsapi">
        </script>
        <script type="text/javascript">
            // Load the visualization API, using the 'corechart' package within it.
            google.load("visualization", "1", {
                packages: ["corechart"]
            });
            var chart;
            // Define a function to draw the chart.
```

```
var drawChart = function() {
    // Create a data table (initially empty).
    var data = new google.visualization.DataTable();
    // Define the columns in the table.
    data.addColumn('string', 'Day');
    data.addColumn('number', 'Cookies');
    data.addColumn('number', 'Cakes');
    // Specify the number of rows in the table.
    data.addRows(3);
    // Now add the data into each cell of the table.

    // Row 0
    data.setValue(0, 0, 'Monday');
    data.setValue(0, 1, 90);
    data.setValue(0, 2, 75);
    // Row 1
    data.setValue(1, 0, 'Tuesday');
    data.setValue(1, 1, 40);
    data.setValue(1, 2, 65);
    // Row 2
    data.setValue(2, 0, 'Wednesday');
    data.setValue(2, 1, 60);
    data.setValue(2, 2, 35);

    // Find an element in the page to draw the chart into.
    chartElement = document.getElementById('chart');
    // Create a chart object.
    chart = new google.visualization.ColumnChart(chartElement);
    // Draw it!
    chart.draw(data, {
        width: 500,
        height: 300,
        title: 'Bakery Sales',
        vAxis: {
            minValue: 0,
            maxValue: 100
        }
    });

    // Add an event listener for onmouseover.
    // It sets the hover-text paragraph on the page to show
    // the row and column.
    google.visualization.events.addListener(chart, 'onmouseover',
    function(event){
        document.getElementById('hover-text').innerHTML =
            event.row + ' ' + event.column;
    });

    // Add an event listener for onmouseover.
    // It clears the hover-text paragraph.
    google.visualization.events.addListener(chart, 'onmouseout',
    function(event){
        document.getElementById('hover-text').innerHTML = "";
    });
```

```
            // This event listener shows various details about
            // the cell/column being clicked.
            // Columns are selected by clicking the legends.
            google.visualization.events.addListener(chart, 'select',
            function(){
                var selectData = chart.getSelection(),
                    message = '',row,column;
                for(var i=0; i<selectData.length; i++) {

                    var info = selectData[i];
                    row = info.row;
                    column = info.column;
                    // If both row and column are set,
                    // then a specific cell is selected.
                    if (row !== undefined && column !== undefined) {
                        message += 'cell[' + row + ',' + column + ']=' +
                        data.getValue(row, column) + ', ';
                    }
                    // Otherwise, just show the row...
                    else if (row !== undefined ) {
                        message += 'row=' + row + ', ';
                    }
                    // or column.
                    else if (column !== undefined ) {
                        message += 'column=' + column + ', ';
                    }
                }
                alert (message);
            });
        }
        // Wait for the API loaded event to happen, then draw the chart.
        google.setOnLoadCallback(drawChart);
    </script>
</head>

<body>
    <!-- This is the element into which the chart will be drawn. -->
    <div id="chart"></div>
    <!-- This paragraph text will change with the hover events. -->
    <p id="hover-text"></p>
</body>
</html>
```

CHAPTER 9

Reaching the Small Screen with jQuery Mobile

Web-enabled mobile devices have opened up a plethora of development options for programmers and designers. With so many mobile platforms available, covering all bases and developing native applications for each mobile operating system is not practical. A nonexhaustive list of mobile operating systems includes:

- iOS
- Symbian
- Android
- BlackBerry OS
- Windows Mobile
- webOS

Each of these operating systems has its own development environment and programming languages. For example, Apple's iOS uses the Cocoa development environment and the Objective-C programming language, whereas Android is built on Linux with development in Java. Unfortunately, the smallness of the devices belies the complexity of the underlying software. Even if we ignore the prospect of having to learn another programming language, we're still faced with large and complex operating systems that provide a significant learning curve in and of themselves.

To eke out the best performance from mobile devices and to make best use of their hardware facilities, we'd ideally develop using the native operating systems and programming languages of the platform. However, where absolute performance is not crucial, development time is limited, and multiplatform support is desired, there is an alternative. Using your usual web development tools—JavaScript, HTML, and CSS—you can develop applications that offer much of the look and feel of native software, but without the overhead and learning curve. However, it's important to be realistic about what is possible with this method of development: JavaScript is not the fastest programming language, and within the context of a low-powered mobile device, it can be even slower. Even modern facilities like Canvas may have performance issues on all but the highest-end mobile devices. It would certainly be difficult to develop a fast-moving mobile arcade game without going native. However, as is usually the case, we can expect mobile JavaScript performance to improve as new, more powerful devices are released.

In this chapter, we will focus on the development of a simple game application, *TilePic*, that is suitable for mobile devices. It will use the new jQuery Mobile library to provide a more native-application feel.

jQuery Mobile

With jQuery having established itself as the most popular JavaScript library, it was a natural development for it to go mobile. jQuery Mobile is built on top of jQuery to provide a unified user interface across all popular mobile devices. With a 12 KB compressed size (on top of jQuery), it has modest bandwidth requirements. At the time of this writing, the library is at version 1.0 Alpha 3. Platform support is like a who's who of the mobile operating system world:

Apple iOS (3.1–4.2)
Tested on iPhone, iPod Touch, and iPad

Android (1.6–2.3)
All devices tested on the HTC Incredible, Motorola Droid, Google G1, and Nook Color

BlackBerry 6
Tested on Torch and Style

Palm webOS (1.4)
Tested on Pre and Pixi

Opera Mobile (10.1)
Android

Opera Mini (5.02)
iOS and Android

Firefox Mobile (beta)
Android

For the up-and-coming beta release (at the time of this writing), support is planned for BlackBerry 5, Nokia/Symbian, and Windows Phone 7.

Web developers are used to supporting several browsers, such as Internet Explorer, Firefox, and Safari. On mobile, things are even more confusing due to the number of platforms and their own associated browsers. Despite this challenge, jQuery Mobile aims for full support (CSS and JavaScript), or near-full support, on the native browsers on each platform. Other less well-supported browsers will degrade gracefully to plain old HTML and simple CSS where required.

jQuery facilitates easy searching and manipulation of page elements to help you achieve the desired functionality of your web applications. You must create any additional user interface elements from scratch, or by using third-party plug-ins or extension libraries like jQuery UI. jQuery Mobile has a higher-level approach: it takes clean, semantic HTML and turns it into a rich, mobile-optimized browsing experience with very little additional work on your part. In reality, it is a mobile user interface library built on top of jQuery. It makes extensive use of the HTML5 data- attribute to change the behavior and appearance of page elements. For example, the following simple code creates the button shown in Figure 9-1:

```
<a href="#" data-role="button" data-icon="delete">Delete</a>
```

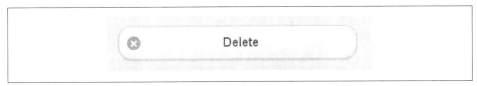

Figure 9-1. jQuery Mobile button

The HTML5 data- attribute allows you to attach arbitrary data to DOM elements, and is typically accessed in jQuery like this:

```
value = $('#myelement).attr('data-mydata');   // value = contents of data-mydata.
```

In the DOM, you specify an element using a data- attribute like this:

```
<div id='myelement' data-mydata = '99' ></div>
```

The data- attribute is becoming more popular, and this increases the possibility of namespace collisions, in which the same data- attribute name is used for different purposes (for example, in your own code and in an external library). A simple solution is to always include a unique identifier when using the data- attribute. For example, data-myuniqueid-icon would not clash with jQuery Mobile's use of data-icon.

The HTML5 data- attribute will validate with the WC3 validator only if you correctly set the page doctype to HTML5 using <!DOCTYPE html>. In addition to mobile-friendly user interface elements, jQuery Mobile provides the following mobile functionality:

- Mobile-like page transitions
- Tap, swipe, and orientation events
- Accessibility features
- Responsive layouts that adapt to device orientation
- Theming framework
- Ajax page loading and history management

TilePic: A Mobile-Friendly Web Application

Using jQuery Mobile, we will create a mobile-friendly application—a game called *TilePic* (Figure 9-2). *TilePic* is a simple sliding-picture puzzle game with a few extra options and features to add longevity and interest. It is a good example of what's realistic in terms of a graphical web application running on average mobile hardware. We could be more ambitious if developing for higher-end devices only, but for the sake of example, we will concentrate on creating an application that works acceptably on as many devices as possible.

Figure 9-2. TilePic, a simple mobile-friendly sliding puzzle game

TilePic Game Description

TilePic works as follows:

1. The user is presented with a main menu screen (Figure 9-3).

2. The user chooses any one of three images.

3. The user selects the number of tiles to split the image into: 9, 16, or 25.

4. The user taps the Play button to start and is presented with the selected image split into tiles, which are randomly ordered to jumble the picture up. A faint watermark

of the complete image is visible beneath the tiles to make the game a little easier (as shown earlier in Figure 9-2).

5. The user tries to correctly reassemble the picture, moving the tiles around by tapping them. At any time, the user can return to the main menu to select another image and/or difficulty level.

 The application will automatically move multiple tiles—a whole row, for example—where appropriate. This feature makes the game less tiring to play; rather than having to tap every tile in a row to move the whole row, the user only needs to tap the last tile in the row.

6. Once all the tiles are rearranged correctly, the user is congratulated and the complete image is displayed without the tiling. A Main Menu button gives the user the option to return to the original screen (Figure 9-4).

Figure 9-3. TilePic main menu screen

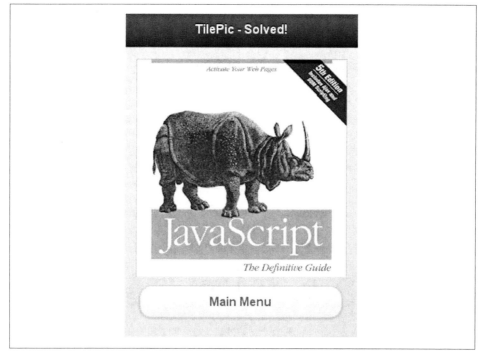

Figure 9-4. Puzzle solved!

TilePic Game Code

The entire *TilePic* application is wrapped in an anonymous function to guarantee full encapsulation of variables and functions. This ensures that nothing within the application appears in the global scope, thus minimizing the chance of clashes with external libraries and code (see the section "TilePic page layout" on page 226, later in this chapter).

Application-wide variables

We define several application-wide variables:

```
var tileSize,   // Tile size in pixels.
    numTiles,   // Number of tiles, e.g. 4 = 4 by 4 grid.
    tilesArray, // An array of tile objects.
    emptyGx,    // X position of empty tile space.
    emptyGy,    // Y position of empty tile space.
    imageUrl;   // Url of image to tile.
```

The tile object

The `tileObj` object encapsulates all the data and functionality for a single tile. It includes a reference to the actual DOM element of the tile (`$element`) and the current grid position of the tile (`gx` and `gy`). The original, unshuffled position of the tile (`solvedGx` and `solvedGy`) is stored, and we can compare this against the current position to see whether the tile is "solved." We use the `move()` method to move a tile (with or without animation) to a new position in the grid. We animate using the jQuery `animate()` method, and it accepts the new tile coordinates as the destination `left` and `top` properties of the tile element

The `checkSolved()` method performs a simple comparison to see whether the tile's current grid position is equal to its original grid position, thus indicating that the tile is "solved." We store a reference to the tile object in the tile DOM element using the jQuery `data()` method. This allows us to easily access the tile object when responding to events bound to its DOM element.

```
// tileObj represents a single tile in the puzzle.
// gx and gy are the grid position of the tile.
var tileObj = function (gx, gy) {
    // solvedGx and solvedGy are the grid coordinates
    // of the tile in its 'solved' position.
    var solvedGx = gx,
        solvedGy = gy,
        // Left and top represent the equivalent css pixel positions.
        left = gx * tileSize,
        top = gy * tileSize,
        $tile = $("<div class='tile'></div>"),

        that = {
            $element: $tile,
            gx: gx,
            gy: gy,

            // The move() method makes a tile move to a new grid position.
            // The use of animation is optional.
            move: function (ngx, ngy, animate) {
                that.gx = ngx;
                that.gy = ngy;
                tilesArray[ngy][ngx] = that;
                if (animate) {
                    $tile.animate({
                        left: ngx * tileSize,
                        top: ngy * tileSize
                    }, 250);
                } else {
                    $tile.css({
                        left: ngx * tileSize,
                        top: ngy * tileSize
                    });
                }
            }
        },
        // The checkSolved() method returns true if the tile
```

```
        // is in the correct 'solved' position.
        checkSolved: function () {
            if (that.gx !== solvedGx || that.gy !== solvedGy) {
                return false;
            }
            return true;
        }
    };
    // Set up the tile element's css properties.
    $tile.css({
        left: gx * tileSize + 'px',
        top: gy * tileSize + 'px',
        width: tileSize - 2 + 'px',
        height: tileSize - 2 + 'px',
        backgroundPosition: -left + 'px ' + -top + 'px',
        backgroundImage: 'url(' + imageUrl + ')'
    });
    // Store a reference to the tileObj instance
    // in the jQuery DOM tile element.
    $tile.data('tileObj', that);
    // Return a reference to the tile object.
    return that;
};
```

Checking whether the puzzle is solved

The checkSolved() function iterates through all the tiles, calling their individual check
Solved() methods. If any of the tiles is not solved (that is, if any tile is not at its original
start position), then the entire puzzle is not solved. The function is called whenever the
user moves a tile.

```
// The checkSolved() function iterates through all the tile objects
// and checks if all the tiles in the puzzle are solved.
var checkSolved = function () {
    var gy, gx;
    for (gy = 0; gy < numTiles; gy++) {
        for (gx = 0; gx < numTiles; gx++) {
            if (!tilesArray[gy][gx].checkSolved()) {
                return false;
            }
        }
    }
    return true;
};
```

Moving tiles

The application needs to determine several factors when the user clicks a tile, including
the clicked tile's distance from the empty space and the direction in which tiles should
move. Possible scenarios are:

- The clicked tile is immediately above, right, below, or left of the empty space. In
  this case, the tile should move into the empty space.

- The clicked tile is not immediately next to the empty space, but is in the same row or column. In this case, the clicked tile and all tiles up to the empty space in the row or column should shift toward the empty space.
- Neither of the two preceding cases is true, in which case the clicked tile cannot move.

With a little thought, it's possible to come up with a solution that works for all cases. Figure 9-5 illustrates the concept applied to handle the different types of tile movement.

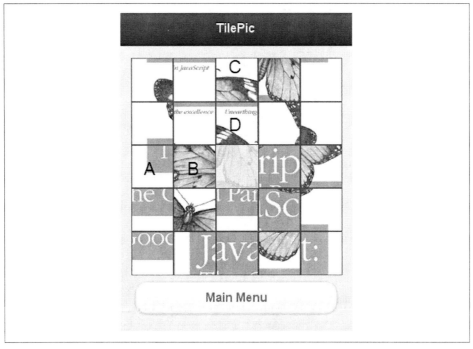

Figure 9-5. Tile movement

For the middle row, assuming the user clicked tile A, we would do the following:

1. Establish that the clicked tile is on the same row as the empty space (in this case, true; otherwise, finish).
2. Establish the direction (`dir`) from the clicked tile (tile A) to the empty space (`dir = 1`).
3. Set a starting grid position (`x`) to be the same position as the empty tile less `dir` (`x = 1`).
4. Get the tile at the current position (tile B), and move it by `dir`.
5. Repeat step 4 (moving to the left) until the position (`x`) is equal to the position of the clicked tile less `dir`. In this example, the next tile would be tile A.

6. Finally, set the empty space position to be the same as the position of the clicked tile at the time of clicking.

For vertical movement of tiles C and D, the concept is exactly the same, but movement and tests take place along the vertical axis instead.

```
// When a tile is clicked on, the moveTiles() function will
// move one or more tiles into the empty space. This can be done
// with or without animation.
var moveTiles = function (tile, animate) {
    var clickPos, x, y, dir, t;
    // If empty space is on same vertical level as clicked tile,
    // move tile(s) horizontally.
    if (tile.gy === emptyGy) {
        clickPos = tile.gx;
        dir = tile.gx < emptyGx ? 1 : -1;
        for (x = emptyGx - dir; x !== clickPos - dir; x -= dir) {
            t = tilesArray[tile.gy][x];
            t.move(x + dir, tile.gy, animate);
        }
        // Update position of empty tile.
        emptyGx = clickPos;
    }
    // If empty space is on same horizontal level as clicked tile,
    // move tile(s) vertically.
    if (tile.gx === emptyGx) {
        clickPos = tile.gy;
        dir = tile.gy < emptyGy ? 1 : -1;
        for (y = emptyGy - dir; y !== clickPos - dir; y -= dir) {
            t = tilesArray[y][tile.gx];
            t.move(tile.gx, y + dir, animate);
        }
        // Update position of empty tile.
        emptyGy = clickPos;
    }
};
```

Shuffling the tiles

The shuffle() function chooses a random tile in either the same column or row as the empty space, and then calls the moveTiles() function on it. Using the modulo operator (%) ensures that the tile chosen is not the empty space (a wasted shuffle), and is always a valid tile within the confines of the grid.

```
// Randomly shuffles the tiles, ensuring that the puzzle
// is solvable. moveTiles() is called with no animation.
var shuffle = function () {
    var randIndex = Math.floor(Math.random() * (numTiles - 1));
    if (Math.floor(Math.random() * 2)) {
        moveTiles(tilesArray[emptyGx][(emptyGy + 1 + randIndex) % numTiles], false);
    } else {
        moveTiles(tilesArray[(emptyGx + 1 + randIndex) % numTiles][emptyGy], false);
    }
};
```

The shuffle() function performs only one random movement of tiles, and must be called multiple times to truly shuffle the tiles.

TilePic setup code

The setup() function performs various cleanup and setup operations before each game, including:

- Removing tiles from the picture frame if they exist from a previous game.
- Creating the watermark guide image within the picture frame.
- Creating new tiles (but it does not place a tile in the bottom right).
- Setting the position of empty space to the bottom right of the picture frame.
- Shuffling the new tiles.

```
// Initial setup. Clears picture frame of old tiles,
// creates new tiles, and shuffles them.
var setup = function () {
    var x, y, i;
    imageUrl = $("input[name='pic-choice']:checked").val();
    // Create a subtle watermark 'guide' image to make the puzzle
    // a little easier.
    $('#pic-guide').css({
        opacity: 0.2,
        backgroundImage: 'url(' + imageUrl + ')'
    });
    // Prepare the completed 'solved' image.
    $('#well-done-image').attr("src", imageUrl);
    // Remove all old tiles.
    $('.tile', $('#pic-frame')).remove();
    // Create new tiles.
    numTiles = $('#difficulty').val();
    tileSize = Math.ceil(280 / numTiles);
    emptyGx = emptyGy = numTiles - 1;
    tilesArray = [],
    for (y = 0; y < numTiles; y++) {
        tilesArray[y] = [];
        for (x = 0; x < numTiles; x++) {
            if (x === numTiles - 1 && y === numTiles - 1) {
                break;
            }
            var tile = tileObj(x, y);
            tilesArray[y][x] = tile;
            $('#pic-frame').append(tile.$element);
        }
    }
    // Shuffle the new tiles randomly.
    for (i = 0; i < 100; i++) {
        shuffle();
    }
};
```

TilePic events

The `bindEvents()` function is called only once on page load to bind the appropriate events to elements in the page. It binds the 'tap' event to the picture frame, as this is more efficient than attaching 'tap' to each tile.

When a user clicks a tile element, the event will bubble up to the surrounding picture frame, and at this point, we can access the element's `tileObj` object via the jQuery `data()` method. The `moveTiles()` function is then called to move the tile(s) in the appropriate way. Finally, a call to `checkSolved()` tests whether the puzzle is solved and, if so, redirects to a page displaying a "Well Done" message.

The `bindEvents()` function also binds a click event to the play-button link to ensure that the `setup()` function is called when a new game is started.

```
var bindEvents = function () {
    // Trap 'tap' events on the picture frame.
    $('#pic-frame').bind('tap',function(evt) {
        var $targ = $(evt.target);
        // Has a tile been tapped?
        if (!$targ.hasClass('tile')) return;
        // If a tile has been tapped, then move the appropriate tile(s).
        moveTiles($targ.data('tileObj'),true);
        // Check if the puzzle is solved.
        if (checkSolved()) {
            $.mobile.changePage("#well-done","pop");
        }
    });

    $('#play-button').bind('click',setup);
};
```

TilePic page layout

```
<!DOCTYPE html>
<html>
<head>
    <meta http-equiv="Content-Type" content="text/html; charset=utf-8">
    <title>TilePic - A jQuery Mobile Game</title>
    <script src="http://code.jquery.com/jquery-1.5.min.js"></script>
        <script type="text/javascript">
        $(function() {

            var tileSize,   // Tile size in pixels.
                numTiles,   // Number of tiles, e.g. 4 = 4 by 4 grid.
                tilesArray, // An array of tile objects.
                emptyGx,    // X position of empty tile space.
                emptyGy,    // Y position of empty tile space.
                imageUrl;   // Url of image to tile.

            // tileObj represents a single tile in the puzzle.
            // gx and gy are the grid position of the tile.
            var tileObj = function (gx, gy) {
                /*** CODE REMOVE FOR CONCISENESS ***/
```

```
        };

        // The checkSolved() function iterates through all the tile objects
        // and checks if all the tiles in the puzzle are solved.
        var checkSolved = function () {
            /*** CODE REMOVE FOR CONCISENESS ***/
        };

        // When a tile is clicked on, the moveTiles() function will
        // move one or more tiles into the empty space. This can be done
        // with or without animation.
        var moveTiles = function (tile, animate) {
            /*** CODE REMOVE FOR CONCISENESS ***/
        };

        // Randomly shuffles the tiles, ensuring that the puzzle
        // is solvable. moveTiles() is called with no animation.
        var shuffle = function () {
            /*** CODE REMOVE FOR CONCISENESS ***/
        };

        // Initial setup. Clears picture frame of old tiles,
        // creates new tiles, and shuffles them.
        var setup = function () {
            /*** CODE REMOVE FOR CONCISENESS ***/
        };

        var bindEvents = function () {
            /*** CODE REMOVE FOR CONCISENESS ***/
        };

        bindEvents();
        setup();

    });
</script>

<link rel="stylesheet"
    href="http://code.jquery.com/mobile/1.0a3/jquery.mobile-1.0a3.min.css" />
<script
        src="http://code.jquery.com/mobile/1.0a3/jquery.mobile-1.0a3.min.js">
    </script>

<style type="text/css">
    label img {
        margin-right:10px;
    }

    #pic-frame {
        width:280px;
        height:280px;
        position:relative;
        left:0px;
        top:0px;
    }
```

```
        #pic-guide {
            position:absolute;
            backround-repeat:no-repeat;
            width:100%;
            height:100%;
        }

        .tile {
            border:1px solid;
            position:absolute;
        }

        #well-done {
            position:relative;
        }

    </style>
</head>
<body>

    <!-- Menu page -->
    <div id="menu" data-role="page">
        <div data-role="header" data-backbtn="false">
            <h1>
                TilePic
            </h1>
        </div>
        <div data-role="content">
            <div id="pic-choice" data-role="fieldcontain">
                <fieldset data-role="controlgroup">
                    <legend>
                        Choose Picture:
                    </legend>

                    <input type="radio" name="pic-choice" id="pic-choice-1"
                        value="rhino.jpg"    checked="checked" />
                    <label for="pic-choice-1">
                        <img width="32" src="rhino.jpg" />
                        Rhino
                    </label>

                    <input type="radio" name="pic-choice" id="pic-choice-2"
                        value="butterfly.jpg" />
                    <label for="pic-choice-2">
                        <img width="32" src="butterfly.jpg" />
                        Butterfly
                    </label>

                    <input type="radio" name="pic-choice" id="pic-choice-3"
                        value="otter.jpg" />
                    <label for="pic-choice-3">
                        <img width="32" src="otter.jpg" />
                        Otter
                    </label>
```

```
                </fieldset>
            </div>
            <div data-role="fieldcontain">
                <label for="difficulty" " class="select ">Choose Difficulty:</label>
                <select name="difficulty " "" id="difficulty">
                    <option value="3">
                        Easy (9 Tiles)
                    </option>
                    <option value="4" selected="1">
                        Normal (16 Tiles)
                    </option>
                    <option value="5">
                        Hard (25 Tiles)
                    </option>
                    </select>
            </div>
            <a id="play-button" href="#game" data-role="button">Play!</a>
        </div>
    </div>

    <!-- Game page -->
    <div id="game" data-role="page" data-backbtn="false">
        <div data-role="header" data-backbtn="false">
            <h1>
                TilePic
            </h1>
        </div>
        <div data-role="content">
            <div id="pic-frame">
                <div id="pic-guide">
                </div>
            </div>
            <a href="#menu" data-role="button">Main Menu</a>
        </div>
    </div>

    <!-- Well done popup page -->
    <div id="well-done" data-role="page">
        <div data-role="header" data-backbtn="false">
            <h1>
                TilePic - Solved!
            </h1>
        </div>
        <div data-role="content">
            <img id="well-done-image" width="280" height="280" />
            <a href="#menu" data-role="button">Main Menu</a>
        </div>
    </div>

</body>
</html>
```

PhoneGap

PhoneGap is a suite of multiplatform native libraries that take regular web applications and hide them inside a native application "wrapper." This enables you to distribute and sell web applications as if they were native applications on multiple mobile formats. However, although PhoneGap is undoubtedly useful, it is not a one-click-wonder solution that will convert web applications into best-selling native applications with no effort on your part. There are a few points to consider when using PhoneGap:

- PhoneGap will not improve a web application's performance. If your web application is slow, it will still be slow after being made native with PhoneGap.
- You'll need to install the desired platform's software development kit along with the relevant PhoneGap library. This is not a trivial task in some cases and can be tricky to get working.
- If applicable, you'll still be required to go through the desired platform's approval process and pay any fees to release a web application wrapped with PhoneGap.

The next chapter will demonstrate how to convert our *TilePic* application into a native Android application using PhoneGap.

CHAPTER 10

Creating Android Apps with PhoneGap

In the previous chapter, we developed a mobile-friendly web application using jQuery Mobile. In this chapter, we'll convert the very same mobile application into a native Android mobile application using PhoneGap. At first glance, converting a humble JavaScript application into a native Android application seems like a miraculous metamorphosis: native Android apps are usually written in Java, Java is not JavaScript, and you can't convert from one to the other. How does PhoneGap manage this? In fact, PhoneGap's apparent magical abilities lie within the Android system itself. Android provides a facility called WebView that allows native applications to display regular web content. This includes the ability to execute JavaScript within the web content as normal.

One exciting feature of WebView is that it also allows interaction between a native Android application and the web content within the WebView. This is extremely useful, both for Android developers wanting to display and interact with web content within their applications and for web developers wanting to take advantage of Android device features like cameras and accelerometers. Essentially, PhoneGap is an Android application that uses a WebView for your web content, and also provides a JavaScript library for accessing some of the facilities of the Android device itself.

Other flavors of PhoneGap work in a similar way. For example, the Apple iPhone version of PhoneGap uses the iOS system's UIWebView facility internally. Regardless of the underlying implementation, the PhoneGap JavaScript library provides a consistent interface to the device's features.

This chapter explains how to install PhoneGap for Android on a Windows system using the Eclipse development environment. At the time of this writing, PhoneGap has variants for Apple's iOS, BlackBerry, Palm webOS, Windows 7 Mobile (coming soon), and Symbian. All of the variants will require you to install the appropriate development environment.

Installing PhoneGap

Web developers are used to installing JavaScript libraries in a jiffy by including a simple script tag at the top of an HTML page. Installing PhoneGap and the other associated applications and files is a more laborious process. Some of the required elements may already be installed on your system, but this chapter assumes that a clean install of all elements is required. Here's a breakdown of the steps involved:

1. Install the Java Development Kit (JDK). This differs from the Java Runtime Environment (JRE) that is typically installed on systems. The JRE allows Java programs to be run on a system, while the JDK contains all the resources for actually developing Java applications (and also contains the JRE). Remember, PhoneGap is actually a native Android Java application, and that's why Java development must be enabled on your system.

2. Install the Android Software Development Kit (SDK) for windows. This download enables you to install all the desired Android platform versions, tools, and utilities, including a virtual device manager and an Android device emulator that allows you to test applications without actually having the device hardware.

3. Install the Eclipse Integrated Development Environment (IDE). This is the preferred IDE for Java and includes a code editor, debugger, project organization facilities, and many other tools for making Java application development easier.

4. Install the Android Development Tools (ADT) plug-in for Eclipse. This leverages Eclipse's Java development tools and turns it into an Android IDE with everything that you need for full-blown Android development.

5. Install PhoneGap itself. This is by far the smallest download!

Installing the Java JDK

You can find the latest Java JDK on the Oracle website at *http://www.oracle.com/tech network/java/javase/downloads/index.html*. This address may change in the future, but just search for "download java jdk" in Google, and you should be fine.

Click the leftmost Java link to download the JDK (Figure 10-1). Select the platform required (e.g., Windows), and agree to the terms of the license agreement. The download filename will be presented as a link (e.g., *jdk-6u24-windows-i586.exe*), and is approximately 75 MB in size (as opposed to about 15 MB for the JRE; this is one way to check whether you are downloading the correct file). Once the file has downloaded, simply double-click it to install.

Figure 10-1. Downloading the Java JDK

Installing the Android SDK

To download the Android SDK, visit *http://developer.android.com/sdk/index.html*.

For Windows systems, the recommended file to download is the Windows installer version (*installer_r10-windows.exe* at this writing). This will install the base software tools for Android development, aka the Android SDK Manager (ASM). The ASM includes its own tools for installing and managing updates of the desired Android platforms and other components (Figure 10-2). The full suite of Android platforms and components can take a while to download in the ASM, but you only need to do it once, downloading updates as and when they become available.

In addition to the regular Windows application window you expect, the ASM opens a command-line window (aka DOS box). No need to panic; this is normal. The ASM is actually a convenient Windows wrapper for a suite of Android command-line tools that you can use if desired. In fact, all Android development can be done with a basic text editor and the Android command-line tools, but the Eclipse environment and associated extras can make life a lot easier.

If, when you try to install the ASM, it pops up a message saying that the Java JDK is not found (even though it definitely has been installed), click the back button in the message dialog and try again. This is a workaround for a bug in the ASM installer that can bring up the "JDK not found" message incorrectly.

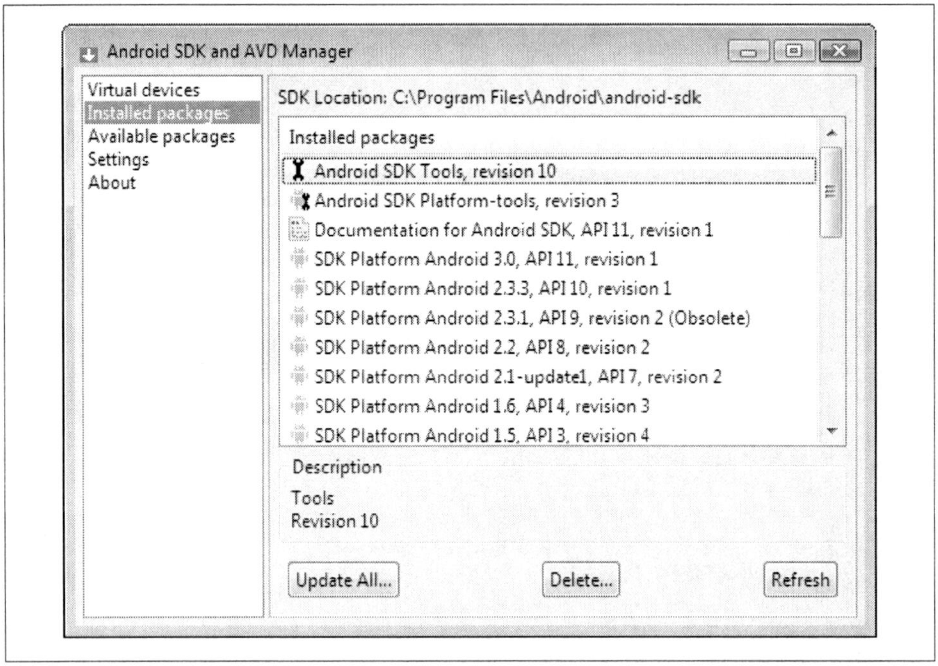

Figure 10-2. Windows Android SDK Manager

Installing Eclipse

Eclipse is a popular programming IDE for many programming languages, and is the recommended choice for Android development. Augmented with the Eclipse Android plug-in, it provides all the tools required to work with Android projects, including those using PhoneGap.

Eclipse comes in several flavors for various programming languages and platforms. We are interested in the Android recommended version, Eclipse Classic (Figure 10-3), which is the Java development version and can be downloaded from *http://www.eclipse .org/downloads/*.

Being a Java application itself, Eclipse will not create any Windows registry entries, program groups, or shortcut icons. It runs entirely from its installation directory via the *eclipse.exe* file. You can create your own shortcut icon to this executable file if desired.

If you are serious about full-blown application development or wish to augment PhoneGap with additional capabilities, there is a huge amount of resources relating to Eclipse development. The following link is a good starting point: *http://www.eclipse .org/resources/*.

Figure 10-3. Eclipse Classic is the one we want

Installing Android Development Tools

Eclipse would be nothing without its plug-ins, and virtually every programming language has an Eclipse plug-in. The plug-ins add language-specific functionality to Eclipse such as syntax highlighting, class browsing, debugging facilities, and much more.

There is no reason why you couldn't do Android development with the regular Java language version of Eclipse, but the most efficient Android development environment is provided by the ADT plug-in.

You can find further information about installing the ADT Eclipse plug-in at *http:// developer.android.com/sdk/eclipse-adt.html*.

The ADT is actually installed from within Eclipse rather than a separate application. There are a few steps involved to install the ADT:

1. Start Eclipse, and then select Help→Install New Software.
2. Click the Add button.

3. In the Add Repository dialog box that appears, enter **ADT Plugin** for the name and the following URL for the location: *https://dl-ssl.google.com/android/eclipse/*. Click OK. The "Work with:" entry should now read "ADT Plugin – *https://dl-ssl.google.com/android/eclipse/*."

   If you encounter problems downloading the ADT plug-in, try using *http://* instead of *https://* for the location.

4. Select the checkbox near Developer Tools and click Next. Eclipse will check the remote ADT files and display a review of the downloads it will perform. Click Next again, accept the terms of the license agreement, and then click Finish. The download and installation will begin. If an "unsigned file" warning appears, just click OK to continue.

5. Finally, restart Eclipse. You're ready for Android development.

All that remains is to install PhoneGap itself.

Installing PhoneGap

PhoneGap isn't actually installed; it just contains a few files that we need to include in this project. You can download Android PhoneGap from *http://www.phonegap.com/start#android*.

Click the Download button for the PhoneGap .zip file, which is approximately 4.5 MB. Extract the file to a directory, ready for inclusion in our project.

Creating a PhoneGap Project in Eclipse

Now that everything has been downloaded and installed, it's time to create a PhoneGap project in Eclipse that's ready for testing on the Android emulator or on a real Android device:

1. Start Eclipse and select File→New→Project.

2. Select Android Project from the New Project dialog.

3. In the New Android Project dialog, enter the details as shown in Figure 10-4. Your default location will be the same as your Eclipse workspace, but you can change this if desired. Choose an Android version that is compatible with one of your virtual Android devices or a real Android device. The package name follows the usual Java rules of package naming—typically, a reverse domain name that is guaranteed unique so it does not conflict with other Java packages.

4. Go to the root directory of the project and create two new directories: */libs* and */assets/www*. (Note that the *assets* directory already exists.)

5. Copy *phonegap.js* from the Android directory in the extracted PhoneGap directory to */assets/www*.

6. Copy *phonegap.jar* from the Android directory in the extracted PhoneGap directory to */libs*.

After you've created the two directories and copied *phonegap.jar* and *phonegap.js*, the project in Eclipse should be structured within the Package Explorer as shown in Figure 10-5.

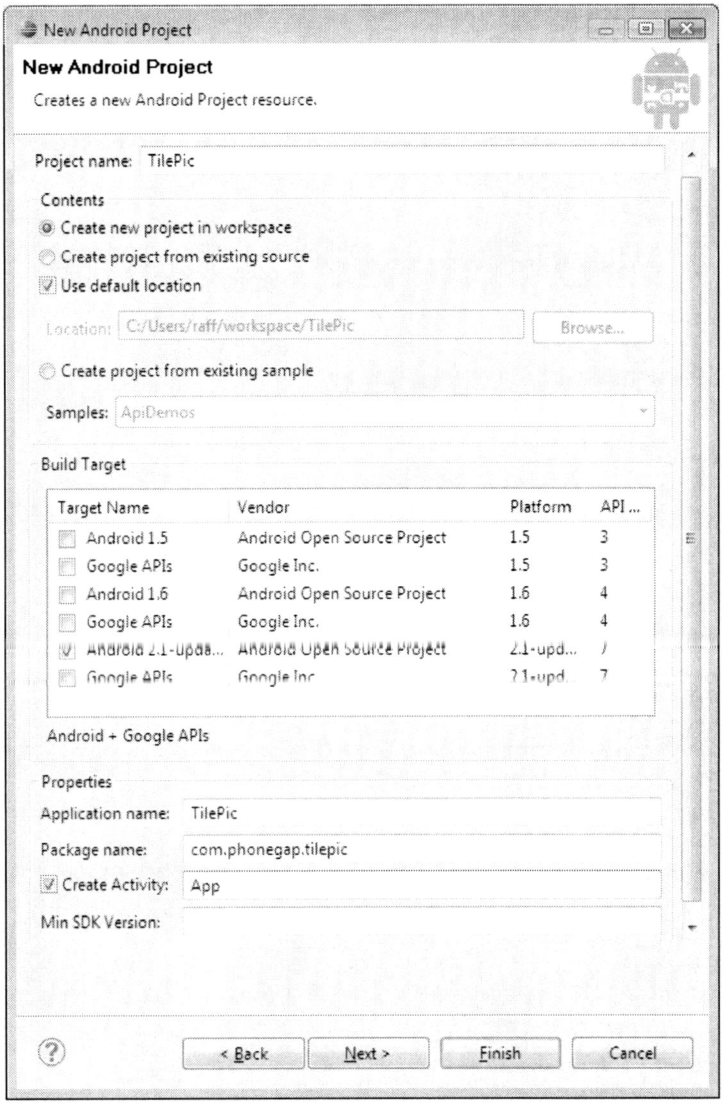

Figure 10-4. The New Android Project dialog

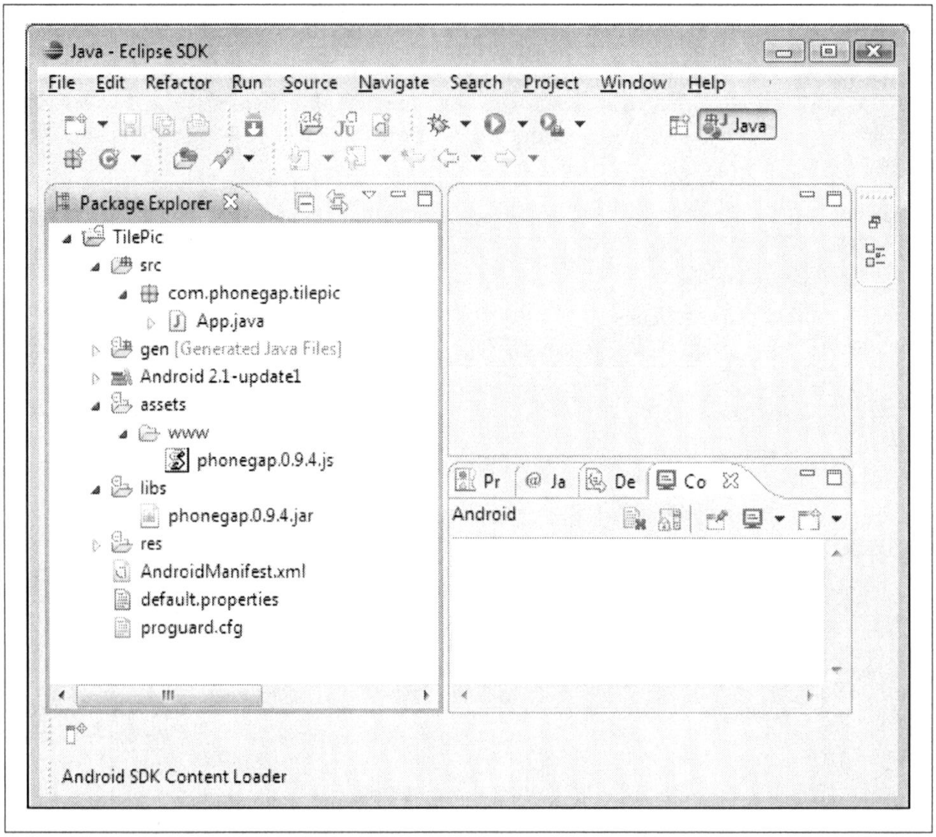

Figure 10-5. Project layout in Eclipse

Altering the App.java File

Double-click the *App.java* file and replace its content with the following code:

```java
package com.phonegap.tilepic;
import android.app.Activity;
import android.os.Bundle;
import com.phonegap.*;

public class App extends DroidGap {
    /** Called when the activity is first created. */
    @Override
    public void onCreate(Bundle savedInstanceState) {
        super.onCreate(savedInstanceState);
        super.loadUrl("file:///android_asset/www/index.html");
    }
}
```

At this point, Eclipse might highlight a few errors. This is because it does not currently know about the PhoneGap Java library in the /libs folder.

To fix this, right-click the /libs folder in the Package Explorer, and then select Build Path→Configure Build Path.

When the "Properties for TilePic" dialog appears, click the Libraries tab, and then click the Add JARs button. This brings up a JAR Selection dialog box that allows you to select the PhoneGap JAR file (Figure 10-6).

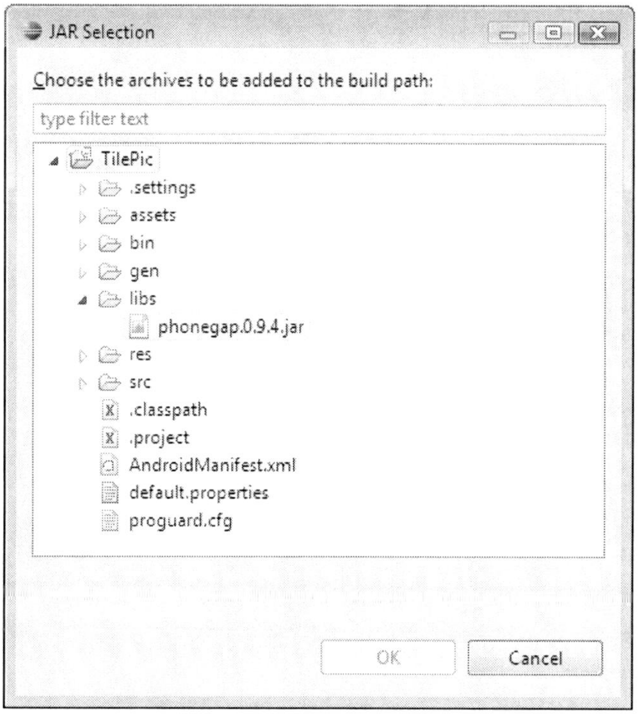

Figure 10-6. Selecting the PhoneGap library for inclusion

Altering the AndroidManifest.xml File

Next, replace the *AndroidManifest.xml* file content with the following code:

```
<?xml version="1.0" encoding="utf-8"?>
<manifest xmlns:android="http://schemas.android.com/apk/res/android"
    package="com.phonegap.helloworld" android:versionCode="1"
    android:versionName="1.0">
    <supports-screens android:largeScreens="true"
        android:normalScreens="true" android:smallScreens="true"
        android:resizeable="true" android:anyDensity="true" />
    <uses-permission
```

```
    android:name="android.permission.CAMERA" />
<uses-permission
    android:name="android.permission.VIBRATE" />
<uses-permission
    android:name="android.permission.ACCESS_COARSE_LOCATION" />
<uses-permission
    android:name="android.permission.ACCESS_FINE_LOCATION" />
<uses-permission
    android:name="android.permission.ACCESS_LOCATION_EXTRA_COMMANDS" />
<uses-permission
    android:name="android.permission.READ_PHONE_STATE" />
<uses-permission
    android:name="android.permission.INTERNET" />
<uses-permission
    android:name="android.permission.RECEIVE_SMS" />
<uses-permission
    android:name="android.permission.RECORD_AUDIO" />
<uses-permission
    android:name="android.permission.MODIFY_AUDIO_SETTINGS" />
<uses-permission
    android:name="android.permission.READ_CONTACTS" />
<uses-permission
    android:name="android.permission.WRITE_CONTACTS" />
<uses-permission
    android:name="android.permission.WRITE_EXTERNAL_STORAGE" />
<uses-permission
    android:name="android.permission.ACCESS_NETWORK_STATE" />

<application android:icon="@drawable/icon"
    android:label="@string/app_name">
    <activity android:name=".App" android:label="@string/app_name"
        android:configChanges="orientation|keyboardHidden">
        <intent-filter>
            <action android:name="android.intent.action.MAIN" />
            <category android:name="android.intent.category.LAUNCHER" />
        </intent-filter>
    </activity>
</application>
</manifest>
```

Creating and Testing a Simple Web Application

We can now create a simple web application to test on the emulator or an actual Android device.

Right-click the *assets/www* folder in the Package Explorer, select New→File, and create a file called *index.html*. Right-click *index.html* in the Package Explorer, and select Open With→Text Editor.

Add the following code into the file:

```
<!DOCTYPE HTML>
<html>
<head>
    <title>TilePic Test</title>
    <script type="text/javascript" charset="utf-8" src="phonegap.js"></script>
</head>
<body>
    <h1>TilePic Test</h1>
</body>
</html>
```

Click the top-level *TilePic* folder in the Package Explorer, and then right-click and select Run As→Android Application. Eclipse will now run the application on either the emulator or, if connected, an actual Android device. The application will display the text "TilePic Test." Well done—you have just created your first PhoneGap Android application!

Testing the TilePic Application

To run the full *TilePic* puzzle game as a native application, copy all the *TilePic* web application files to the *assets/www* folder. The *index.html* test file created earlier will be overwritten with the *TilePic index.html* file. The *assets/www* should contain the files and folders as shown in Figure 10-7.

Run and test *TilePic* by clicking the top-level *TilePic* folder in the Package Explorer, then right-clicking and selecting Run As→Android Application.

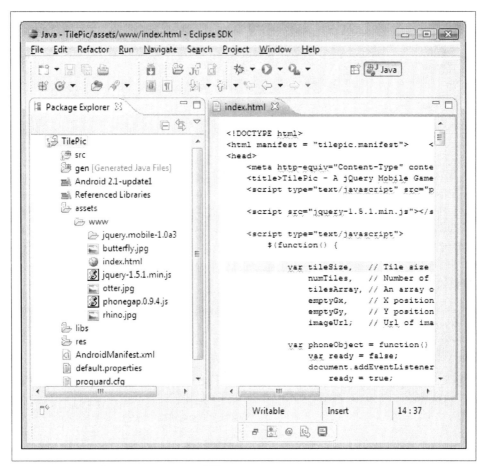

Figure 10-7. Complete TilePic project and file assets

Index

Symbols

3D carousel (see carousel (3D), creating)
3D drawing context for Canvas, 130
& (ampersand)
    binary AND operator
        checking collision flags in Orbit Assault game, 99
    bitwise AND operator, 13
    in URLs, problems with, 199
< > (angle brackets)
    << (binary shift left) operator, 15
    >> (binary right shift with sign) operator, 182
    >> (binary shift right with sign) operator, 15, 150
    >>> (binary shift right with zero fill) operator, 15
* (asterisk), multiplication operator, 15
^ (caret), bitwise XOR operator, 14
$ (dollar sign)
    $.fn.bouncyPlugin.defaults object (example), 37
    $drawTarget variable (example) for jQuery plug-in, 37
    preceding PHP variables, 155
    referencing jQuery object, 20, 36
% (percent sign), modulus operator, 14
. (period), string concatenation operator in PHP, 155
+ (plus sign), preceding values taken from XML file, 65
? (question mark), ?: (ternary) operator, 15
; (semicolon), separating jQuery plug-in from preceding code, 36

/ (slash), division operator, 15
~ (tilde), bitwise NOT operator, 15
| (vertical bar), bitwise OR operator, 14

A

accordion widgets, 72
actual FPS, calculating, 42
add( ) method, adding Orbit Assault game objects to proccess list, 97
addColorStop( ) method, CanvasGradient object, 142, 143
addedItems[ ] array, Orbit Assault game (example), 97
addition and subtraction (on vectors), 170
addText( ) method, graphical chat application (example), 160
Adobe Flash
    Adobe Flash CS5+ Canvas exporter, 127
    Canvas versus, 126
Adobe Illustrator plug-in, All-Canvas, 128
ADT (Android Development Tools), 232
    installing, 235
ajax( ) function, 65
    loading Tiled map via, 65
algorithms, optimizing, 7
alien bombs (Orbit Assault game), 94, 104
    checking for collisions with other game objects, 100
alien invaders (Orbit Assault game), 93, 104, 105
    aliensManager object, 107
    game over when alien reaches bottom of play area, 118
    new wave starting after all aliens are hit, 117

We'd like to hear your suggestions for improving our indexes. Send email to *index@oreilly.com*.

I

id attribute, Canvas elements, 129
IDE (Integrated Development Environment), 232
IE (see Internet Explorer)
image charts (Google Chart Tools), 193, 194, 197–207
  chart terminology, 196
  Chart Wizard, 197
  data formats and chart resolution, 199–203
  using dynamic data, 203–207
image elements, in tile-based image scrolling, 54
imageList parameter, animEffect object (Orbit Assault game), 98
images
  animating sprite images, 26
  drawing bitmap images in Canvas, 138
  loading for 3D carousel, 82
immediate mode API (Canvas), 123
index.html file, creating for TilePic game in Eclipse, 241
indexes
  animIndex variable storing bouncySprite animation image index, 32
  sprite images, converting to pixel offsets, 26
  tile maps, created with Tiled editor, 61
inheritance
  functional, 3
  prototypal, 2
init( ) function, Orbit Assault game (example), 116
initialization, graphical chat application (example), 162–164
initShields( ) function, Orbit Assault game (example), 115
<input> tags, new types in HTML5, 69
installing PhoneGap
  Android SDK, 233
  Eclipse Classic IDE, 234
  Java Development Kit (JDK), 232
  PhoneGap, 236
  required steps, 232
integers, 12
Integrated Development Environment (IDE), 232
interactive charts (Google Chart Tools), 194, 207–214

events, 211
  retrieving event information, 212–214
  example using bakery sales data, 207
  key elements of using visualization API, 209
  stages in drawing, 207
Internet Explorer (IE)
  background image caching in IE6, 46
  Canvas support in IE9, 124
  example code on, xiii
  IE6 Countdown website, 81
  making carousel work with IE 6 or 7, 81
  problems with 32-bit PNG files in IE6, 27
  source code generated by interactive chart, 209
  speed of animation and movement in IE8, 41
interpreted languages, 4
iOS, xiii, 215
  Cocoa development environment and Objective-C programming language, 215
  support of jQuery Mobile, 216
  UIWebView, 231
iPhone, Phone Gap, 231
items, carousel, creating, 83

J

Java Development Kit (JDK), 232
  installing, 232
Java Runtime Environment (JRE), 232
JavaScript
  network socket programming, 154
  optimizing code, 7
  resources for further information, 23
  3D graphcis capabilities, 130
jQuery
  ajax( ) function, 65
    loading Tiled map via, 65
  converting bouncy sprite application to jQuery plug-in, 36–38
  creating 3D carousel widget plug-in, 79
    jQuery plug-in code, 87
  css( ) function, 29
  Mobile library, 216
    creating TilePic game, 218
    mobile functionality, 217
    TilePic game, application-wide variables, 220

controlling for tile scroller, 67
stored in game object velocity vector, 182
spherical solidity, illusion of, 182
SpiderGL library, 130
split( ) function, using on CSV data, 65
sprites
    converting bouncy sprite application to
        jQuery plug-in, 36–38
    creating DHTMLSprite instance for alien
        objects in Orbit Assault game,
        105
    creating DHTMLSprite instance for mystery
        saucer in Orbit Assault game,
        114
    creating DHTMLSprite instance for player
        tank's laser in Orbit Assault game,
        112
    creating DHTMLSprite instance for player's
        tank in Orbit Assault game, 110
    creating using DHTML, 25–36
        encapsulation and drawing abstraction,
            28
        image animation, 26
        minimizing DOM insertion and deletion,
            28
        more dynamic sprite application, 32–36
        simple sprite application, 30–31
        sprite code, 28
    DHTML, replacing with Canvas sprites,
        149
        new CanvasSprite object (example), 150
        other code changes for CanvasSprite
            object (example), 151
    initializing DHTMLSprite instance for
        shields in Orbit Assault game,
        113
    Orbit Assault game (example), arranged in
        single bitmap, 92
squares, drawing using arcTo( ) method in
    Canvas, 134
string concatenation in PHP, 155
strings
    converting numeric array into extended
        encoded string, 202
    converting numeric array into simple
        encoded string, 201
    raw data in XML files treated as, when
        parsing with JavaScript, 65
stroke( ) method, Canvas context, 131, 140

strokeRect( ) method, Canvas context, 130
strokeStyle property, Canvas context, 140
style properties
    optimizing changes for DOM elements, 20
    storing reference for each tile in array for tile-
        based scrolling, 57
subtraction operations (on vectors), 170
sun effect, using radial gradient, 143
SVG (Scalable Vector Graphics)
    Canvas versus, 125
    Canvg JavaScript library, drawing SVG data
        using Canvas, 127
    SVG-to-Canvas converter, 127
    use in interactive charts, 207, 209
Symbian, 215
SYS_keys variable (Orbit Assault game), 96
SYS_process variable (Orbit Assault game)
    alenManager object instance added to, 110
    alien bomb adding itself, 105
    animation effect adding itself to process list,
        99

T

tables (data), 196
    creating visualization API data table, 209
tabs, in jQuery UI widgets, 72
Taito Corporation, 92
tank obejcts, Orbit Assault game player, 110
tank's laser (Orbit Assault game), 94, 112
    checking for collisions with other game
        objects, 100
ternary operator (?.), 15
text
    formats for image charts, 199
        basic text, 200
        extended encoding format, 202
        simple encoding format, 201
        text format with custom scaling, 201
    in graphical chat application, 160
textScroller object, graphical chat application
    (example), 160
ThemeRoller application, 75
themes, jQuery UI, 71, 74
throttling graphical updates in JavaScript, 38
thrust vector, adding to rocket's velocity, 183
tile-based image scrolling
    creating tile maps with Tiled, 61
    ensuring rapid frame rate, 56
    parameters passed to tileScroller object, 57

About the Author

Raffaele Cecco is a veteran software developer from the European video games industry. He served as Technical Director at London-based software studio, King of the Jungle Ltd., where he created software for clients such as Hasbro and Virgin. He has also worked with web technologies and retail e-commerce systems.

Colophon

The animal on the cover of *Supercharged JavaScript Graphics* is a maned sheep, or Barbary sheep.

The Barbary sheep (*Ammotragus lervia*) is a relatively large species of caprid, or goat-antelope. It is native to Northern Africa and can now be found in southeastern Spain, the southwestern US, and parts of Mexico. These desert-dwelling grazers are also known as *aoudad* or *auddan*.

The Barbary sheep is adapted to hot, dry, and barren areas. It takes in most of its water through the plants it eats, but will drink and bathe in water if it's present. Its large, curved horns contain a rich blood supply, which helps keep it cool in the hot, dry desert. In addition to its horns, the Barbary sheep is characterized by a sandy-brown, bristly coat and long hair on the chest, front legs, and throat.

Barbary sheep, like most desert-dwelling animals, seek shade during the day and are most active at dawn and dusk, when it's cooler. They are expert climbers and jumpers and can ascend and descend extremely steep slopes; this ability to out-climb humans makes them difficult to hunt. Because they dwell in areas with little to no cover, their coloring helps them elude predators. In North Africa, they were preyed upon by the caracal, Barbary lion, and Barbary leopard, but today, their main threat comes from humans.

Despite their agility, hunting has depleted the Barbary sheep population in Africa; however, their introduction into the wild of the southwestern US in the 1950s led to a slight increase in population. The Barbary sheep is currently on the International Union for Conservation of Nature's Red List of vulnerable species due to its population of between 5,000 and 10,000 animals and due to a predicted 10 percent population decline over the next 15 years (as a result of hunting and loss of habitat).

The cover image is from *Riverside Natural History*. The cover font is Adobe ITC Garamond. The text font is Linotype Birka; the heading font is Adobe Myriad Condensed; and the code font is LucasFont's TheSansMonoCondensed.

Get even more for your money.

Join the O'Reilly Community, and register the O'Reilly books you own. It's free, and you'll get:

- $4.99 ebook upgrade offer
- 40% upgrade offer on O'Reilly print books
- Membership discounts on books and events
- Free lifetime updates to ebooks and videos
- Multiple ebook formats, DRM FREE
- Participation in the O'Reilly community
- Newsletters
- Account management
- 100% Satisfaction Guarantee

Signing up is easy:

1. **Go to: oreilly.com/go/register**
2. **Create an O'Reilly login.**
3. **Provide your address.**
4. **Register your books.**

Note: English-language books only

To order books online:
oreilly.com/store

For questions about products or an order:
orders@oreilly.com

To sign up to get topic-specific email announcements and/or news about upcoming books, conferences, special offers, and new technologies:
elists@oreilly.com

For technical questions about book content:
booktech@oreilly.com

To submit new book proposals to our editors:
proposals@oreilly.com

O'Reilly books are available in multiple DRM-free ebook formats. For more information:
oreilly.com/ebooks

O'REILLY®

Spreading the knowledge of innovators   oreilly.com

Have it your way.

CPSIA information can be obtained at www.ICGtesting.com
Printed in the USA
BVOW081421280312

286294BV00006B/59/P

9 781449 393632